THE NATURE OF PERCEPTION

The Nature of Perception

JOHN FOSTER

OXFORD

UNIVERSITY PRESS

OXFORD

UNIVERSITY PRESS

Great Clarendon Street, Oxford OX2 6DP

Oxford University Press is a department of the University of Oxford
It furthers the University's objective of excellence in research, scholarship,
and education by publishing worldwide in

Oxford New York

Athens Auckland Bangkok Bogotá Buenos Aires Calcutta
Cape Town Chennai Dar es Salaam Delhi Florence Hong Kong Istanbul
Karachi Kuala Lumpur Madrid Melbourne Mexico City Mumbai
Nairobi Paris São Paulo Singapore Taipei Tokyo Toronto Warsaw

with associated companies in Berlin Ibadan

Oxford is a registered trade mark of Oxford University Press
in the UK and in certain other countries

Published in the United States
by Oxford University Press Inc., New York

© John Foster 2000

The moral rights of the author have been asserted

Database right Oxford University Press (maker)

First published 2000

British Library Cataloguing in Publication Data
Data available

Library of Congress Cataloging in Publication Data
Data available

ISBN 0–19–823769–3

1 3 5 7 9 10 8 6 4 2

Typeset by Invisible Ink
Printed in Great Britain
on acid-free paper by
Biddles Ltd.
Guildford & King's Lynn

To Rachel, Gerard, Richard, and Alice

CONTENTS

Contents

PART ONE

THE RESHAPING OF THE ISSUE

1 THE TRADITIONAL ISSUE

What is the nature of perception—the sensory perception of items in the physical world by human subjects?

By tradition, there are three general theories. First, there is *direct realism*. This accepts a realist view of the physical world: it takes the physical world (the world of physical space and material objects) to be something whose existence is logically independent of the human mind, and something which is, in its basic character, metaphysically fundamental. And, within this realist framework, it takes our perceptual access to the physical world to be direct. Second, there is the *representative theory* (or *representative realism*). This too accepts a realist view of the physical world. But it sees this realism—in particular, the claim of mind-independence—as putting the world beyond the reach of direct perception. Thus, in place of the claim that our perceptual access to the physical world is direct, it insists that the perceiving of a physical item is always mediated by the occurrence of something in the mind which represents its presence to us. Finally, there is *idealism*. This agrees with the representative theory in holding that direct perceptual awareness does not reach beyond the boundaries of the mind, but manages to combine this with the insistence that our perceptual access to the physical world is nonetheless direct. What enables it to combine these seemingly irreconcilable views is that it abandons physical realism. Thus it takes the physical world to come within the reach of direct perceptual awareness by taking it to be something which is logically created by facts about human sensory experience, or by some richer complex of facts in which such sense-experiential facts centrally feature.

Of these three traditional positions, the idealist option is likely to strike us, initially, as just absurd. This is not merely because it is an affront to 'common sense'—an outright rejection of something which we ordinarily take for granted. It is also, and more importantly, because it seems that our very concept of the physical world requires it to be something external to, and ontologically independent of, the human mind. For reasons which will emerge, I think that such a dismissal of idealism is too hasty. But, for the time being, I am going to put the idealist option on one side, and, in company with almost all other current philosophers, look at the issue of perception in the framework of physical realism.

Within this realist framework, the traditional debate focuses on the issue between direct realism, which takes our perceptual access to the physical world to be direct, and the representative theory, which takes it to be representationally mediated. However, before we can properly deal with this issue, we need to pause to reshape it. For it turns out that there are two crucially different ways in which the claim of direct access can be interpreted; and, for each interpretation, there is a corresponding version of the representative theory to stand in contrast. In other words, what poses as a unitary issue, turns out, on closer examination, to be the conflation of two distinct issues—between two distinct forms of direct realism and the correspondingly distinct forms of the representative theory. We obviously cannot hope to make any progress in our investigation until we have brought the two issues to light and decided the manner in which we are going to address them.

2 THE TWO INTERPRETATIONS

I

We must start by getting clear about the precise point at which the different interpretations of the direct-access claim arise. And, as a first step, I need to introduce and explain two key notions: that of *constitution* and that of *perceptual mediation*. I shall take these in turn.

Let us say that a fact F is *constituted by* a fact F′, or by a set of facts α, if and only if (1) F obtains *in virtue of* the obtaining of F′ (the obtaining of the members of α), and (2) the obtaining of F is *nothing over and above* the obtaining of F′ (the obtaining of the members of α). The relation of *obtaining in virtue of* is to be understood as necessarily asymmetric, so that we cannot envisage a case in which F obtains in virtue of the obtaining of F′ and F′ obtains in virtue of the obtaining of F. This means, in particular, that we cannot speak of a fact as constituted by itself (though, trivially, its obtaining is nothing over and above its obtaining); and, in effect, it means that we cannot speak of a fact as constituted by a set of facts which contain it. I am using the term 'fact' in what I take to be its standard philosophical sense, to signify an aspect of how things are. I could equally well have used the expression 'state of affairs'; my preference for 'fact' is only that it is shorter.

The definition of constitution allows it to occur in two forms, as either a relationship between two facts or a relationship between a fact and a set of facts. In effect, the distinction here is between the case where the constitutive base comprises a *single* fact and the case where it comprises a *plurality* of facts. I say 'in effect', because, technically, a set of facts could contain only one member. But to envisage a case in which a fact F is constituted by the set whose sole member is a fact F′ is to envisage a case which would be more naturally described as one in which F is constituted by F′.

It is easy to find examples of both forms of constitution. A range of clear-cut cases of single-fact constitution is provided by the relationship between the instantiation of a generic (determinable) property and the instantiation of some specific (determinate) form of it. Thus if an object is scarlet, then the fact of its being (generically) red is clearly constituted, in the relevant sense, by the fact of its being (specifically) scarlet: the generic colour-fact obtains in virtue of, and its obtaining is nothing over and above, the obtaining of the more specific. A range of clear-cut cases of multi-fact constitution is provided by the relationship between the weight-relationship between two objects and their individual weights. Thus if John weighs twelve stone and Mary weighs ten stone, the fact of John's being heavier than Mary is clearly constituted, in the relevant sense, by the combination of the fact that John weighs twelve stone and the fact that Mary weighs ten stone: their weight-relationship obtains in virtue of, and its obtaining is nothing over and above, the combination of the separate weight-facts about them. Any case of multi-fact constitution can, of course, be automatically recast as a case of single-fact constitution by simply replacing the plurality of facts by their conjunction; or at least this can be done if the plurality is finite. But all this shows is that a case of single-fact constitution is only *interestingly* of a single-fact form if the single fact in question is *not* explicitly or implicitly conjunctive in that way.

Where a fact is constituted by a plurality of facts, I shall also speak of it as 'breaking down' or 'decomposing' into those facts. So, in the example above, the weight-relationship between John and Mary (John's being heavier than Mary) can be said to *break down*, or *decompose*, into the facts about their individual weights—the facts which in combination constitute that relationship.

Two other things should be noted. First, there are cases of *constitutive overdetermination*, where a single fact is separately constituted in two ways. For example, given any pair of facts, that p and that q, the disjunctive fact that either p or q is separately constituted by each of these facts on its own. Second, it will be convenient to construe the relation of *obtaining in virtue of*, as it features in the definition of constitution, in a way which excludes forms of redundancy in the constitutive base. Thus if F obtains in virtue of the obtaining of F′, then we are not to speak of F as obtaining in virtue of the obtaining of the conjunction of F′ and some further fact, or in virtue of the obtaining of some plurality of facts which includes F′. And if F obtains in virtue of the obtaining of the members of α, we are not to speak of it as obtaining in virtue of the obtaining of the members of some larger set which includes α. This means, in particular, that, in cases of constitutive overdetermination, we are not to speak of the fact which is doubly constituted as also constituted by the combination of the facts, or sets of facts, which are separately constitutively involved.

With the notion of constitution in place, I can now explain the notion of *perceptual mediation*. It often happens that the perceiving of one thing is wholly channelled through the perceiving of another. This occurs when, for some subject S, time t, and items x and y,

(1) S perceives x at t;

(2) S perceives y at t;

(3) S's perceiving of x at t breaks down into (is constituted by the combination of) his perceiving of y at t and certain additional facts;

and

(4) these additional facts do not involve anything further about S's perceptual condition at t (anything over and above what is already covered by S's perceiving of *y*). In other words, in combining with the fact of S's perceiving of y, they do not add further perceptual facts, about S at t, to the constitutive base.

It is this phenomenon that I call 'perceptual mediation'; and, in cases where it obtains, I speak of the perceiving of the relevant y as *perceptually mediating* the perceiving of the relevant x, and the perceiving of x as *perceptually mediated by* the perceiving of y.

Perceptual mediation can assume a number of forms (or putative forms) according to the nature of the additional facts involved—the facts which combine with the perceiving of the one item to constitute the perceiving of the other. We shall be looking at these different forms in due course. At present, it is best to confine our attention to a very simple type of case. Thus suppose Pauline is looking at an apple on the table. She sees the apple (A), and, in that sense, sees the *whole* apple. But she does not see *the whole of* (*every part of*) A: the only part which is strictly visible to her is a certain portion (P) of A's surface. In consequence, her seeing of A breaks down into (is constituted by the combination of) her seeing of P and the fact that P is a portion of A's surface. And this means that her seeing of P perceptually mediates her seeing of A in the sense defined. We can take the example one stage further. The relevant portion of A's surface, like A itself, is a temporal continuant—something which persists through time. But, at each moment when Pauline sees this portion, she sees it, not as it is at the various stages of its history, but only as it is *at that moment*—or strictly, given the time it takes for light to travel from the surface of the apple and get visually registered, she sees it as it was at a *fractionally earlier* moment.[1] This means that, just as Pauline's seeing of A is perceptually mediated by her seeing of P, so, at any particular moment, her seeing of P is perceptually mediated by her seeing of a certain momentary stage (time-slice) of it. For it means that, at each such moment, her seeing of P breaks down into (is constituted by the combination of) her seeing of the relevant momentary item and the fact that this item is a momentary stage of P. Obviously, we could apply this same two-stage analysis to *any* instance of seeing a material object—to yield any number of further cases in which the seeing of the whole object is perceptually mediated by the seeing of a part, and the seeing (at a particular moment) of this part is perceptually mediated by the seeing of a time-slice.

In considering cases of perceptual mediation, it must always be borne in mind that the relationship holds between *facts* of perceiving, not *acts* (concrete events) of perceiving. Thus when we say that a subject's perceiving of one thing is perceptually mediated by his perceiving of another, we are saying that the *fact* of his perceiving the first thing is constituted by the *fact* of his perceiving the second, together with certain additional facts of the relevant sort. What makes this point particularly crucial is that, in cases of perceptual mediation, the relevant acts (concrete events) of perceiving will often be the same. Indeed, they will *always* be the same in cases where the

---

[1] Even this is an over-simplification, since the distance from surface to visual system is not constant over surface-points.

additional facts do not involve anything further about the subject's psychological condition at the relevant time. Thus, in the case of Pauline, while the fact of her seeing A is perceptually mediated by the fact of her seeing P, and the fact of her seeing P is in turn perceptually mediated by the fact of her seeing the relevant P-stage, there is only one act (one concrete event) of seeing involved. Thus the act of seeing the momentary item qualifies as an act of seeing P, in virtue of the item's being a stage of P; and the act of seeing P (which is itself identical with the act of seeing the P-stage) qualifies as an act of seeing A, in virtue of P's being a portion of A's surface.

II

The direct realist claims that our perceptual access to the physical world is direct. Now, in making this claim, he is not wanting to deny that there are cases of perceptual mediation of the sort that we have just been considering. He is not wanting to deny that, in a case like Pauline's, the seeing of the whole object is perceptually mediated by the seeing of the part, and the seeing of the persisting part is perceptually mediated by the seeing of the relevant stage. Nor is he wanting to deny that there is a variety of other types of case, which we have not yet discussed, in which the perceiving of one physical item is perceptually mediated by the perceiving of another. What he is wanting to claim is that our perceptual contact with things in the physical world becomes direct at the point where there is no further perceptual mediation within the physical domain. Thus let us say that a subject S *Φ-terminally perceives* an item x if and only if x is a physical item and S perceives x and there is no other physical item y such that S's perceiving of x is perceptually mediated by his perceiving of y. Then the direct realist's claim is exclusively concerned with the nature of physical-item perceiving *at the point of Φ-terminality*. His claim is that Φ-terminal perceiving—perceiving not subject to any further perceptual mediation within the physical domain—is direct. In making this claim, he is assuming that, in any case of physical-item perception, there *is* a point of Φ-terminality—that the series of physical-domain mediational links is not, in the direction of the perceiver, infinitely regressive. But this assumption is surely safe enough. In the case of Pauline, indeed, which represents a whole class of analogous cases, we have already, it seems, identified the Φ-terminal point. For there is surely no physical item which she sees more immediately than the relevant time-slice of the portion of the apple's surface.

It is at this point that the different interpretations of the direct realist position arise. For the claim that Φ-terminal perceiving is direct can be understood in two ways. On each construal, the claim is concerned with excluding, at the point of Φ-terminality, a certain form of mediation. But the two forms of mediation involved—the two senses in which the perceptual relationship is taken to be unmediated—are crucially different.

In the context of our recent discussion, the most obvious way of understanding the claim of directness would be as excluding any further form of *perceptual* mediation—as claiming that where someone Φ-terminally perceives a physical item x, there is no further item y such that his perceiving of y perceptually mediates his perceiving of x. In other words, if we speak of perceiving which is *not* subject to perceptual mediation as *perceptually direct*, then the most obvious way of understanding the claim would be as a claim of perceptual directness in this sense. Such a claim would not be trivial. For although, by definition, Φ-terminal perceiving cannot be perceptually mediated by the perceiving of something *physical*, it does not follow that it cannot be perceptually mediated by the perceiving of something *non*-physical—something which is not an ingredient of the world of physical space and material objects.

Thus interpreted, the claim of directness is not trivial. But it will only be of philosophical interest if there is some identifiable position which we might think of adopting and which the claim excludes—some definite way in which we might come to suppose that perceptual contact with the physical world involves this further stage of mediation. And, in fact, there is a major tradition in the philosophy of perception which espouses just such a view. For it holds that whenever a subject perceives a physical item, his perceiving of it is perceptually mediated by an awareness of something which only exists in his own mind. At first sight, such a view is likely to strike us as very strange: it does not ordinarily occur to us that our access to the physical world might be mediated in that sort of way. Nonetheless, there are a number of considerations which could lead us to take the view seriously, and although this is not the moment to discuss them in any detail, it will be helpful to mention one in particular, as a way of shedding a little more light on the content of the view itself. This consideration is concerned with the phenomenon of hallucination.

In cases of hallucination, or at least the kind of hallucination that presently concerns us, the subject has an experience which is subjectively just like that of perceiving a physical item, though without there being any physical item which is perceived—an experience which is not physically perceptive, but which is introspectively indistinguishable from one which is. Now it is at least *tempting* to say that a crucial part of what enables the hallucinatory experience to replicate the subjective character of an ordinary perception is that, although not physically perceptive, it does genuinely bring some sensible object before the mind. Thus, in the case of visual hallucination, it is tempting to say that a crucial part of what enables it to replicate the subjective character of ordinary (physical-item) seeing is that, although nothing physical is seen, there is a real array of colours visually before the mind—an array which poses as, and invites the subject to take it to be, an ingredient of the physical world. Likewise, in the case of auditory hallucination, it is tempting to say that a crucial part of what enables it to replicate the subjective character of ordinary (physical-item) hearing is that, although nothing physical is heard, there is a real sound or complex of sounds auditorily before the mind—an item which, again, poses as, and invites the subject to take it to be, an ingredient of the physical world. But if there are indeed such qualitative items before the mind—items which, *ex hypothesi*, are not themselves ingredients of the physical world—they will presumably have to be entities which are internal to the subject's awareness—entities which have, and can have, no existence outside the context of the awareness directed on to them. And once we have come to accept the presence of these internal objects of awareness in the case of *hallucination*, it then becomes tempting to recognize their presence in the case of *perception—physical-item* perception—too. For if perception and hallucination have the same subjective character, the simplest and most obvious way of accounting for this would be to suppose that they also have, at the fundamental level of description, the same psychological character through and through, and that what distinguishes the two types of case is simply that, where the experience is physically perceptive, it stands in some appropriate qualitative and causal relationship to the external environment. In this way, we could be led to the conclusion that, even in the case of physical-item perception, what is immediately before the mind is an object which is internal to the subject's awareness, and that contact with the external environment is achieved by perceptual mediation—as something constituted by the perceiving of this internal object, together with additional facts of the relevant kind. The basic idea would be that, by standing in the appropriate qualitative and causal relations to a certain physical item, the internal object would serve to represent it—in something like the way in which a photograph can serve to represent an earlier photographed scene, or the playing of a tape can serve to represent an earlier recorded conversation—and that this representation would then suffice to put the subject and the item into perceptual contact.

This position constitutes the representative theory of perception in its classic empiricist form, and, from Locke onwards, it has been widely endorsed by philosophers in the empiricist tradition. Some of those who have endorsed it have preferred to restrict the terms 'perception' and 'perceptual awareness' to the relationship between the subject and the *physical* item, and to use such terms as 'sensing' and 'sensory awareness' for the subject's relationship to the items in his mind. And so, while accepting that the mental items are what the subject is *immediately aware of*, they prefer to avoid speaking of them as what he *immediately perceives*. But this is just a variation in terminology. For the purposes of our present discussion, we can still represent these philosophers as accepting a thesis of perceptual mediation in the sense defined, and as taking the internal objects of awareness to be the things whose occurrence plays the relevant mediating role.

Now when the direct realist claims that, at the point of Φ-terminality, our perceptual contact with the physical world is perceptually direct, it is precisely this form of the representative theory that he is wanting to exclude. He is insisting that the perceiving of the relevant physical item is not subject to perceptual mediation, and the point of this insistence is to rule out this traditional empiricist alternative, which takes the perceiving of the item to be mediated by the occurrence of an internal object of awareness, which represents it. This gives us, then, our first way of construing the direct realist position and the issue between it and the representative theory. Direct realism, thus construed, claims that Φ-terminal perceiving is always perceptually direct; and, in appropriate opposition, the representative theory claims that such perceiving is always perceptually mediated by the perceiving, or sensing, of something in the mind—something whose existence is necessarily confined to the context of the subject's own awareness.

For the sake of precision, there is something which I should now add, though its significance will only become apparent later. As I have so far characterized it, the relevant version of the representative theory takes the immediate objects of perception to be entities which are internal to the subject's awareness; and I have taken this to mean that, on each perceptual occasion, the immediate object is something which has, and can have, no existence outside the context of the particular episode of awareness directed on to it. However, although this is certainly the *standard* way in which this form of the representative theory is held, it is not the only possibility. For it is also possible for the theorist to construe the relevant objects as a special category of *universals*—as things which are capable of occurring to different subjects and on different occasions. And, on this construal, we would have to say that what is tied to the context of the subject's awareness on a given occasion is not the *existence* of the relevant object, but only a certain *occurrence*, or *realization*, of it. The availability of this construal will become crucial at a certain stage in our investigation. But, at present, it will only tend to undermine our understanding of the situation if we try to take it into account. And so, until the critical stage is reached, I shall simply put the point on one side, and continue to think of the relevant theory in its standard form—with the objects tied, in their existence, to particular subjects at particular times.

III

The issue we have just identified is concerned with the scope of perceptual mediation: it is the issue of whether, at the point where perceptual mediation terminates in the physical domain, our perceptual contact with the physical world is perceptually direct, or is rather subject to a further stage of such mediation, involving the perceiving, or sensing, of items in the mind. But *perceptual* mediation is not the only form of mediation which could be thought of as relevant. For philosophers who agree that Φ-terminal perceiving is not subject to any further form of *perceptual* mediation, may still differ over whether it is subject to mediation *in a broader sense*, and this difference of view can also be represented as an issue between a kind of direct realism and a kind of representative theory. Let me explain.

Suppose we have a subject S who perceives a physical item x at a time t. Then let us say that S's perceiving of x at t is *psychologically mediated by his being in Σ* if and only if

(1) Σ is a psychological state;

(2) Σ is not, in itself, x-perceptive (i.e. being in Σ does not, on its own, logically suffice to put one in perceptual contact with x);

(3) S's perceiving of x at t breaks down into his being in Σ at t and certain additional facts;

and

(4) these additional facts do not involve anything further about S's psychological condition at t (anything over and above what is already covered by S's being in Σ). In other words, in combining with the fact of S's being in Σ, they do not add any further psychological facts, about S at t, to the constitutive base.

In a similar vein, let us say that S's perceiving of x is *psychologically mediated* (*tout court*) if and only if there is some state Σ such that it is psychologically mediated by his being in Σ, and that S's perceiving of x is *psychologically direct* if and only if it is not psychologically mediated. I should mention here that when I speak of a 'state', I always mean a *type*-state, not a *token*-state. In other words, a state, in my terminology, is a sort of universal—something which, at least in typical cases, is capable of being realized in different things and at different times.[2] I should also stress that states, as I construe them, can be relational, so that we can speak of the psychological state of seeing a particular apple or of being in love with a particular person.

Now it is with respect to psychological mediation that the further issue, between a kind of direct realism and a kind of representative theory, is to be defined. Suppose S Φ-terminally perceives a physical item x. If we claim that S's perceiving of x is *perceptually* mediated, we shall also have to accept that it is, *eo ipso*, *psychologically* mediated too. For if the perceiving is perceptually mediated, then it must break down into the occurrence of an internal object of awareness and certain additional facts of the relevantly restricted kind; and this will mean that there is a psychological state Σ, which is either simply the state involved in the awareness of the internal item (if the additional facts do not include additional psychological factors), or is this state together with some enrichment (if the additional facts *do* include additional psychological factors), such that S's perceiving of x is psychologically mediated by his being in Σ. But crucially, this point does not hold in reverse. Thus if we claim that S's perceiving of x is *psychologically* mediated, this does not commit us to saying that it is, *eo ipso*, *perceptually* mediated. For we might want to say that the perceiving is psychologically mediated by S's being in a state which is not itself perceptual—a state which does not involve the occurrence of a perceptual object in the mind. For example, we might want to say that what psychologically mediates the perceiving of x is not the occurrence of some internal object of awareness (or that, together with certain other psychological factors), but the subject's acquiring of a certain belief, or complex of beliefs, about the current state of his environment.

It is this which creates the possibility of an alternative interpretation of direct realism and its conflict with the representative theory. The direct

---

[2] I say 'at least in typical cases', because it is possible for a state—a type-state—to be defined in a way which restricts its capacity for realization to just one thing, or to just one time, or, indeed, to just one thing at one time. For example, the state of *being taller both than anyone else at any time and than anyone at any other time* can at most be realized by one person at one time.

realist claims that our perceptual access to the physical world is direct, and, given that there are uncontroversial cases of perceptual mediation within the physical domain, this boils down to the claim that *Φ-terminal* perceiving is direct. But, now, instead of taking this claim to mean that Φ-terminal perceiving is always *perceptually* direct—not subject to *perceptual* mediation—we could take it to mean, more strongly, that such perceiving is always *psychologically* direct—that it is not subject to *psychological mediation in any form*. And correspondingly, instead of taking the representative theory to be claiming, restrictively, that Φ-terminal perceiving is always *perceptually* mediated—a mediation which involves the occurrence of a perceptual object in the mind—we could take it to be claiming, more flexibly, that it is always *psychologically mediated in some form*—without commitment to whether the psychological state involved is itself (wholly or partly) perceptual. It might be thought that, in formulating this more flexible position, I should at least have represented it as insisting that Φ-terminal perceiving is psychologically mediated in some *representational* form; for the claim can hardly count as a version of the *representative* theory unless it restricts the relevant forms of psychological mediation to ones which involve *representation*. But this is not, I think, a point of real substance. If the realization of the psychological state succeeds in mediating *perceptual contact* with the physical item in question, it is bound to be something that we can think of as in some way representing (in some way serving to convey the presence of) that item to the subject involved. At least, this is bound to be so once we have agreed that psychological representation does not have to take the perceptual—as it were pictorial—form of the classic empiricist version of the theory. In any case, however we care to label it, it is the flexible position *as I have actually formulated it*—the position which simply claims that Φ-terminal perceiving is psychologically mediated—that will be relevant to our concerns.

IV

The traditional issue between direct realism and the representative theory has now turned into—or turned out in reality to be—*two* issues. Thus, on the one hand, there is the issue between a weaker, more modest version of direct realism, which claims merely that Φ-terminal perceiving is *perceptually* direct (not subject to perceptual mediation), and a narrower, restrictive version of the representative theory, which claims, in opposition, that such perceiving is *perceptually mediated* (psychologically mediated in a way which involves the occurrence of a perceptual object in the mind). Let us label these positions *weak direct realism* (WDR) and the *narrow represen-tative theory* (NRT). On the other hand, there is the issue between a stronger, full-blooded version of direct realism, which claims that Φ-term-inal perceiving is *psychologically* direct (not subject to psychological mediation of any kind), and a broader, more flexible version of the repre-sentative theory, which claims, in opposition, that such perceiving is *psy-chologically mediated in some way* (without commitment to whether the psychological state involved is itself perceptual). Let us label these positions *strong direct realism* (SDR) and the *broad representative theory* (BRT).

An acceptance of the stronger version of direct realism (SDR) would automatically commit us to an acceptance of the weaker version (WDR), and an acceptance of the narrower version of the representative theory (NRT) would automatically commit us to an acceptance of the broader version (BRT). And so, a fortiori, SDR (standing in opposition to BRT) and NRT (standing in opposition to WDR) are themselves incompatible. But, crucially, WDR and BRT—the weaker version of direct realism and the broader version of the representative theory—can be consistently com-bined, since there is the option of saying that Φ-terminal perceiving is psy-chologically mediated, but in a non-perceptual way. It is because of this that our discernment of the different versions of direct realism and the rep-resentative theory counts as a *reshaping* of the traditional issue, rather than as just an *elaboration* of it. If each version of each of the traditional pos-itions turned out to be incompatible with each version of the other, the traditional issue would remain as something well defined, and the discov-ery of the different versions would just be the discovery that the traditional positions—on each side of a clear-cut divide—were capable of further sub-division. The new issues to emerge would not be *between* direct realism and the representative theory, but *within* them. As it is, the traditional issue has shown itself to be *ill* defined, there being no clear-cut divide between the positions which feature in it; and, in its place, we have to put the two prop-erly defined issues which we have just identified, each with its own precise conception of how the distinction between directness and mediation is to be drawn.

In our quest for an understanding of the nature of perception, each of these issues is crucial to our concern, and will need to be addressed at some point. But the first thing we have to decide is the order in which to take them. Either order would be procedurally possible. Thus, on the one hand, we could start by considering the conflict between the weaker version of direct realism (WDR) and the narrower version of the representative theory (NRT). If NRT emerged the winner, this would automatically settle the other issue in favour of BRT, since NRT entails BRT. If WDR emerged the winner, we could then turn our attention to the consequential issue of whether we should hold the direct realist position in its full-blooded (SDR) form or combine the weak direct realist view with the acceptance of some non-perceptual form of psychological mediation (in accordance with BRT). On the other hand, we could start with the conflict between the stronger version of direct realism (SDR) and the broader version of the representative theory (BRT). If SDR emerged the winner, this would automatically settle the other issue in favour of WDR, since SDR entails WDR. If BRT emerged the winner, we could then turn to the question of the precise form of psychological mediation involved, and, in particular, of whether we should hold the representative theory in its narrow, perceptual-mediational, form (NRT) or combine it with the weak version of direct realism (WDR).

Although both these investigative procedures are available, and would end up covering the same ground, the second is clearly preferable. This is because the range of positions left open by BRT forms a natural genus, whereas those left open by WDR do not. Thus the BRT-positions all have in common the positive feature that they take Φ-terminal perceiving to be psychologically mediated in some way—the difference between them only concerning the nature of the psychological state involved; whereas what the WDR-positions have in common is the negative feature that they exclude perceptual mediation at the point of Φ-terminality—a feature which could take the very different forms of a full-blooded direct realist view (denying psychological mediation altogether) or a type of representative account which postulates psychological mediation of a non-perceptual kind. Since it would be awkward having to deal with such contrasting positions at the second stage of the investigation, it is more natural and more rational to begin by considering the issue between SDR and BRT—the issue of whether there is psychological mediation at all—and then, should it arise, turn to the consequential issue of the form of mediation involved. This, at any rate, is the procedure I shall follow.

3 SDR AND BRT

I

The issue on which we shall be focusing, then, in the first phase of our investigation, is that between the strong, full-blooded version of direct realism (SDR), which claims that Φ-terminal perceiving is always psychologically direct, and the broad, flexible version of the representative theory (BRT), which claims that such perceiving is always psychologically mediated. BRT could equally be formulated as the claim that *all* physical-item perceiving (whether Φ-terminal or not) is psychologically mediated. For any psychological mediation which applies at the point of Φ-terminality is bound to apply to the perceiving of any further (perceptually more remote) physical item which the Φ-terminal perceiving perceptually mediates (though if the perceptual mediation involves some additional psychological factor, the relevant Σ will have to be suitably expanded). The only point in restricting the formulation of BRT to the Φ-terminal case is that it is exclusively in relation to this case that the conflict with SDR arises.

This conflict is over the question of whether, at the point of Φ-terminality, the perceptual relationship between the subject and the relevant physical item decomposes in a certain way. In claiming that it is psychologically mediated, BRT is claiming that this relationship breaks down into (is constituted by the combination of) two components, the one consisting in the subject's being in some more fundamental psychological state—a state which is not, in itself, perceptive of the relevant physical item—the other comprising certain additional facts, but ones which do not involve anything further about the subject's psychological condition at the relevant time. In claiming that the perceptual relationship is psychologically direct, SDR is claiming that it does *not* decompose in this way—that it does *not* break down into these two types of component in the way that BRT envisages. So the two positions are diametrically opposed, one asserting the universal obtaining of the relevant kind of decomposition, the other asserting its universal absence.

Although, thus defined, SDR only formally excludes *this particular form* of decomposition—the decomposition definitive of psychological mediation—an acceptance of SDR would, in effect, involve accepting something stronger. Thus it would, in effect, involve accepting that, at the psychological level of description, Φ-terminal perceiving does not decompose in any way at all—that where someone Φ-terminally perceives a physical item, his perceptual relationship with it does not break down into any plurality of facts which are wholly or partly concerned with his psychological condition. Indeed, it would in effect involve accepting that, at the psychological level, the perceptual relationship is something fundamental—something which is not subject to constitution of any form. The only qualification here—though the significance of this will only emerge later—is that the SDR-theorist does have the option of saying that the bare fact of

perceptual contact, or of sense-modally specific contact, is constituted by
a further perceptual fact of an experientially richer or more determinate
kind—a fact of which the fact of contact can be thought of as either an
integral element or a determinable version. But even this does not affect
the basic point. For, whether he pursues this option or not, the theorist is
still obliged to say that, *in some suitably specified form*, the Φ-terminal perceptual relationship, is psychologically fundamental.

As I have indicated, this fundamentalist view of the Φ-terminal relationship is not something which, in the way I have defined it, SDR *formally
entails*: formally, the theory only excludes those forms of constitution
which yield psychological mediation. But the point is that, with the exception allowed for—an exception which is not in fact in conflict with the fundamentalist view—there are no other constitutional options that one
could begin to take seriously. Once someone has excluded the form of constitution definitive of psychological mediation, he cannot, in practice,
avoid recognizing the Φ-terminal relationship (suitably specified) as a fundamental aspect of the psychological situation. From now on, I shall simply assume that this fundamentalist view is an integral part of the
SDR-position.

This said, there is one important respect in which the fundamentalist
implications of SDR must not be exaggerated. In denying that Φ-terminal
perceiving is psychologically mediated, the SDR-theorist has indeed to recognize it as *psychologically* fundamental—fundamental *at the psychological
level of description*. But he does not have to take it to be fundamental *absolutely*. For his acceptance of SDR as the correct account of what perception
is *in its own psychological terms* leaves him free to adopt a reductive account
of the psychological facts themselves. It leaves him free to claim that the
facts of perception are ultimately constituted by facts of a non-psychological kind; and it leaves him free to endorse a similar account for psychological facts quite generally. The main option here would be to adopt some
form of strong and comprehensive materialism, which takes all psychological facts to be ultimately constituted by *physical* facts—for example,
about the physiology and functioning of the human organism, and the
interaction of the organism with the physical environment. This reductive
approach to mentality is not, of course, the exclusive prerogative of SDR:
it is equally available under BRT, and, indeed, certain forms of BRT-
account may be thought positively to facilitate it. The only point in under-
lining its availability to the SDR-theorist is that this is something which his
fundamentalist claim at the psychological level is liable to obscure.

In taking the Φ-terminal relationship to be psychologically fundamental, the SDR-theorist is not, then, excluding a reductive account of mentality itself, and this is something which it is crucial to bear in mind if we are to have a correct understanding of the nature of his position. At the same time, we should not expect this point to feature very prominently in our subsequent discussion. The issue between SDR and BRT is, in itself, to do with how things stand at the psychological level—with how the perceptual relationship is to be understood in its own psychological terms. It is inevitable that, for the most part, the considerations which bear on this issue will be ones which arise at that same level—considerations which do not relate to the question of the metaphysical status of the psychological realm itself. Even so, the availability of the reductive approach will be of relevance in one area of our discussion, as we shall shortly see.

II

There are two final preliminary points that I need to make, though not ones which are in any way connected.

The first concerns the implications of BRT. BRT, as I have said, takes the Φ-terminal perceptual relationship to break down into two components, one of which is the subject's being in a certain psychological state—a state which is not, in itself, perceptive of the relevant physical item—and the other of which comprises certain additional facts, but ones which do not involve anything further about the subject's psychological condition at the relevant time. Now, in requiring the relevant psychological state to be one which is not, in itself, perceptive *of the relevant physical item*—one which does not, on its own, suffice to put the subject into perceptual contact *with that item*—BRT is, in effect, requiring it to be one which is not, in itself, *physically perceptive at all*—to be a state which is logically capable of realization without there being *anything physical* perceived. This is not because there is any *general* difficulty in understanding how a state which is, in itself, physically perceptive could be mediationally involved in the perceiving of a physical item of which it is not in itself perceptive. For a state which is in itself perceptive of one physical item might be mediationally involved in the perceiving of another. But once we have reached the point of Φ-terminality—the point where there is no further physical item which is more immediately perceived—the only way in which the psychological state which is fundamentally involved in the perceiving of the relevant physical item could turn out to be in itself physically perceptive would be by being, in itself, perceptive of that item.

The second point concerns the framework of our discussion. I have already stressed that, for the time being, I am taking for granted the truth of physical realism. But, in turning to the issue between SDR and BRT, there is one other assumption which I shall provisionally make. For I shall provisionally assume that, whichever of these theories gives the right account of it, we do have genuine perceptual access to the physical world, and that, specifically, under this access, physical items become perceptible to us in just those kinds of circumstance, and by the use of those sense organs, that we ordinarily suppose—so that, for example, the relationship in which I now stand to the piece of paper on which I am writing is one of genuine seeing, and the relationship in which I now stand to the voices of the children in the garden is one of genuine hearing. Theoretically, this common-sense assumption could turn out to be false. For it is conceivable that the relationship in which we stand to the things which we suppose ourselves to perceive should fail to meet the requirements implicit in our actual concept of perception. But while this is a possibility which we may need to consider at some point, it will be convenient if, for the time being, we put it on one side, and work with the presumption that our perceptual capacities are what we ordinarily take them to be.

PART TWO

AN EXAMINATION OF STRONG DIRECT REALISM

1 THE ISSUE BEFORE US

I

For the time being, we are taking for granted the framework of physical realism—the view that the physical world is something whose existence is logically independent of the human mind, and something which is, in its basic character, metaphysically fundamental. Within this framework, the tradition offers two rival views of the nature of physical-item perception. Thus, on the one hand, there is the direct realist position, which claims that our perceptual access to the physical world is direct. And, on the other hand, there is the representative theory, which claims that our perceptual contact with physical items is always mediated by some form of mental representation. We saw, in Part One, that this traditional issue needs to be reshaped, since the claim of direct access is open to two crucially different interpretations, and, for each of the resulting versions of direct realism, there is, in appropriate opposition, a corresponding version of the representative theory. As a result, the traditional issue has turned into two issues: an issue between a *weak* (or *modest*) version of direct realism (WDR) and a *narrow* (or *restrictive*) version of the representative theory (NRT); and an issue between a *strong* (or *full-blooded*) version of direct realism (SDR) and a *broad* (or *flexible*) version of the representative theory (BRT). For reasons which I explained, it is the second of these issues—between SDR and BRT—that we need to consider first.

The conflict between these two positions is over the question of whether physical-item perceiving is subject to a certain form of decomposition. We have agreed to speak of a subject as *Φ-terminally* perceiving a physical item when he perceives that item and when there is no other physical item which (in relation to his perceiving of the first) he perceives more immediately.

Then BRT claims that Φ-terminal perceiving is always *psychologically mediated*. This means that, for any subject S, physical item x, and time t, if S Φ-terminally perceives x at t, then there is a psychological state (type-state) Σ, which is not in itself x-perceptive, such that S's perceiving of x at t breaks down into (is constituted by the combination of) two components: one component consists in S's being in Σ at t; the other comprises certain additional facts, though ones which do not involve anything further about S's psychological condition at t. In contrast, SDR claims that Φ-terminal perceiving is always *psychologically direct*. This means that, for any subject S, physical item x, and time t, if S Φ-terminally perceives x at t, then S's perceiving of x at t does *not* break down into two components in this BRT-way: it is *not* constituted by the combination of S's being in this sort of psychological state and these sorts of additional fact. The reason why BRT counts as the *broad* (or *flexible*) version of direct realism is that, apart from requiring it to be not, in itself, perceptive of the relevant physical item, it does not impose any conditions on the nature of the mediationally relevant psychological state, whereas the narrow (or restrictive) version, NRT, requires this state to involve the occurrence of an internal object of awareness. And the reason why SDR counts as the *strong* (or *full-blooded*) version of direct realism is that it rules out psychological mediation of any kind, whereas the weak (or modest) version, WDR, only rules out that special kind of mediation postulated by NRT.

As we noted, BRT could equally be formulated as a claim about *all* cases of physical-item perceiving, not just those that are Φ-terminal, since any form of psychological mediation which applies at the point of Φ-terminality is bound to apply to the perceiving of any further physical item which the Φ-terminal perceiving perceptually mediates. And, as we also noted, in excluding the decomposition definitive of psychological mediation, an acceptance of SDR in effect involves taking the Φ-terminal perceptual relationship to be something *psychologically fundamental*; and, from now on, we are assuming this fundamentalist view to be an integral part of the SDR-position. Finally, we noted that, in requiring the psychological state which is mediationally involved in Φ-terminal perceiving to be one which is not, in itself, perceptive *of the relevant physical item*, BRT is in effect requiring it to be one which is not, in itself, *physically perceptive at all*—a state which can be realized without there being *anything physical* perceived.

Having identified the issue that immediately concerns us, we must now turn to the task of trying to resolve it. Of course, this resolution need not take the form of simply establishing the truth of one of the rival theories and refuting the other. For it might turn out that Φ-terminal perceiving comes in two quite different forms, and that one of these forms requires an account along the lines of SDR, and the other requires an account along the lines of BRT. We cannot assume in advance that the truth will be tidy.

II

Of the two rival theories, SDR is likely to strike us, initially, as the more attractive option. This is partly because it is the view of 'common sense'— the view which is implicit in what we take for granted prior to philosophical reflection. Thus we ordinarily think of our perceptual awareness as reaching out to its external targets in a wholly straightforward way—a way which would not leave room for any kind of decomposition at the psychological level. Indeed, as we shall see, our ordinary view of the situation commits us to accepting SDR in an especially strong form. But there is also another and more significant factor which puts SDR in a favourable light. For when we do philosophically reflect on the situation, our first response is to wonder how we can even make sense of the BRT-account. What BRT claims is that, when someone Φ-terminally perceives a physical item, his perceptual contact with it breaks down into his being in a certain psychological state and certain additional facts. The psychological state is one which is not, in itself, perceptive of the relevant physical item, and this means, in practice, one which is not, in itself, physically perceptive at all. At the same time, the additional facts, whatever they comprise, do not involve anything further about the subject's current psychological condition. But if the psychological state does not, in itself, secure perceptual contact with the physical world, and if the additional facts add nothing further to the subject's psychological condition, it is hard to see how the subject's awareness can be thought of as reaching beyond the boundaries of his own mind, and so hard to see how his relationship with the relevant physical item can be thought of as genuinely perceptual. Of course, this is just how things strike us *initially*, on a quick glance at the situation set out in broad terms: it could well turn out that the difficulty evaporates once we reflect on things in more depth and in greater detail. But what at least has to be acknowledged is that, in this initial perspective, SDR presents itself as the more promising approach.[1]

---

[1] It has also, in recent years, gained considerable ground over its rival in philosophical esteem. Among those philosophers whose views we can see as implicitly endorsing it are Paul Snowdon and John McDowell (though, in the case of McDowell, it is not always easy to disen-

Despite its initial attractions, my own view is that SDR is mistaken, and this is the conclusion which I shall be trying to establish in the present phase of our discussion. The main focus of this phase will be on a certain aspect of the experiential content of perception; and the basic thrust of my argument will be that SDR cannot provide a satisfactory account of the nature of this aspect and of the role it plays, or the place it occupies, in the obtaining of the perceptual relationship. But before I turn to this, I want to consider an argument which attacks SDR from a quite different direction. In general conception, the argument coincides with one which has been strongly defended by Howard Robinson in a recent book, though the issue to which he explicitly relates it is not quite the same as the SDR–BRT conflict on which we are focusing here.[2] I too deployed the argument in an earlier book, and explicitly in relation to the present issue, and saw it then as decisive.[3] In the context of the present discussion, the pursuit of this topic will form something of a digression. But I regard the argument as sufficiently interesting in its own right to merit a detailed examination.

The argument will focus on the phenomenon of hallucination, and on how we should understand its distinction from genuine perception. A hallucinatory episode, in the sense that concerns us, is an experience which is subjectively like (introspectively indistinguishable from) an event of genuine (physical-item) perception, but in which no physical item is actually perceived. Obviously, the rival theories will see the distinction between perception and hallucination in quite different ways. BRT takes the psychological states which are fundamentally involved in perception to be ones which are not in themselves physically perceptive, and hence to be states which are logically capable of occurring in both perception and hallucination. So the BRT-theorist will say that, at least for one category of hallucinations, there is no difference between the psychological character of perceptual and hallucinatory events at the fundamental level of descrip-

tangle his views about the directness of *perception* from his views about the directness of *perceptual knowledge*). Thus see Paul Snowdon, 'Perception, vision, and causation', *Proceedings of the Aristotelian Society*, 81 (1980–1), 175–92, and John McDowell, 'Criteria, defeasibility, and knowledge', *Proceedings of the British Academy*, 68 (1982), 455–79. Both articles are reprinted in J. Dancy (ed.), *Perceptual Knowledge* (Oxford: Oxford University Press, 1988), in McDowell's case with certain revisions and additions.

[2] Howard Robinson, *Perception* (London: Routledge, 1994), ch. VI. See also his 'The general form of the argument for Berkeleian idealism', sect. IV, in J. Foster and H. Robinson (eds.), *Essays on Berkeley* (Oxford: Oxford University Press, 1985). A primitive version of the argument is found in C. D. Broad, 'Some elementary reflexions on sense-perception', *Philosophy*, 27 (1952), 3–17, though without his wholehearted endorsement.

[3] In my *Ayer* (London: Routledge & Kegan Paul, 1985), 147–9, 161.

tion. SDR, in contrast, holds that, at the point of Φ-terminality, the perceptual relationship is something psychologically fundamental. So the SDR-theorist will say that the psychological states which are fundamentally involved in perception are radically different from those involved in hallucination. He will say that such states are in themselves physically perceptive and are therefore logically incapable of realization in the context of hallucination. It is on this sharp contrast between the views of BRT and SDR that the argument turns.

2 THE CAUSAL ARGUMENT

I

Imagine that we have a minute radio-controlled device which can be attached to someone's optic nerves (perhaps, strategically, at the point of the optic chiasma), and which, thus located, can be used by an external operator to exercise full control over the neural signals which pass to the brain. This means that when the device is activated and the operator has assumed full control, the light which enters the subject's eyes has no influence on his central nervous system: the neural signals which pass to the brain are wholly determined by the functioning of the device, which in turn is fully controlled by the radio signals which the operator (no doubt with the assistance of a powerful computer) transmits to it. Now let us suppose that, without his knowledge, the device has been implanted in a particular subject, Henry, and that one afternoon, Henry is sitting on a river bank, with the controller discreetly watching events from a nearby cottage. Initially, the device is switched off, and, with his visual system working normally, Henry happens, at a certain moment, to catch sight of a salmon as it leaps out of the water. A little later, Henry's gaze is fixed on the spot where he saw the salmon leap, and the controller, judging this to be an opportune moment, switches on the device and programmes it to produce neural signals exactly like those which were photically produced by the encounter with the salmon, and its surroundings, on the earlier occasion. (How he manages to engineer this exact neural match need not concern us; if necessary, we could suppose that he succeeds, at least partly, by chance.) Let us also assume, what is perfectly plausible, that the neural signals on the two occasions have exactly the same effect on Henry's brain, so that, down to the last detail, the relevant brain state involved in the seeing of the salmon on the first occasion is reproduced on the second.

Now, following through this thought-experiment, what should we expect to happen, psychologically, as a result of the controller's intervention? Well, given their exact similarity to what occurred earlier, it seems reasonable to assume that the artificially induced neural signals and the brain responses they elicit will produce a visual experience which subjectively matches the earlier perception, so that it will be with Henry, subjectively, exactly as if he sees a qualitatively identical salmon making a qualitatively identical leap. But, crucially, it also seems reasonable to suppose that, in addition to *subjectively* matching (to being *introspectively indistinguishable*), the two resulting mental episodes will be, at the fundamental level of description, of *exactly the same psychological type*— instances of *exactly the same psychological state*. For, granted that the relevant neural factors are qualitatively the same on the two occasions, and assuming that we hold constant all the other relevant factors pertaining to the subject's current bodily and psychological condition, there seems to be nothing in the causal influences at work which might lead to a difference in psychological outcome. But we know that, on the second occasion, the visual experience is purely hallucinatory: there is no salmon there to be seen; and, in any case, with the device activated, the subject's visual access to his external environment is automatically severed. So, if we suppose that the psychological states which are fundamentally involved on the two occasions are the same, we have to conclude that the state involved on the first occasion, in the context of seeing the salmon, is not *in itself* physically perceptive: it is not one whose realization, on its own, suffices for the perception of a physical item. And this forces us to say that the visual contact with the salmon, or with that momentary stage of the relevant salmon surface-portion which is Φ-terminally seen, breaks down into two components in accordance with BRT—one component consisting in Henry's being in this further, and not in itself physically perceptive, psychological state, the other comprising certain additional facts, but ones which do not involve anything further about his psychological condition at the relevant time. These additional facts will presumably, at least in part, be to do with the qualitative relationship of the state to the external environment, and with the causal role of the environment, and, in particular, of the relevant portion-stage of the salmon, in bringing about the relevant realization of this state in Henry.

Now this is just one case. But if it is sound, the reasoning involved will presumably apply with equal force to *any* case of physical-item perception, since, for any such case, we could envisage a similar device and tell a similar story. So we have, here, a model for a quite general argument against the

SDR-account and in favour of BRT. This argument can be set out as follows:

1. For any physical-item perception, we can envisage a situation in which, by artificially inducing the same causally relevant neural conditions in the same subject on a subsequent occasion (these conditions covering both the process in the sensory nerves and the resulting brain response), we bring about a subjectively matching (introspectively indistinguishable) hallucination. Moreover, we can envisage this without departing from reasonable assumptions about how the world actually works.

2. Given the coincidence of the neural factors involved on the two occasions, and of all other simultaneous bodily and psychological factors that might be causally relevant, it is reasonable to suppose that the outcomes themselves would be, at the fundamental level of psychological description, of exactly the same psychological type.

3. SDR is committed to saying that the psychological state which is fundamentally involved in any instance of perception is, in itself, physically perceptive—a state whose realization, on its own, suffices for the perceiving of a physical item. For if the state were not in itself physically perceptive, the Φ-terminal perceptual relationship would have to decompose in the psychologically mediational way postulated by BRT.

4. But, trivially, the psychological state involved in any case of hallucination is not in itself physically perceptive, since there is no physical item which is even perceived.

5. So the supposition that, in the case envisaged, the two psychological outcomes would be, at the fundamental level of description, qualitatively the same commits us to rejecting SDR and offering a BRT (psychologically mediational) account of the perceptual relationship involved.

Let us refer to this as the *Causal Argument from Hallucination*, or, for short, the *Causal Argument*.

This argument may be thought to have certain echoes of a line of reasoning which I mentioned in Part One—a line of reasoning on which we passed no judgement, but which was envisaged as something which might at least *tempt* us to accept the narrow—classic empiricist—version of the representative theory.[4] The temptation turned on two suggestions, which formed, as it were, the tentative premises of the reasoning. The first was that what enables hallucination to replicate the subjective character of physical-item perception is that, while not physically perceptive, it at least brings a real sensible object before the mind—an object which, given that it is not an ingredient of the physical world, would have to be thought of as internal to the subject's own awareness. The second suggestion was that, given that perception and hallucination have the same subjective character—that they cannot be distinguished from the standpoint of introspection—it is plausible to think of them as having the same psychological character through and through. Put together, the two suggestions invite us to accept, as the conclusion which they jointly yield, that, even in the case of perception (*physical-item* perception), what is immediately before the mind is an internal object of awareness, and that any contact with the external environment is channelled through the occurrence of this object in a perceptual-mediational way.

Now it is important to recognize that the Causal Argument, while indeed containing certain *echoes* of this line of reasoning, differs from it in two crucial respects. The first point of difference is that it is arguing for a weaker conclusion. For, instead of offering support for the *narrow* version of the representative theory, it only seeks to vindicate the *broader* (more flexible) version—the version which insists on psychological mediation, but does not impose any conditions on the nature of the mediating state involved. And, in consequence, it does not require us to accept the first of the suggestions which featured in the other line of reasoning—that hallucination involves the bringing of some real sensible object before the mind. The second point is that, instead of just relying (as in the other reasoning) on the supposed plausibility of assuming that, where mental episodes have the same subjective character, they have the same psychological character through and through, the Causal Argument focuses on a situation where there is an additional and special reason for expecting the perceptive and hallucinatory episodes to be of exactly the same psychological kind, namely that they are generated by neural conditions of exactly the same kind. This is crucial. If it were just a matter of his opponent insisting, in the abstract, that there is no room for psychological differences where there are no subjective differences, the SDR-theorist would find it easy to demur.

---

[4] Part One, Section 2, II.

And, indeed, his own account of the psychological nature of perception would give him a rationale for doing so. For if the Φ-terminal relationship is psychologically fundamental, and if the physical item perceived is external to the mind, we can hardly expect the full nature of the psychological situation, when that relationship obtains, to be introspectively transparent; and, of course, it would be blatantly question-begging just to invoke a principle of transparency as a way of excluding SDR from the start.[5] But what the theorist has to accept, in a case like that of Henry, seems altogether more problematic. To maintain his account of perception, he has to insist, here, as quite generally, that the psychological states which are fundamentally involved in perception and hallucination are different (since otherwise the perceptual relationship would have to decompose in the psychologically mediational way); but he is now forced to apply this result to a case where, on the face of it, the factors which are directly causally involved in bringing about the perceptive and hallucinatory events are exactly the same. And it is this which makes his situation, prima facie, so awkward.

The difficulty, it must be stressed, is not just that what is envisaged violates the principle of *same type of proximate cause, same type of immediate effect*. If this were all that was involved, the SDR-theorist need not be too concerned. After all, there are other familiar cases, drawn from particle physics, where this principle, or putative principle, seems not to hold—where it seems that the same conditions can, on different occasions, give rise to different outcomes. If God can play dice with fundamental particles, why not with mental responses too? But what is particularly problematic in the present case is that the way in which this principle fails (or seems to fail) is systematic with respect to something else. For the nature of the psychological event which the central-nervous process produces does not just vary: it varies, in a regular way, with how the process itself was brought about. Thus let us continue to focus on the case of Henry. Whenever the device is switched off, the subject is able to see things in the normal way: light from the environment enters his eyes, sets up the relevant process in his central nervous system, and makes the scene before him visible. Whenever the device is activated and the nervous processes are wholly controlled by the operator, any resulting experiences are, at best, hallucinations

---

[5] This is not to deny that such a principle (sometimes in a modified form) has been widely accepted by philosophers. Descartes, indeed, took introspective transparency to be the defining feature of the mental (*cogitatio*). Thus see his *The Principles of Philosophy*, Part 1, Principle IX, in *The Philosophical Writings of Descartes*, trans. J. Cottingham, R. Stoothof, and D. Murdoch, vol. I (Cambridge: Cambridge University Press, 1985).

(I say 'at best' because, even to qualify as hallucinations, the experiences are required to have the subjective character of genuine perception). So, for a given relevant type of central-nervous process, the SDR-theorist has to say that this process *always* issues in one type of psychological event (the real-ization of a psychological state which is in itself physically perceptive) when it is brought about in the normal, light-induced way, and *always* issues in a different type of psychological event (the realization of a psy-chological state which is not in itself physically perceptive) when it is brought about in the artificial, device-induced way. It is this which makes the situation for the theorist so difficult. By the time the psychological event is due to be produced, there is no physical record of how the process was started. So by what mechanism does the mind adjust its response to fit the character of the remote cause? How, as it were, does the mind know whether the central-nervous process was caused in the normal or the arti-ficial way before selecting its response? On the face of it, the right conclu-sion to draw is the one drawn by the Causal Argument—that the type of psychological event produced by a given type of process does not vary in accordance with how that process was itself brought about, and that, even in the case of perception, the psychological state which is fundamentally involved is one that is not in itself physically perceptive. And this would require us to say that, whenever there is perceptual contact, it breaks down into the relevant types of component in the manner stipulated by BRT.

Thus expounded, the Causal Argument looks compelling. And, as I indi-cated at the outset, there was a time when I thought it so myself and invoked it to justify a rejection of SDR. Subsequent reflection, however, has led me to alter my estimate of its worth. The reasons for this shift are what I shall shortly elaborate. But first, I want to take note of a quite different way in which it might be thought that the argument can be resisted.

II

In my explication of it in Part One, I drew attention to the fact that, although it takes the Φ-terminal perceptual relationship to be something *psychologically* fundamental, SDR does not exclude the possibility of a reductive account of mentality itself—an account which claims that psy-chological facts, or some relevant subset of them, are ultimately constituted by non-psychological facts.[6] Now, in general, as I remarked, we should not expect the availability of this reductivist option to have much relevance to

[6] See Part One, Section 3, I.

the issues that concern us. After all, the dispute between SDR and BRT turns on how things are to be construed *at the psychological level*, and, for the most part, the considerations which bear on it are bound to be ones which arise *at this level*. But, with respect to the present issue, the availability of the option does, in fact, make a significant difference. For there is a way in which the SDR-theorist could pursue the option which would entirely dispose of the Causal Argument. It is not that *all* forms of psychological reduction would be of assistance to him here. For some—indeed, some of the most familiar—are themselves committed to BRT. This is true, for example, of the case where the reduction is effected by a behaviourist analysis of psychological states, since the psychological states involved in perception and hallucination are not distinguishable in behavioural terms. But there is one particular way of pursuing the reductive approach which is available to the SDR-theorist and which would enable him to side-step the Causal Argument altogether.

To see what this is we need to start by spelling out just why it is that the Causal Argument does not raise any problems *for BRT*. The reason is not that BRT does not recognize, in any sense, a psychological difference between perception and hallucination; how could anyone deny that the state of *genuinely* perceiving something is different from the state of *merely seeming* to perceive something? The reason is, rather, that BRT does not see this difference as pertaining to the states that are *psychologically fundamental*. Thus the BRT-theorist will say that, in the case where they subjectively match, the perceptual and hallucinatory events have the same fundamental psychological character, and that the difference in their perceptive status derives from other (non-psychological) factors—in particular, from the different ways in which the events have been brought about. So, in the case of Henry, he will say that the event of seeing the salmon and the subsequent hallucinatory episode are events of the same fundamental psychological type, but that the first qualifies as perceptive and the second as hallucinatory because of the different ways in which the optical nerve firings leading up to them have been induced—in the one case, by light from the salmon, retinally registered in the normal way, in the other, by the use of the device. There is no opportunity for a deployment of the Causal Argument because there are no differences of psychological outcome at the fundamental level of description.

Now the way in which the SDR-theorist could exploit the reductivist option is, in effect, by replicating this BRT-approach at the sub-psychological level. The account he would need to advance involves three claims. The first would be a claim of token-identity. It would assert that each mental event, or at least each mental event of the relevant (perceptual or hallu-cinatory) kind, is (is identical with) an event in the subject's brain. Note that, being merely an assertion of *token*-identity—identifying particular mental events with particular physical events—this claim does not imply that the psychological character of a relevant event is, or is an aspect of, its physical character. Nor even does it imply that, within the relevant class of events, similarities and differences in psychological and physical character are correlated. The second claim would be that the psychological character of a mental event, or a mental event of the relevant kind, is not something metaphysically fundamental, but something wholly constituted by certain physical facts about it. It is this claim which makes the relevant account *reductive*. Token-identity itself would allow the psychological and physical aspects of mental events to enjoy the same metaphysical status. But the additional claim of constitution represents the psychological aspects as metaphysically derivative from the physical: it represents them as obtain-ing in virtue of, and their obtaining as nothing over and above, the obtain-ing of the physical. The third claim is an elaboration of the second. It is that, within the relevant class of mental events, part of what gives a particular event its psychological character are facts about the way in which it has been brought about, and, in particular, the nature of that phase of the causal process leading up to the relevant neural process. It is this claim which allows a replication of the approach of BRT. Thus, as in the case of BRT, it allows one to say that, given an event of perceiving, part of what makes it perceptive of the relevant physical item is the fact that the causal process leads back, in an appropriate way, to that item, and correspond-ingly, that one way in which a mental event can be rendered hallucinatory is by there being no such physical item to which the causal process appro-priately leads back. The crucial difference between the BRT and the reduc-tive cases is that, whereas under BRT the distinction between what is derivative and what is fundamental occurs at the psychological level, on the reductive account it becomes a distinction between what obtains at the psychological level and what obtains physically. And this means that, unlike the BRT-theorist, the reductivist can insist that, at the psychological level, the states fundamentally involved in perception and hallucination are dif-ferent. It is this which makes the approach available to the proponent of SDR.

It is clear why adopting this reductive account would immediately side-step the Causal Argument. On the one hand, when we focus on the situa-tion at the metaphysically fundamental level—the level of what obtains and occurs physically—there is no difference in outcome in the perceptive and hallucinatory cases. The same type of neural process gives rise to the same type of brain event, whether the process has been brought about in the normal (perception-yielding) way, or by some form of artificial intervention, as in the case of the device. On the other hand, when we focus on how things work out psychologically, we do discern a difference in the type of outcome, and indeed one which is fundamental relative to the psychological framework of description. But the difference does not present itself as in any way problematic, since it is immediately attributable to a difference in the underlying physical factors by which the relevant psychological facts are constituted. Thus, in the case of Henry, if P is the perceptual event and H the hallucinatory, then P and H would have the same intrinsic physical character (in line with what we would expect, given the absence of any difference in the character of their proximate physical causes). But P would qualify, psychologically, as a seeing of the salmon, in virtue of the role of the salmon in bringing it about, while H would qualify as a mere hallucination, because of the absence of any physical item which plays such a role. And, in accordance with the needs of SDR, this psychological difference would count as fundamental at the psychological level of description.

There is no denying, then, that, by adopting the envisaged account, the SDR-theorist would entirely avoid the challenge of the Causal Argument: there would be no more opportunity for the deployment of such an argument in this new situation than there was in the case of BRT. What still has to be decided is whether the account is acceptable in other ways. And this promises to be a much more complex and controversial question.

One bar to any *immediate* endorsement of the account is that, even if we are happy with mental reductivism as such, we have not yet been given a proper idea of how the envisaged forms of constitution are supposed to work. Two areas in particular—both concerned with the perceptual case—call for a much more detailed explication of the constitutional situation if there is to be any prospect of seeing what is envisaged as acceptable.

In the first place, we would need to be told how, in the case of perception, the claim of constitution can be given a rationale without its resulting in a version of BRT. The *obvious* way of trying to understand how a brain event could qualify as physically perceptive in virtue of certain physical facts about it would be to see these facts as logically generating the perceptual fact in two stages. At stage one, a certain subset of the facts would suffice to endow the event with a certain representational character—with the property of representing a certain type of environmental item or situation. This stage would most likely be achieved by deploying some kind of functionalist analysis of the representational properties in question, so that an event would be thought of as having such a property in virtue of the typical functional role of events of its intrinsic type in the subject's causal system. At stage two, the event would derive its perceptive status (as the perceiving of a certain physical item) from the combination of its representational character and certain further physical facts—facts in which the properties of the relevant physical item and its causal role in bringing about the event would prominently feature. But, on the face of it, this way of trying to understand the constitutional situation would result in a version of BRT. For it seems that the assignment of a representational character to the brain event at stage one would allow us to think of the subject as being in a correspondingly representational psychological state (a state which represented a certain type of environmental item or situation, without being in itself physically perceptive); and then what is envisaged at stage two could be recast as a claim of psychological mediation, to the effect that the subject's perceiving of the relevant physical item is constituted by his being in this psychological state, together with the other physical facts. Now it may be that there is some other way of making sense of the constitutional situation—a way which sustains an SDR rather than a BRT position at the psychological level. Thus perhaps there is some way of seeing how a brain event could qualify as perceptive *without* giving it a representational character. Or perhaps there is some way of making sense of its representational character as something *sub*-psychological—so that the psychological level is only reached once the perceptive status is in place. But if there are alternatives, we would need to have them spelt out before we could begin to take the reductive proposal seriously.

The second area where there is a particular need for more elaboration relates to a point that came up earlier. When we first turned to the issue between SDR and BRT, we noted that one of the factors which makes SDR initially the more attractive option is that it is not clear how we can even make sense of what BRT envisages.[7] For if the psychological states which are fundamentally involved in cases of supposed perception are not, in themselves, physically perceptive—if they are equally capable of occurring in the context of hallucination—it is hard to see how we can think of the subject's awareness as genuinely reaching to the external environment at all. Now, at the time, it seemed that SDR would not be subject to a similar worry, precisely because it postulated a perceptual relationship which was psychologically fundamental. The reaching out to the external environment was thought of as something secure in its own right, without having

---

[7] Part Two, Section 1, II.

to be sustained by more fundamental factors. But, by combining his fundamentalist thesis at the psychological level with a reductive account of the psychological facts themselves, the SDR-theorist would alter the character of the intuitive situation. For if the psychological relationship with the environment is ultimately constituted by physical facts in the way envisaged, there is the same prima facie difficulty in seeing how it can qualify as genuinely perceptual. How can we think of the subject's awareness as genuinely reaching out to the environment if, in the final analysis, the only fundamental connection between it and him is causal? What would justify the claim that the physical factors secure a genuine *perceptual* link, rather than simply allowing for the acquisition of environmental information? These queries may well have answers—as their counterparts may under BRT. But the answers will have to be in place before there is any chance of our finding the proposed account acceptable.

In both these ways, then—and others too—we would need to be given a much fuller account of how the reductivist approach is supposed to work before we could think of accepting it. But even if this account is available, there remains the more fundamental issue of the correctness of mental reductivism itself. Certainly, the quest for a reductive account of mentality has become very fashionable in recent years, mainly because the alternative is thought to generate insuperable problems—for example, about our epistemological access to the minds of others, and about our understanding of how mind and body causally interact. But, against this, it is also widely acknowledged that reductivism faces its own difficulties. Perhaps the chief of these is that it is hard to see how any version of it could hope to do justice to the subjective character of our mental lives—to what it feels like, from the inside, to be a conscious subject and to undergo specific forms of conscious state. And, of course, the area of perception and hallucination is a paradigm locus for the deployment of this objection, since the subjective aspects of these forms of mentality are particularly conspicuous. Now all this is a large and complex topic, and clearly one which I cannot hope to deal with, in any detail, in the context of the present investigation. If I am to be able to give proper attention to the specific topic of perception, I am forced, in this context, by and large, to put the general issues of the mind on one side. On the other hand, these issues are ones which I have discussed and tried to settle elsewhere, in a book which attempts to establish a radically dualist conception of the mind, and to discredit the various forms of reductivist and materialist alternative.[8] The arguments of that book are

---

[8] In my *The Immaterial Self* (London: Routledge, 1991). I should stress, as I do in that book,

ones which I still fully endorse. So, although I cannot pursue the issue of reductivism here, I am content simply to appeal to those arguments, and draw the appropriate conclusion. As I see it, then, the reductive proposal has to be rejected, because mental reductivism of any kind can be shown to fail.

This, then, is my verdict on the reductivist approach. As it happens, it is not something on which I need to put any great weight in the context of the present discussion. If, as once, I wanted to defend the Causal Argument and use it as a weapon against SDR, then the rejection of the reductive response to it would be crucial, and this, in turn, might depend on showing that any reductive account of mentality is misconceived. But this is no longer my situation. For, as I shall shortly explain, I now think that, even when we consider the issue in purely psychological terms—leaving aside any question of the status of mentality itself—the Casual Argument fails. And although I still consider SDR to be mistaken, I shall be relying on a quite different form of argument to refute it.

The reason why I have paused to draw attention to the reductivist option is for the light it sheds on the dialectical situation. What it reveals is that the Causal Argument only has a chance of succeeding against a background in which a certain way of construing the relevant forms of mentality has already been excluded; and, in this way, it brings out a crucial limitation on what the argument on its own can hope to achieve. This limitation was not apparent at the start, when our attention was confined to how things presented themselves in the perspective of the psychological framework; and it is something which proponents of the argument are liable to miss.

III

Let us assume that the reductive response to the Causal Argument fails. The question which we must now consider is whether there is any other response which the SDR-theorist can make—one which does not require him to think of the relevant forms of mentality as reducible to something else, one which does not require him to step outside the psychological framework in which the argument itself is formulated. As we left things earlier—before our digression into the reductivist issue—the argument was looking powerful: what the theorist was obliged to envisage seemed

---

that a dualist conception *of the mind* falls short of *full* dualism, since it leaves open issues about the nature and status of the physical world. Thus it is compatible with mentalist and idealist accounts of the physical world.

very hard to accept. But we can hardly claim to have looked at the situation in any depth.

Two points, I think, are initially clear, and set the constraints for any form of response that might prove acceptable. First, if his position is to retain any plausibility, the SDR-theorist does indeed have to find some explanation of why the same type of neural process has different types of outcome in the two types of case. It is true that there would be nothing *logically* incoherent in just insisting on the difference in outcome, but leaving it unexplained, or (still more brazenly) denying that it is capable of explanation at all. But such a response would not leave his position credible. Whether or not it is ultimately conclusive, the Causal Argument reveals a major problem for his position, and, if he wants to be taken seriously, the theorist has to find some way of eliminating, or at least diminishing, it. Secondly, any satisfactory explanation of why the single type of neural process has different types of outcome in the two types of case must, in some way, represent the nature of the outcome not merely as *varying with*, but as *depending on*, the nature of the remote cause. It is true that we can envisage, in the abstract, other possibilities: for example, it could be claimed that the correlation between type of outcome and type of remote cause was the product of a pre-established harmony, Leibniz-style. But, in practice, any form of explanation other than one which postulates some kind of dependence of the nature of the outcome on the nature of the earlier causal circumstances, would not be a serious contender.

So, given these constraints, can the theorist find a satisfactory account of the situation—an effective line of defence against the argument? It seems to me that he can. In fact, the account which I have in mind is one which is already suggested by the very structure of the problem which confronts him, though its claim to merit serious consideration may not be initially apparent.

The problem, as we have said, is that the psychological outcome varies, in a regular way, according to whether the neural process which leads up to it is brought about by the normal or by the artificial method; and since the neural process does not contain any record of the way in which it was caused (otherwise it would not be exactly the same type of process in the two cases), there seems to be no room for a mechanism by which the correlation between the type of outcome and the type of remote cause could be ensured. Now, for a theorist who is determined to hold his ground, there is, in the abstract, an obvious response available. For he can say that, although the remote cause does not stamp its character on the *intervening process*, it causally affects the outcome *directly*. In other words, he can claim

that, at the point when the psychological event is about to occur, the factors which directly contribute, causally, to its occurrence and character
include not just the current state of the brain, but also certain aspects of
the preceding causal process, including, crucially, certain aspects of the way
in which the neural process leading up to the realization of the brain state
has itself been brought about. This would mean that there was, after all, no
violation of the principle *same type of proximate cause, same type of immediate effect*, since what we have hitherto been describing as the remote cause
would become *directly* relevant to the outcome, and therefore an element
of the *proximate* cause. More precisely, the process which leads up to the
neural process would play a double causal role. It would still continue to
play, in the straightforward way, the role of what brings about the neural
process, and, on that score, would indeed count as the *remote* cause with
respect to the psychological outcome. But it would also, as part of the
whole physical causal process leading up to the event in the brain, combine
with this event to exert a direct influence on the psychological outcome—
in particular, to fix it as something perceptive or as something hallucinatory—and, on that score, would count as part of the *proximate* cause.

Once again, we can best illustrate what is envisaged by focusing on the
pair of episodes in the case of Henry. On the first occasion, light from the
salmon, and from the relevant surroundings, passes through the subject's
eyes and induces a certain pattern of retinal responses; these induce a certain pattern of firings in the optic nerves, which in turn induce the realization of a certain brain state; the realization of this state is immediately
followed (or perhaps accompanied) by an event of visual perception, the
seeing of the salmon. On the second occasion, radio signals are transmit-
ted by the controller and induce a certain pattern of responses in the
device; these induce a pattern of firings in the optic nerves exactly like the
pattern which occurred on the first occasion, and these firings in turn
induce the realization of the same brain state; this is immediately followed
(or accompanied) by an event of visual hallucination, which subjectively
matches the earlier perception. Let us call the earlier causal process from
salmon to brain event 'C_1', and the later causal process from controller to
brain event 'C_2'. What is being envisaged, then, is that the character of the
psychological outcome in the two episodes is determined by the combination of the character of what occurs in the brain (which holds constant
between them) and the character of the relevant causal process (which
varies)—so that, on the first occasion, the realization of the relevant brain
state, together with the fact that this realization has been brought about by
a causal process of the C_1-type, causes Henry to see the salmon (the psy-

chological state involved being in itself physically perceptive), while, on the second occasion, the realization of exactly the same brain state, together with the fact that this realization has been brought about by a causal process of the C2-type, causes Henry to have a hallucinatory experience, as of seeing a salmon (the psychological state involved being not in itself physically perceptive). So although the relevant brain state does not preserve the information about whether its realization has been induced by the normal or by the artificial method, the very causal history leading up to its realization—including, crucially, that part of the causal history leading up to the optical-neural process which precedes it—is taken to be a directly causally relevant factor in determining what kind of psychological event ensues.

This is what the determined theorist can say. And at least there can be no denying that it offers an explanation of what needed to be explained—of why the nature of the psychological outcome varies, systematically, according to the way in which the neural process is brought about. Its prima facie drawback is that the causal mechanism it postulates, by way of explanation, seems bizarre. Everything else we know about the world suggests that causation does not work in this sort of way: it always works in a way which is not only temporally *directed* (from earlier to later), but temporally *continuous*, so that earlier events only have an influence on non-contiguous later events by affecting the chain of events that intervene. The idea that earlier events may have a *direct* influence on what happens after a temporal interval—an interval in which any record of the relevant features of those earlier events has been lost—seems very strange, and perhaps hardly credible. In short, it might be thought that, while the account explains the correlation, and so in that respect removes a source of puzzlement, it does so in a way which creates its own unacceptable puzzle—the puzzle of how the earlier causal history could have the sort of influence attributed to it.

But we must be careful here. It is true that, by the standards of how causation generally works, the account proposed is highly unusual. But, even before this account is imposed on it, the situation which the SDR-theorist postulates has certain distinctive features which should alert us to the possibility that our ordinary modes of causal explanation may fail to apply.

There are two relevant points here. One is simply that the area of reality to which the envisaged situation belongs is different from that which provides our ordinary paradigms of causation. These paradigms, in relation to which the postulated causal mechanism seems strange, are drawn exclusively from the *physical* realm: they concern the ways in which one physical event or set of conditions brings about another. But the situation for which the theorist is seeking an account concerns the relationship between the physical and the *mental*—between the types of physical process leading up to perception and hallucination and the nature of the psychological outcome itself. It is clearly unwarranted just to *assume* that forms of causality which are operative in the physical realm will be operative in the psychophysical realm as well. The psychophysical case needs to be examined on its merits.

The other point, and the more crucial one, is that, even when we put aside the problem raised by the Causal Argument, it turns out that the special form of causation envisaged, however strange-seeming in the abstract, is just what we would expect in the case of perception as the SDR-theorist construes it. This is a complex point, and we shall need to unpack it in stages.

In standard cases of causation, when some physical object is caused to come into a certain state, and when the state in question is the one that is *fundamentally* involved (so that the object's being in it is not constituted by its being in some further state, together with certain additional facts), this state does not consist in, or inherently include, a relationship to something earlier. In the domain of such cases—the standard cases—we would indeed be surprised, and perhaps perplexed, if we came across an instance in which (as it seemed) the object's coming into the relevant state directly causally depended not just on conditions obtaining at the time, but also on the nature of the process leading up to them. But in the case of perception, as the SDR-theorist construes it, the situation is quite different. The subject is caused to come into a psychological state which, even in its fundamental form, is inherently a relationship with an earlier item—a state which, on its own, suffices to put the subject into perceptual contact with a physical event or object-stage at an earlier time. And this does not just mean that the relevant state is one which cannot be realized without putting the subject into contact with *some* earlier physical item. It means that there is a *particular* earlier item of which the state is, in itself, perceptive; for it is precisely the Φ-terminal *relationship* (between the subject and the perceived physical item) which is held to be psychologically fundamental—to be what resists decomposition at the psychological level. It is hardly surprising that this aspect of the situation should make a crucial difference to our expectations about the nature of the causal process involved.

Part of the difference is contained in the merely logical point that, if a psychological state is inherently (in itself) perceptive of a particular earlier item, then nothing could directly bring about a realization of this state unless it included, or operated in a field of conditions which included, the existence of that item. For, without the existence of the item, there would be no such state to be even a candidate for realization. But there is also a more significant factor. For any subject and time, there is a multiplicity of physical items which are available for Φ-terminal perception by that subject at that time. Given that a particular item gets perceived, it is natural to suppose that there is something which causally accounts for the selection. And if we accept that the psychological state involved is *inherently* perceptive of the relevant item, and so accept that the existence of the item has, in any case, to be included in, or in the contextual conditions accompanying, anything which directly brings about a realization of the state, then it is natural to envisage this item as playing a direct role in that selection. It is natural to envisage it as making a direct causal contribution to the realization of the relevant state, and as doing so, in particular, in a way which ensures that the state which gets realized is perceptive of *it*, rather than of something else—a way which targets the subject's perceptual awareness on to itself. But not only is this what it is natural to envisage, given the theory of perception involved; it is also, crucially, just what is needed, from the standpoint of the theory, to make sense of the actual facts of human perception. After all, the form of the targeting of Φ-terminal perceptions on to physical items is, over the domain of cases, highly systematic: which item gets perceived is predictable on the basis of the environmental situation and the nature of the causal process from the environment to the subject's sensory system. For example, it is predictable that the momentary stage of a physical object which is Φ-terminally seen on any occasion is precisely that stage whose illumination is responsible for the causally relevant photic input to the eye, and thereby responsible for the causally relevant events in the subject's nervous system. Clearly this sort of regularity is not just accidental: it must have some explanation. But presumably, from the standpoint of SDR, the explanation must turn crucially on the kind of direct causal role which the relevant item plays in the targeting of the perceiving on to it. The predictability of the targeting must in some way flow from the predictability of the special influence which the item itself exerts.

But granted that the SDR-theorist has to see the perceived item as playing a direct causal role in the targeting of the perception on to it, the crucial question now is: what form would this role take? What specific contribution should we envisage the theorist as assigning to the item? Well, in part, this contribution could turn on the mere qualitative fit between the item and the content of the psychological state. For it could be that, independently of the role of the item, the other factors which directly causally bear on the psychological outcome fix the qualitative content of the state in a way which restricts its perceptive potential to objects of a certain type—a type to which the item in question conforms. But even if this qualitative restriction is part of the explanation, it cannot be the whole story, since, it will not, typically, suffice to limit the potential targets of the perceiving to just one thing. Thus while, on a given occasion, Henry Φ-terminally sees a particular portion-stage of the salmon's surface, there are obviously many other momentary items—in particular, different but qualitatively indistinguishable portion-stages drawn from the same salmon—which are qualitatively just as appropriate. And, of course, the same point would apply to almost all other cases of perception. Nor can we make up the extra factors here by merely taking account of how the various candidate-items are spatiotemporally related to the subject. For, by focusing on circumstances involving such things as mirrors or telescopes—not to mention the more complicated cases of televisions and telephones—it is easy to envisage situations where what is Φ-terminally perceived does not stand to the subject in what would normally count as the appropriate spatiotemporal relationship, and also to envisage situations where something with the appropriate character and spatiotemporal location is not what is Φ-terminally perceived. And, in any case, even where the spatiotemporal relationship involved in a perception is of the normally appropriate type (normally appropriate, that is, relative to the qualitative content of the perception and the character of the perceived item), the significance of this relationship, as a factor in the targeting, is clearly dependent on its role in facilitating the right kind of *causal* link. This is why, in the case of visual perception, the greater the spatial distance between the Φ-terminally perceived item and the subject, the greater the temporal distance too. Thus, when we survey the night sky, the star-stages which are currently visible to us are ones which are sufficiently earlier to have a causal impact on our current senses—even if there are other stages, of the appropriate type and in the same direction, which are temporally closer.

How then can the theorist account for the targeting? How can he see the relevant item as appropriately featuring in the conditions which causally suffice for a perception of it? The answer is now surely clear. He must invoke, and appropriately apply, the very account which we have already envisaged as his response to the Causal Argument. Thus he must say that, whenever someone Φ-terminally perceives a physical item, the nature of the psychological event which occurs directly causally depends not only on the brain state whose realization immediately precedes it, but also on the whole causal process from item to brain; and he must say that, as a crucial aspect of this direct dependence, the role of the item as the initiator of the process is (or is in the context of certain other factors) what is causally responsible for its role as perceptual object—responsible for ensuring that the resulting perception is a perception *of it*. In its original context, this way of envisaging the causal situation struck us as bizarre. But though it is strange by the standards of ordinary causation, it turns out to be so in a way which, quite independently of the problem raised by the Causal Argument, exactly fits, and satisfies the needs of, the distinctive nature of the psychological phenomenon whose causation is at issue. We should think of it, then, not as something which the theorist is *driven* to accept, as a desperate remedy against this argument, but as an integral part of the way in which he already understands the psychological nature of the perceptual relationship—as part and parcel of what is involved in his taking this relationship to be, at the point of Φ-terminality, psychologically fundamental.

In its earlier form, of course, this account was not just concerned with the case of perception, but with the case of hallucination too: it was an attempt to explain why the same type of central nervous process gives rise to different types of psychological outcome according to the way in which the process is itself brought about. But if the account is successful for the case of perception, it *eo ipso* has application to the case of hallucination as well. Thus if the psychological state involved in perception is always in itself perceptive of a particular physical item, and if a causally indispensable part of what directs the subject on to a particular target is the fact that a particular physical item plays a certain type of causal role in bringing about the relevant brain event, then the lack of that sort of causal factor—there not being any physical item which plays that sort of role—is bound to have a causal influence in the other direction. It is bound to ensure that, whatever the subjective character of the experience produced, no physical item is perceived—not even if there happens to be a physical item of the appropriate type in the appropriate place.

There would still be the question of what psychological nature the theorist should ascribe to such hallucinatory experiences. His theory commits him to saying that, even at the fundamental level of psychological description, they differ in character from episodes of perception. But should he take them to be merely depleted versions of what takes place in perception—a hallucinatory state coinciding with the subjective component of a perceptive state? Or should he rather think of them as involving some additional *sui generis* element, such as the occurrence of an internal object of awareness? The first of these approaches would, I think, be the more attractive one from the theorist's standpoint. For given that there is a wide range of quite different hallucinogenic ways of bringing about the relevant types of neural process, and that the only interesting thing which they have in common is their deviance from what is involved in the case of perception, it seems more natural to think of these ways as only having a *negative* influence on the psychological outcome. But this is not an issue which we need to pursue at this stage. Nor could we sensibly do so. For whatever account of hallucination the theorist adopts will have to fit in with, and be conditioned by, his account of the experiential content of perception—a topic which we shall be considering in its own right presently.

In conclusion, then, it seems to me that, notwithstanding the *prima facie* force of the Causal Argument, the SDR-theorist does have a reasonable line of defence, and one which he can employ without having to invoke any kind of reductive account of the relevant forms of mentality. He can explain the seemingly puzzling difference in the psychological outcomes by insisting that, contrary to initial appearances, these outcomes are *directly responsive* to differences in the causally relevant conditions (so that there is no departure from the expectation of *same type of proximate cause, same type of immediate effect*); and he can do this in a way which, even if strange by the standard of our ordinary causal paradigms, is consonant with his own distinctive view of the nature of perception. It might be retorted that, in being thus consonant, this response would just serve to bring out the method in the theorist's madness: the strangeness of his causal hypothesis would just reflect, and underline, the strangeness—*unacceptable* strangeness—of his conception of the perceptual relationship. But if this is so, it still needs to be demonstrated: there would have to be some independent argument to show that the relevant conception was unacceptable. And, indeed, so far from being under a prima facie cloud, this conception has, as we noted at the outset, the support of both our ordinary ways of thought and our first reflective intuitions. Clearly, the onus is on those who would reject it to point out its faults.

IV

Finally, we can now see, in retrospect, that the initial plausibility of the Causal Argument was an artefact of the way in which it was presented. The argument was formulated with a specific reference to the distinction between perception and hallucination, and, as things were presented, this focus seemed appropriate. Thus the problem for the SDR-theorist seemed to be that, on the one hand, his theory commits him to saying that the psychological states fundamentally involved in perception are in themselves perceptive, and hence different from the states involved in hallucination, while, on the other, the neural processes which lead up to the occurrence of the perceptive and hallucinatory psychological episodes could well be qualitatively identical, since the hallucinatory episodes could be brought about by inducing the normal processes in a deviant way. And it then seemed difficult for the theorist to explain the mechanics of this—the same type of neural process issuing in different types of psychological outcome, and the difference in outcome systematically correlating with the differ- ence in the character of the remote cause. But what this presentation of the issue concealed was that the very factors which seem to create the problem are already present in the sphere of perception itself. For it is not just that SDR takes the psychological states which are fundamentally involved in perception to be in themselves *perceptive* (of some physical item or other). It takes them to be perceptive *of particular items*: it claims that, for each relevant state Σ, there is a specific physical item x, such that Σ is, in itself, perceptive (Φ-terminally perceptive) *of x*. And this means that, from the SDR-standpoint, the sort of situation which arises with respect to the dis- tinction between perception and hallucination also arises, routinely, with respect to the distinction between different perceptions. For it means that, even where the causal processes from item to brain are qualitatively iden- tical on two occasions, the psychological outcomes will be qualitatively dif- ferent, simply because the two psychological states involved will be inherently perceptive of different things. If the Causal Argument had been initially viewed in this broader perspective, it would never have seemed compelling. For, as it occurs in the perceptual context, the situation does not create even a prima facie problem for the theorist. Rather, it serves to make clear the sort of causal account that his distinctive understanding of perception requires—an account which sees the whole causal process, from item to brain, as directly responsible for the nature of the perceptual outcome, and, in particular, sees the identity of the initiating item as causally fixing the identity of the perceptual target. This is an account which the theorist can accept, without embarrassment, prior to any issue over the treatment of hallucination, and can then suitably deploy, to dis- pose of the Causal Argument, once this issue has been raised.

3 CONTACT AND CONTENT

I

SDR has survived the Causal Argument. And, as we noted earlier, it will strike us, initially, as more attractive than its decompositionalist rival, hav-

ing the support of both our ordinary ways of thought and our first reflective intuitions. Nonetheless, as I have already indicated, I hold the position
to be mistaken, and its being so is the conclusion for which I shall now, in
a series of stages, be arguing. The new line of argument will have a very different style from the one which we have been considering. Whereas the
Causal Argument offered itself as a *knock-down* objection to SDR—focusing simply on the SDR-thesis as such—the strategy of the new argument
will be to consider the range of different ways in which the thesis could be
developed (the various specific SDR-accounts of perception available), and
show that none of them is satisfactory. This will be a more laborious way
of trying to discredit the position, but I hope, for that reason, more effective.

What I shall try to show is that, however it is developed, SDR cannot
provide a satisfactory account of the experiential content of a perception,
and of how this content relates to the achieving of perceptual contact. By
the *experiential* content of a perception, I mean that content which gives
the perception its subjective character—its character as introspection
reveals it, or purports to reveal it. So two perceptions with the same experiential content must have the same subjective character—they must be
introspectively indistinguishable. It is important, however, that we do not
just *equate* the experiential content of a perception with its subjective character. For while the experiential content is what *makes* (*renders*) it introspectively with the subject thus and so, it does not *consist in* its being
introspectively with him thus and so. And indeed, prior to investigation,
we need to leave open the possibility of there being different types of experiential content which have the same subjective character. This is particularly important when considering a theory such as SDR. As we have already
seen, the SDR-theorist is bound to think that the psychological states which
are fundamentally involved in perception and hallucination are of different kinds, even when they subjectively match; and we need to leave open
the possibility that this supposed difference in psychological character will
involve some difference in the character of their experiential content.
Indeed, it seems almost inevitable that it will.

My argument will focus on a particular form of experiential content—
a form which I call 'phenomenal' content. I must start by explaining what
this is.

II

Whenever someone perceives a physical item, he perceives it—or at least
perceives whatever it is that he Φ-terminally perceives—under a certain

sensible appearance. Thus when Pauline sees the apple, it (or the relevant Φ-terminally seen portion-stage) visually appears to her as a roughly hemispherical patch of a certain size and colouring, located at a certain distance in front of her. Likewise, when I take a bottle of milk out of the refrigerator, the bottle (or the relevant portion-stage) tactually appears to me as a cold, smooth, hard surface, of a certain curvature. Quite generally, whenever a subject Φ-terminally perceives a physical item, it sensibly appears to him in a certain way—a way which represents it as having a certain sensible character drawn from qualities associated with the relevant sense-realm, and, typically, as having a certain (though perhaps only generically specified) location relative to his own body or current position. The point of saying that the subject perceives the item *under* this sensible appearance is that the appearance is, on its mental side, part of the very *content* of the perception: the item's appearing in a certain sensible manner is one and the same as the subject's perceiving it in a certain psychological manner. Obviously, this form of perceptual content qualifies as *experiential* in the relevant sense.

Now it is this form of experiential content that I speak of as 'phenomenal'. In other words, the phenomenal content of the perceiving is the mental reciprocal of the item's sensible appearance: it is the item's sensible appearance taken from the other direction—what embodies this appearance in its mental aspect. It is, we might say, how, in the perceiving of that item, the subject is *sensibly appeared to*. Notice that, as I am understanding the notion, sensible appearance is, by definition, a form of *perceptual* (*physical-item* perceptual) appearance: it is always and necessarily the appearance of *what is Φ-terminally perceived*. And correspondingly, phenomenal content is, by definition, a form of *perceptual* (*physical-item* perceptual) content—always and necessarily the content of *Φ-terminal perceiving*. In consequence, we cannot, in my terminology, speak of there being sensible appearance or phenomenal content in the case of *hallucination*, even though perception and hallucination have the same subjective character. This does not rule out the possibility of saying that, at the fundamental level of psychological description, the psychological states involved in perception and hallucination are of the same kind and have experiential content of the same kind. Certainly this will be the claim of BRT. But it does mean that, whatever kind of content occurs in hallucination, we cannot, as it occurs in that context, describe it as *phenomenal*, or as the mental embodiment of how things *sensibly appear*.

Sensible appearance is exclusively a form of perceptual appearance. But not all forms of perceptual appearance count as *sensible*. Thus, in the case of Pauline, it may be that, as well as appearing to her as something with a certain shape, size, and colouring, the item she Φ-terminally sees appears to (is seen by) her as *part of the surface of an apple*; and this further aspect of how things visually appear goes beyond what is purely sensible. Likewise, the item which I Φ-terminally feel may appear to me not just as something with a certain smoothness, hardness, and curvature, but as *part of the surface of a milk-bottle*; and again this further aspect of how things perceptually appear transcends the purely sensible. Sensible appearance is a *special kind* of perceptual appearance; and correspondingly, phenomenal content is a *special kind* of perceptual content. Exactly what makes them special is not something which we can hope to deal with adequately at this stage: their distinctive character will only become fully clear as the outcome of our philosophical investigation. Nonetheless, there are certain distinctive features of sensible appearance which it is possible to identify in advance, without prejudging the philosophical outcome; and there are three, in particular, which I think it will be helpful to draw attention to at this point, as a way of throwing light on the investigative project.

One way in which sensible appearance differs from other forms of perceptual appearance is that the range of qualities which are available to feature in its content (which are logically capable of forming elements of how things sensibly appear) is of a narrowly circumscribed kind. Thus, for any sense-realm R, the qualities available for R-sensible appearance fall into two groups. One group, which is not, as such, distinctively linked with R, comprises qualities of a spatial or temporal kind—qualities such as shape and size, spatial patterning, subject-relative location, duration and succession. Thus the sensibly apparent shape of the relevant portion-stage Φ-terminally seen by Pauline will be drawn from this group; likewise, if someone hears a cuckoo, the sensibly apparent temporal pattern of the two sounds belongs to this group too. The other group comprises qualities which are not spatial or temporal, but which have a special relationship to R—a relationship which makes them, in some sense, distinctively *R*-qualities. Thus if R is the visual realm, the relevant group will comprise colours, and aspects of colour, and if R is the auditory realm, it will comprise sounds, and aspects of sound. The exact nature of the special relationship involved is not something which we can specify at this stage: it is one of the things which must await the outcome of our philosophical investigation. All I shall say at present (though here again the detailed discussion will only come later) is that where a quality stands in this special relationship to a certain sense-realm, a proper understanding of the nature of that quality involves—and distinctively involves—knowing what it is (or would be) like, subjectively, to encounter it in the experiential content of perceptions in that realm, or in the content of experiences which are subjectively like such perceptions. So it is only by knowing what it is subjectively like to encounter colours in the content of *visual* experiences, and sounds in the content of *auditory* experiences, that we can fully grasp their nature.

It should be noted that, although, in the way I have demarcated it, the first group of qualities (the spatial and temporal) does not, *as a group*, have any distinctive link with the relevant sense-realm, I am not excluding the possibility that some of its members have such a link, and, in particular, stand in the same special relationship to it as the qualities which occur in the second group. For example, in the case of the visual realm, I am leaving open the possibility that the group contains, amongst other things, distinctively *visual* qualities of shape and spatial patterning—qualities which are distinctively equipped to provide the spatial arrangement of *colour*, and which stand in the same special relationship to this realm as colours themselves.

Sensible appearance, then, draws its qualitative content exclusively from these two sources—from qualities of a spatial or temporal kind, and from qualities which, while not spatial or temporal, stand in the relevantly special relationship to the sense-realm involved. And this distinguishes such appearance, as a general type, from other forms of appearance, whose qualitative options are not thus restricted. It does not, however, yield a complete test of whether an instance of perceptual appearance qualifies as sensible. For although the options for non-sensible appearance are not relevantly restricted, it may happen that a non-sensible appearance draws its content exclusively from qualities of the restricted kind. For example, if someone inspects a white flower in his garden at night, when its sensible appearance is as something grey, and if he is familiar with how it sensibly looks in daylight, then the flower may still, in a certain sense, look white to him—the same sense in which, say, a ripe plum might look sweet to someone, or a pile of manure might look smelly. And this would be an instance of a *non-sensible* appearance, but one whose qualitative content (whiteness) is equally suitable for *sensible* appearance in the relevant realm. So, while the fact that an appearance draws its qualitative content partly from some source beyond the two specified groups is enough to show that it is not sensible, the fact that it does not draw on such an additional source is not enough to show that it is.

A second way in which sensible appearance differs from other forms of perceptual appearance is that it is the only form which has any essential involvement in Φ-terminal perceiving. This is so in a double sense. In the first place, it is so in a *general* sense, in that it is logically possible for there to be instances of Φ-terminal perceiving in which the only appearance involved is sensible, but not logically possible for there to be instances of such perceiving in which the only appearance is non-sensible. Thus we can envisage an instance of seeing in which the Φ-terminal object is merely seen under a sensible appearance—seen as an item of a certain shape, size, and colouring, in a certain subject-relative location. But we cannot envisage an instance of seeing in which the Φ-terminal object is merely seen under a non-sensible appearance—for example, as a portion or portion-stage of a certain sort of material object. For, without an underlying sensible appearance, the item would simply not be visible at all, and so would not be perceptually available as something to which some other form of appearance was attached. Secondly, the point applies to instances of Φ-terminal perceiving *taken individually*, in that, given any such instance, the perceptual contact with the relevant object would be unaffected if all the elements of non-sensible appearance were eliminated, but could not survive the complete elimination of sensible appearance. Thus let us assume that, in the case of Pauline, the Φ-terminal object not only (sensibly) appears to her as a roughly hemispherical patch of colour at a certain distance in front of her, but also (non-sensibly) appears to her as part of the surface of an apple. Then the non-sensible element of appearance is not needed for the perceptual contact: it could be eliminated (without replacement) without affecting her visual contact with the item itself. But the sensible appearance is crucial, since, without this appearance, or something of the same general sort in its place, the item would simply not be visible to her at all, and so would not be something which she was able to see in the relevantly apple-like way. The two applications of the underlying point are not, of course, independent. For part of what is involved in each application entails part of what is involved in the other. Thus the fact that, in each individual case, the elements of non-sensible appearance are not required for Φ-terminal contact entails that it is logically possible for Φ-terminal perceiving to occur without such elements. And conversely, the fact that it is logically impossible for Φ-terminal perceiving to occur without sensible appearance entails that, in each individual case, the sensible appearance involved plays an essential, or at least non-redundant, role.

In insisting that only sensible appearance has any essential involvement in *Φ-terminal* perceiving, I am allowing for the possibility of cases in which some other form of appearance is essentially involved in the securing of contact with items which are perceptually *more remote*—cases in which a subject's contact with one physical item is perceptually mediated by his contact with another, and where some aspect of how the more immediate object non-sensibly appears to him plays a role in the mediation. Such a possibility does not, I think, arise for the types of perceptual mediation which we have so far cited—the types exemplified by the case of Pauline. In these sorts of case—the seeing of a spatially extended object by seeing one of its parts, and the seeing of a persisting object by seeing one of its stages—the mere mereological relationship between the physical items involved seems sufficient to effect the mediation. But there are also, arguably, some quite different types of case, where it is much more plausible to think of non-sensible appearance as playing an essential role. For example, if someone detects the approach of a train by hearing the bell ring on the platform, and if we are happy to describe this as a case of actually *hearing* the approach of the train, it is plausible to think that his perceptual contact with this approach partly depends on the fact that he hears the bell *as the signal of it*—in other words, on the fact that the bell *appears to him* as such a signal. This is not, however, an issue which we need to settle now. The whole topic of perceptual mediation within the physical domain is something which we shall be discussing in detail later.[9]

There is one final distinctive feature of sensible appearance which I want to mention at this stage. It concerns the distinctive *subjective* character of such appearance—the distinctive introspective impression which it makes on the perceiving subject.

Let us say that an item x is *directly presented to* a subject S, or that S is *presentationally aware of* x, if and only if x is psychologically related to S in a way which satisfies three conditions. First, the relationship is such as to make x available for demonstrative identification by S. In other words, it brings x before S's mind in a way which allows him to pick it out as 'this item' (of which he is now conscious, and on to which he directs his attention), or at least in a way which would allow him to do this if he had the conceptual resources needed for such demonstrative thought (resources which he might lack if he is very young or mentally handicapped). Second, the relationship is such as to display certain aspects of x's character, or character and S-relative location, in a way which makes them immediately available for cognitive scrutiny—though, once again, S's capacity to take advantage of this availability would depend on his having the requisite conceptual resources. (The satisfying of this second condition would not, of course, be something separate from the satisfying of the first: the item would not be available for demonstrative identification in the relevant way

---

[9] In Part Four.

if there were no aspects of its character on display, and the relevant aspects would not be on display if the item were not thus available for demonstrative identification.) Third, and crucially, the relationship is wholly non-representational. It does not, in itself, involve the use of concepts, symbols, or images, as a psychological means of registering x's presence or the relevant (displayed) aspects of its character (character and location). Rather, the item and the relevant aspects are before S's mind in a mode of absolute ontological immediacy, forming, in their own ontological person, the very content of his awareness. In saying that the *aspects* are before S's mind in this ontologically immediate way, I mean, of course, the aspects as *concretely realized*—in their form *as aspects of the character of x.*

Now the relevant point about sensible appearance is that it carries the subjective impression of being directly presentational in this sense. It gives the subject the impression that the item he Φ-terminally perceives is before his mind in this qualitatively transparent and ontologically immediate way, with the qualitative content of the appearance exactly covering those aspects of the item's character and relative location which are seemingly displayed, and with the item and these aspects seeming to form the very content of his perceptual awareness. Thus, in as much as the portion-stage which she Φ-terminally sees sensibly appears to her as a roughly hemispherical patch of a certain size and colouring, located at a certain distance from her, Pauline is given the impression that just such an item is directly presented to her, in that locational perspective, and displaying just such qualities of shape, size, and colour. And in as much as the relevant portion-stage of the bottle sensibly appears to me as a cold, smooth, hard surface, of a certain curvature, I too am given the impression that just such an item is directly presented to me, in the relevant sort of physical contact with my body, and displaying just such qualities of temperature, texture, hardness, and shape. Moreover, this subjective aspect of sensible appearance is something which distinguishes it from other forms of appearance. Thus let us assume, as before, that what Pauline Φ-terminally sees additionally appears to her as part of the surface of an apple. Then, whatever this further appearance involves, it does not give her the impression that the item's being of this sort is something presentationally displayed—with the same kind of ontological immediacy as the display of its colour and shape. She herself, presumably, would, on introspective reflection, at once concede that, however automatic and immediate her recognition of this state of affairs, it is an aspect of how she (or how her experience) *interprets* the situation, rather than something which can be simply read off—as it were cognitively

copied from—a pre-interpreted 'given'. Of course, on *philosophical* reflection, she might be led to the conclusion that sensible appearance too is, or
is partly, a matter of interpretation, rather than just the transparent display
of some aspect of the physical situation; and, for all we have said, such a
conclusion might be right. All we are insisting on, at the moment, is that
sensible appearance carries the *subjective impression* of being directly presentational in the relevant way, whether or not this impression is correct.

This throws light on something else. We noted earlier, as one of the factors which makes it initially attractive, that SDR is implicit in our ordinary,
pre-reflective view of the nature of perception—that we ordinarily think
of our perceptual awareness as reaching out to its external targets in a
wholly straightforward way, which excludes any kind of decomposition at
the psychological level. Given the presentational feel of sensible appearance, we can now understand why this is so. On the one hand, it is only to
be expected that, prior to philosophical reflection, we will tend to think of
perception in a way which accords with how it subjectively strikes us; and
since perception is always under a sensible appearance, this will mean
thinking of it as presentational. On the other hand, to think of perception
as directly presenting its Φ-terminal objects is implicitly an endorsement
of SDR. For if the Φ-terminal relationship psychologically decomposed, so
that the fundamental psychological state was not, in itself, perceptive of the
relevant physical item, then it would not bring this item before the mind
in a way that was ontologically immediate—a way which allowed the item
itself, and the relevant aspect of its character, to form the content of the
subject's awareness. In short, given that perception is always under a sensible appearance, and that sensible appearance carries the subjective
impression of being presentational, it is only to be expected that a presentationalist construal will come to characterize our ordinary modes of
thought, and thus bring with it an implicit commitment to SDR. This is
not to say that, in our ordinary thinking, we *always* construe perception as
presentational: we are sometimes conscious of factors which show that the
impression of a presentational awareness is mistaken—the obvious case
being when we realize that the sensible appearance is not accurate. The
point is simply that, because it coincides with how things subjectively
seem, the presentationalist construal becomes established as the *normal*
mode of construal—the construal which tends to occur in the absence of
other relevant factors; and, as such, it comes to shape our ordinary basic
understanding of the nature of perception prior to philosophical reflection.

III

Whenever a subject Φ-terminally perceives a physical item, he perceives it under a certain sensible appearance. The *phenomenal content* of the perceiving is, as I have said, that aspect of its experiential content which embodies this appearance. It is the sensible appearance taken from the other direction—the manner in which the item sensibly appears, redescribed as the manner in which the subject perceives it. Any acceptable theory of perception has to be able to offer an adequate account of the nature of such content and of its relation to perceptual contact—an account of what, ultimately, phenomenal content is, and what place it occupies, or role it plays, in the obtaining of the perceptual relationship between the subject and the physical item. In one way or another, this issue will occupy our attention for most of the book. At present, my main concern is in pursuing the issue *in relation to SDR*, to see whether an adequate account of contact and content can be provided within its framework.

Let us focus on the issue in the context of the particular example of Pauline and the apple. Still more narrowly, let us focus on Pauline's Φ-terminal seeing, at a particular time t, of a particular momentary portion-stage, L, of the apple's surface. And, to provide for the relevant factor of phenomenal content, let us suppose that she sees L, at t, in the specific phenomenal manner M—M being what thus coincides (taken from other direction) with the manner in which L sensibly appears to her at t. So, focusing on this particular case, let us now consider what account might be given of the relevant instance of phenomenal content—of Pauline's seeing M-ly—and of how this content and the visual contact with the relevant physical item—her Φ-terminal seeing of L—fit together.

We should begin by taking note of three points that are uncontroversial. First, although Pauline at t sees L *M-ly*, it is logically possible for someone to see L, and to see it Φ-terminally, in a different phenomenal manner. For example, if Pauline herself had seen L from a different distance, or under a different illumination, or through shape-distorting lenses, the item would have taken on a different visual appearance and thus given rise to a different phenomenal content. From this it follows that the fact of Pauline's being in the relevant phenomenal state (of her seeing something M-ly) involves something genuinely additional to the fact of her Φ-terminally seeing L. The fact of phenomenal content is not wholly covered by the bare fact of visual contact. Let us call this *Point A*. Secondly, although Pauline, at t, sees *L* M-ly, it is logically possible for someone to see some other physical item in the same phenomenal manner. For example, if there is no change in the character of the apple or the conditions of observation, Pauline herself might well, over the next few minutes, see a whole series of successive portion-stages without any change in the character of the sensible appearance, and so without any change in the phenomenal manner of the seeing. From this it follows that the fact of Pauline's seeing L (that particular physical item) involves something genuinely additional to the fact of her being in the relevant (M-ly seeing) phenomenal state. The fact of that specifically targeted contact is not wholly covered by the bare fact of phenomenal content. Let us call this *Point B*. Thirdly, although the facts of contact and content are thus different—indeed, with each fact involving something genuinely additional to the other—they relate to a single concrete psychological event. It is not a matter of two things going on in Pauline's mind, simultaneously but ontologically separately—the seeing of the item and the having of a certain kind of phenomenal experience. It is a matter of one thing occurring which has both a perceptive and a phenomenal aspect—the event of seeing a particular item L in a particular phenomenal manner M. This, indeed, is simply a consequence of how the notion of phenomenal content has been defined. Let us call this *Point C*. These three points are, as I have said, uncontroversial, and so they are points which any philosophical account of the situation is obliged to accommodate. And, of course, although, as thus formulated, they only apply to the specific case of Pauline at t, exactly analogous points, with the same uncontroversial status, would hold for any other case of Φ-terminal perceiving.

It is not difficult to see how the three points would be accommodated by BRT. BRT claims that, whenever someone perceives a physical item, his perceptual contact with it breaks down into (is constituted by the combination of) two components, one of which consists in his being in some further, more fundamental, psychological state—a state which is not in itself perceptive of that physical item—and the other of which comprises certain additional facts, though not involving anything further (over and above his being in that state) about the subject's psychological condition at the relevant time. Applying this claim to the case of Pauline, the BRT-theorist will see both the fact of contact (Pauline's seeing *of* L) and the fact of content (Pauline's seeing *M-ly*) as decomposing into more fundamental (and the *same* more fundamental) factors at the psychological level. Thus he will say that there is an experiential state E, which is not in itself physically perceptive (a state which it is logically possible to be in without there being any physical item which one perceives), such that both the fact of Pauline's seeing L at t and the fact of her seeing M-ly at t are constituted by her being in E at t, together with certain additional facts of the relevantly restricted sort—facts such as the qualitative relationship of E to L and the causal role of L in bringing about the relevant realization of E. This account respects the point (Point A) that the fact of content (Pauline's seeing something M-ly) involves something genuinely additional to the fact of contact (her Φ-terminal seeing of L), since it allows for a situation in which contact with L is mediated by the realization of a different experiential state. Likewise, it respects the point (Point B) that the fact of contact involves something genuinely additional to the fact of content, since it allows for a situation in which contact with something else is mediated by the realization of the same experiential state. Finally, because it recognizes only a single *fundamental* psychological fact, it ensures (Point C) that there is only one concrete psychological event—an event which is, in its fundamental description, that of Pauline's being in the relevant experiential state, but which qualifies as an event of her seeing L M-ly (and so, a fortiori, as an event of her seeing L and as an event of her seeing M-ly) in virtue of the relevant additional facts.

These, of course, are just the bare bones of the BRT-account. All the details—concerning the nature of the more fundamental experiential state and the nature of the additional facts—would need to be filled in; and, for any such filling, there would still be the question of whether the account was correct—of whether it provided the right characterization of the nature of contact and content and the relationship between them. All this we shall look into in Parts Three and Four. At the moment, as I have indicated, our main concern is with the situation of *SDR*. *Ex hypothesi*, the SDR-theorist cannot take over the BRT-account, since his position denies that the Φ-terminal perceptual relationship decomposes in that kind of way. So what would be the right approach from his standpoint?

One option which is formally available—and theoretically this would be his simplest approach—would be to take the bare fact of perceptual contact, or, strictly, sense-modally specific perceptual contact, as what is psychologically fundamental, and construe the fact of phenomenal content as something constituted by the combination of contact and other factors. Let us speak of this as the *perceptualist strategy*. Thus, in the case of Pauline, the perceptualist would say that the bare fact of her Φ-terminally seeing L at t covers all that is relevant in her fundamental psychological condition at t, and that the fact of her seeing L *M-ly* at t, and a fortiori the fact of her seeing *some* physical item M-ly at t, are constituted by the bare fact of visual contact, together with certain additional facts—facts not involving anything further about her psychological condition at t. Obviously, this approach would be in line with SDR, since it explicitly recognizes the Φ-terminal relationship as psychologically fundamental. And it would also allow the SDR-theorist to accommodate the three uncontroversial points. In the case of Points A and C, the accommodation would be automatic: thus since it takes the content-fact to be constituted by the *combination* of the contact-fact and certain further facts, it automatically represents the content-fact as involving something genuinely additional to the contact-fact; and likewise, it straightforwardly ensures that there is only one psychological event—an event which is fundamentally that of the subject's perceiving the relevant item, but which qualifies as an event of perceiving in a certain phenomenal manner in virtue of the additional facts. In the case of Point B, the accommodation could be arranged by adding the appropriate claim. Thus the theorist could insist, as an essential feature of what he is envisaging, that if someone were, through the same sense-modality, Φ-terminally to perceive another relevantly similar physical item (for example, in Pauline's case, to see a different but qualitatively identical stage of the same apple), and if all the other additional factors involved were qualitatively the same, then the derivative fact of content (constituted by the fact of perceptual contact, together with the additional facts) would be qualitatively the same as well—a perceiving of a different item in exactly the same phenomenal manner. This would ensure that the fact of contact involves something genuinely additional to the fact of content to which it constitutively contributes.

The perceptualist strategy would be theoretically the simplest approach for the SDR-theorist, but it only takes a little reflection to reveal that it is misconceived. This becomes clear when we turn to the question of how it might be concretely developed. Given the bare fact of contact, what sorts of additional fact would be selected as its constitutive partners? And how would they combine with this fact of contact to yield the fact of content?

Initially, the obvious way of trying to develop the strategy would be by taking the relevant additional facts to divide into three groups, namely,

(1) certain facts about the intrinsic character of the perceived item;

(2) certain facts about the spatial or bodily-contact relationship of this item to the subject at the time of the perceiving;

and

(3) certain facts about the conditions of observation, over and above what is already included in (1) and (2).

Thus, in the case of Pauline, the first group would cover the shape, size, and colouring of L—those intrinsic qualities of L which are capable of featuring in the content of visual sensible appearance; the second would cover the distance and direction of L (or the various points on L) from Pauline-at-t; and the third group would cover such things as the character of the illumination and the nature of the intervening medium between item and eye. The idea would be that, although there is a range of phenomenal manners compatible with the Φ-terminal perceiving of the relevant physical item in the relevant sense-realm, the fact of such perceiving determines the exact phenomenal manner when combined with these further facts.

However, there are two reasons why this proposal does not work. First, it is clear that, even if these additional facts could be thought of as *partly* constitutive of the subject's phenomenal condition, they do not, in conjunction with the fact of contact, suffice to *determine* it. Thus someone whose visual system was appropriately different from Pauline's—for example, someone who was colour-blind or astigmatic—could Φ-terminally see L with the obtaining of exactly similar additional facts, but see it in a different phenomenal manner. Secondly, the contribution which the third group of factors—the conditions of observation—make to the character of the phenomenal content is a *causal*, not a *constitutive* one: their only relevance is that they causally affect the character of the sensory input. Thus if the illumination is dim, as at dusk, this affects the phenomenal manner in which a surface is seen by reducing the quantity of light which it reflects; or if someone is looking at a scene through a pane of red glass, this affects the phenomenal manner of the seeing by filtering out some of the wavelengths of light that would otherwise reach the eye. This is a purely contingent relationship between the conditions of observation and the character of the perceptual experience, and not something which would equip the facts about these conditions to form part of what *constitutes* the relevant experiential fact.

The perceptualist might try to meet the first problem by supplementing the three groups of facts by a fourth group, of *physiological* facts—facts about the structure of the subject's sense-organs and nervous system, and about the particular neural process which led up to the perceptual event. By making these new facts sufficiently detailed, he might hope to exclude the possibility of variation in phenomenal content when all the relevant factors are duplicated. But, of course, this revision would do nothing to answer the second problem—that the conditions of observation only bear on the character of the phenomenal content *causally*. Indeed, it would only serve to exacerbate it, since the additional physiological factors would themselves only contribute to the character of the phenomenal content in a causal way. Admittedly, once the physiological factors had been invoked, the perceptualist could presumably arrange things in such a way that, instead of an exacerbation of the problem, there was only a transference of it to another point. For, presumably, if these new factors were sufficiently detailed to avoid the first problem, they would render any reference to the external conditions of observation redundant. But the point remains that the new facts themselves cannot be regarded as part of what constitutes the subject's phenomenal condition. At least, they cannot be so regarded outside the context of a physicalistically reductive account of the relevant psychological facts. And, even if we thought that such an account was acceptable—and I have indicated that I would reject it myself—it would not be relevant to the pursuit of the perceptualist strategy, which is seeking to characterize the situation at the *psychological level.*

In fact, there is no way in which the second problem for the perceptualist strategy can be avoided, and, in consequence, the strategy has to be abandoned. The only chance of success for the SDR-theorist is by adopting a quite different approach, to which I now turn.

The theorist is trying to give an account of the nature of the facts of contact and content and the relationship between them—an account which is in line with his basic position, and which allows for the three uncontroversial points that we have mentioned. On the approach we have just considered, and found wanting, he took the contact-fact (in its bare-contact form) to be psychologically fundamental, and construed the content-fact as something derivative. What he must do, instead, is to accord both these facts the same status—taking them to be different, but complementary aspects of a single fundamental fact. Thus, in the case of Pauline, he must say that what is psychologically fundamental is the fact of her Φ-terminally seeing L at t M-ly, and that the distinctive contact-fact, of her Φ-terminally seeing L (in some phenomenal manner), and the distinctive content-fact, of her Φ-terminally seeing (something) M-ly, are just different aspects of it. And he must apply this same model to all cases of Φ-terminal perception, taking the fundamental fact to be that of the subject's perceiving a particular item in a specific phenomenal manner, and treating the facts of contact and content as its different aspects. Because the unitary complex fact is what is taken to be fundamental, its relationship with the aspectual facts will be seen as one of single-fact constitution: both these latter facts will be thought of as obtaining in virtue of, and their obtaining as nothing over and above, the obtaining of the unitary fact in which they are integrated.

We can now understand the significance of something which I mentioned in Part One, when first setting out the implications of the SDR-position.[10] I had already noted that, in excluding the form of decomposition definitive of psychological mediation, an acceptance of SDR in effect involves taking the Φ-terminal perceptual relationship to be something psychologically fundamental—something which is not subject to any form of constitution at the psychological level. But I then added a qualification—though not one which affected the basic point. For I said that the SDR-theorist does have the option of saying that the bare fact of Φ-terminal contact is constituted by a further perceptual fact of an experientially richer or more determinate kind—a fact of which the bare contact-fact can be thought of as either an integral element or a determinable version. It is just this option which we are now envisaging the theorist as taking up, by holding the facts of contact and content to be constituted by a single fact, of which they are different aspects. The two aspectual facts can be represented as either *elements* or *determinables* of this single fact, according to how they are formulated. Thus, in the particular example, we may speak simply of Pauline's *seeing L* and of her *seeing M-ly*, which represents the aspectual facts as *elements* of the single fact. Alternatively, we may speak, more elaborately, of Pauline's *seeing L in some phenomenal manner* and of her *seeing some item M-ly*, which represents them as *determinable versions* of the single fact. Which way we care to represent the situation is purely a matter of taste. The crucial point is that it is the single fact—of perceiving a particular item in a specific phenomenal manner—which counts as psychologically fundamental.

Let us speak of this new approach as the *integrational strategy*, because of the way in which it preserves the integrity of the contact–content bond at the fundamental level of psychological specification. It is clear how this strategy complies with the terms of SDR—keeping the Φ-terminal relationship (specified with the requisite richness or determinacy) as something psychologically fundamental. And it is also clear how it immediately accommodates the three uncontroversial points; for each aspectual fact involves something genuinely additional to the other, while relating to a single concrete (contact-cum-content) psychological event. Moreover, with the failure of the perceptualist strategy, there is no other approach which will meet these basic requirements. Whatever our final verdict on his position, this new strategy is the only approach which offers the SDR-theorist any prospect of a satisfactory outcome.

[10] In Part One, Section 3, I.

4 THE PRESENTATIONAL VIEW

I

To have any chance of success, the SDR-theorist has to adopt the integrational strategy—taking the facts of contact and content to be aspects of a single and psychologically fundamental fact, in which they are integrated. But how exactly is this strategy to be pursued? What account should the theorist give of the two factors involved and the manner of their integration? Well, just as there was the more basic division between the perceptualist and integrational strategies, so it now turns out that, within the framework of the integrational strategy, there are two quite different approaches available to the theorist. The difference between them turns on the ontological relationship which is thought to hold between the featuring of qualities in phenomenal content, as aspects of how things sensibly appear, and their featuring in the external reality, as attributes of the item perceived. I shall begin by considering what I take to be the most obvious approach.

As we noted earlier, one of the distinctive features of sensible appearance is that it carries the subjective impression of being directly presentational, in the sense we defined. Now the theorist's most obvious approach would be to say that this subjective impression is in fact *correct*. That is, he could say that, whenever a subject S Φ-terminally perceives a physical item x, x is before S's mind in a way which satisfies the three specified conditions: first, it makes x available for demonstrative identification by S (as 'this thing', of which he is now conscious, and on to which he directs his attention); second, it displays certain aspects of x's character, or character and S-relative location—these aspects being what form the qualitative content of the sensible appearance; and third, it is wholly non-representational: it does not involve the use of concepts, symbols, or images, as a psychological means of registering the presence of x or the relevant (displayed) aspects; rather, x and the relevant aspects are before S's mind in a mode of absolute ontological immediacy, forming the very content of his perceptual awareness. It is this third condition which is the most crucial. Obviously, under any version of SDR, the Φ-terminal object itself must feature, in some irreducible way, in the content of the subject's perceptual awareness—otherwise the perceptual relationship would not be psychologically fundamental. But what the third condition additionally and distinctively ensures is that the content of the awareness embraces the relevant *qualitative* ingredients of the external situation as well. It ensures that the featuring of a quality or relation in the phenomenal content is not something ontologically separate from its external realization in the perceived item (something which merely serves to *represent* that realization), but is rather that realization itself made transparent to the mind—the external qualitative situation becoming experientially present, in perspective, in the content of the perceiving. So, in as much as L looks to Pauline (say) a certain shade of green, the proposal would be that this aspect of her visual experience consists in the fact that L's actual greenness, as thus externally realized, features in the content of her awareness in this ontologically immediate way. Likewise, in as much as this colour visually appears to her as distributed over a certain (roughly hemispherical) array of points, at certain distances and in certain directions from her, this aspect of her experience would be equated with the fact that the actual L-array, at such distances and in such directions, is present in the content of her awareness, with the relevant ontological immediacy, in the perspective of her spatial viewpoint. Quite generally, the proposal would be that, wherever there is Φ-terminal perception, the phenomenal content draws its qualitative ingredients directly from the concrete external situation, so that these ingredients are nothing more than elements of this situation made experientially present, in (where appropriate) the relevant perspective.

Let us call what is being proposed the *presentational view*. This view, as I have said, represents the theorist's most obvious approach. Part of the reason for this is that it coincides with the subjective impression which perceptual experience itself conveys—with the interpretation, as it were, which such experience puts on itself. And, in coinciding with this, it also, as we noted earlier, coincides with what we tend to take for granted in the course of ordinary (pre-philosophically-reflective) life; for our ordinary understanding of the nature of perception tends, not surprisingly, to reflect the way in which things subjectively seem when perceptual experience occurs. But there is also a further factor. For, as well as coinciding with how things subjectively seem, and with what we pre-philosophically tend to take for granted, the presentational view constitutes the simplest, most straightforward way in which the theorist could respond to the challenge of the issue before him, within the limits of what SDR and the integrational strategy allow. Thus we know that, however the situation is to be construed, phenomenal content and perceptual contact have a distinctively intimate relationship: the content is, precisely, and by definition, the phenomenal manner of the perceiving; it embodies the sensible appearance under which the contact is made. Once the BRT-approach has been excluded (so that content cannot be seen as the product of the experiential form in which the perceiving is psychologically mediated), and once the integrational strategy has been put in place, the presentational view is the simplest way of trying to accommodate that intimacy—the most straightforward way of accounting for the manner in which contact and content fit together in the relevantly integrated form. Content becomes simply the qualitative component of the presentational contact—the display of certain features of the external item or situation as part and parcel of its direct presentation.

II

The presentational view is the most obvious position for the theorist to adopt—the position which first suggests itself in the framework of the theorist's basic thesis and the integrational strategy. The trouble is that it is also—and in effect just as obviously—open to a decisive objection. The objection is that it cannot accommodate cases of *non-veridical* perception.

By a case of non-veridical perception, I mean one in which a physical item is genuinely perceived (in contrast with a case of hallucination), but where it is perceived in a phenomenal manner which is, in some respect, at variance with its true character—where the perceived item is not, in that respect, as it sensibly appears. That such cases occur can hardly be denied—at least on the assumption that we perceive physical items at all. A much-cited example is that of the stick in water. The stick is, in reality, straight, and remains so when it is partially immersed in water; but, thus immersed, and because of the refraction of light, it looks bent at the point where it enters the liquid, and this non-veridical look is an aspect of its sensible appearance. Another familiar example is that of the distorting effect of coloured glass. Thus if I look at newly fallen snow through red-tinted spectacles, it will look—sensibly appear—to me some shade of red, even though it is, in reality, pure white. In these examples, the distorting physical factors—the refractive effect of the immersion and the filtering effect of the glass—lie outside the subject's body. There are also examples where the relevant factors lie within—factors which affect the way in which the physical input is processed by the subject's own sensory system. For instance, there is the case of astigmatism, where the apparent shape of what is seen gets systematically affected by a defect in the lens of the eye; and there is the case of colour-blindness, where, as a result of some deficiency in the retinal receptors, certain colours which can be readily distinguished by the normal subject look the same. And, of course, for both categories of distortion—both that where the factors lie *outside* the subject's body and that where they lie *within*—there is a multitude of examples from other sense-realms, though, for the most part, I shall continue to focus on the case of sight.

Whether a perception counts as veridical or non-veridical in a given respect is not, of course, just a function of how its phenomenal content compares with the relevant qualities of the item perceived. It often depends, in addition, on the spatial relation between the subject and the item, since this can affect the requirements of perspective. Thus the correct phenomenal way of seeing a circular object from an oblique angle is not the same as the correct way of seeing it frontally; and the correct phenomenal way of seeing something in the distance is not the same as the correct way of seeing it close to. Here, though, we must be careful to distinguish between the veridical registering of a spatial quality in three-dimensional perspective and a non-veridical registering which merely captures the quality's two-dimensional projection on to the subject's viewpoint. Thus, in a situation where someone is viewing a circular object from an oblique angle, we must not confuse the case in which the orientation of the object relative to the line of vision is itself sensibly apparent, so that the different points on the object are sensibly assigned their correct values of distance, or relative distance, from the subject, and the case in which this orientation is not sensibly registered and the object appears, non-veridically, as an elliptical item directly facing one. Only the first is a case of seeing in perspective in the relevant (veridicality-preserving) sense. Nor, for similar reasons, should we suppose that the diminishing of visual acuity, which is a natural consequence of an increase in the distance of the item from the subject, is a matter of perspective. If someone does not visually register the details of a pattern because he is standing too far away from it, this cannot, except in a loose sense, be described as a case of veridically seeing what is there, but in a perspective suitable to the distance. The only cases where we can properly construe some aspect of phenomenal content as veridical-in-perspective are those where what is perceived is, in the relevant respect, quite strictly as it sensibly appears, but where the appearance records, from the standpoint of the subject (and hence in perspective), some aspect of how the item is spatially related to him.

Another thing which we need to bear in mind, when evaluating the veridicality of a perception, is that the conditions of observation may affect not just the sensible appearance of the perceived item, but its actual character in the relevant respect. Take the case of colour. When I look at snow through red-tinted glasses, this only affects the colour-appearance of the snow: its actual whiteness remains unaffected. But suppose I look at the snow at sunset, when it is illuminated by a reddish light. Again this affects the colour-appearance—perhaps in much the same way as the tinted glasses. But there is also a sense in which it affects the colour of what is illuminated too. Of course, the *pigment* of the snow does not change, and, in that sense, the snow remains white. But there is also a familiar and unproblematic sense in which the surface of the snow can be thought of as actually tinted by the light which falls on it, and, in *that* sense, its colour-appearance would be deemed veridical—an appearance in line with how things really are. A partially analogous point holds for sounds. If someone uses ear-plugs to muffle the sound of a nearby radio, we would ordinarily think of the resulting auditory perceptions as non-veridical with respect to the loudness of the physical sounds he detects: the ear-plugs serve to conceal the true intensity of these sounds, just as tinted glasses may conceal the true character of the external colours. But if the subject puts a blanket over the radio, or moves to a spot further away, we would say, I think, that he has genuinely diminished the loudness in his immediate vicinity, and so is hearing things as they now really are at his auditory viewpoint. Admittedly, in thus discussing the conditions for veridicality in respect of such qualities as colour and sound, we are implicitly assuming a common-sense account of what is involved in the physical realization of these qualities: we are assuming that the sorts of colours and sounds which feature in the content of sensible appearance are the same as the sorts which occur in the physical world. If we were to adopt a Lockean view of such 'secondary' qualities—taking them to be, in their physical realization, nothing but powers to affect human experience—then we would have to deny this assumption, and, in consequence, think of the relevant forms of sensible appearance as involving an element of non-veridicality in all circumstances.[11] And, indeed, there are some familiar and seemingly powerful arguments in favour of this view. In particular, there is the argument that science is able to explain the relevant forms of appearance in terms which do not involve attributing the sensible qualities themselves to the items perceived.

In a number of respects, then, the application of the distinction between veridical and non-veridical perception is complicated, and at certain points philosophically controversial. But, for our immediate purposes, all that matters is that, however generous we may be in our recognition of cases of veridicality, there are some cases of perception which must be regarded as

---

[11] Locke advanced this view in *An Essay Concerning Human Understanding,* ed. A. Campbell Fraser (New York: Dover, 1959), Bk. 2, ch. 8.

non-veridical *on any account*. Thus, even when we make allowance for the fact that the veridical perception of shape has to vary in phenomenal manner to suit the needs of perspective, we cannot deny that a straight stick which looks bent in water does not look the way it really is, or that an astigmatic subject is liable to see physical shape in a genuinely distorted manner. And, even on a common-sense view of physical colour, we cannot deny that the effect of tinted glasses and colour-blindness is to create a real discrepancy between appearance and reality.

What makes these uncontroversial cases of non-veridicality crucial is that, on their own, they suffice to refute the presentational view. Or at least they do so if, as in the way we first formulated it, we take this view to be making a claim about *all* cases of Φ-terminal perception. For, in taking the qualitative ingredients of phenomenal content to be directly drawn from the external situation, the presentational view leaves no room for cases in which the character of the content—embodying how things sensibly appear—is at variance with the character of the perceived item. Phenomenal content (sensible appearance) just is, for the presentationalist, the imprint of the item's actual character, in the relevant perspective, on the percipient's mind. Full veridicality is always ensured, because it is only in so far as there is a veridical awareness of the physical world that there is phenomenal content at all. So the fact that we have to recognize cases of non-veridical perception immediately establishes that the presentational view, as a general theory of perception, is mistaken. On that point, there is no scope for dissent.

III

The fact that there are cases of non-veridical perception forces the SDR-theorist to abandon the presentational view in its *general* form—as a view about *all* cases of Φ-terminal perceiving. But it does not, immediately, force him to abandon the presentational approach altogether. After all, perception is not non-veridical *all the time* and *in every respect*. So it would still be open to him to insist that, being *to some extent* veridical, perception is also *to some extent* presentational. Let us speak of this position as the *modified presentational view*. This modified view, of course, leaves room for a whole range of more specific options, of varying types and strengths, depending on which forms or aspects of perception are accorded the presentational treatment. And here, there are two distinct issues whose outcomes will affect the end result. On the one hand, there is the prior issue of veridicality: in which types of case should the theorist think of perception as veridical? On the other hand, given a demarcation of the cases of veridicality, there is the subsequent issue of which of these cases should be construed in a presentational way. The strongest (i.e. presentationally strongest) version of the modified approach would be one which maximized both the extent of the veridicality and the extent of its presentational construal. It would take perception to be predominantly veridical, with non-veridicality as just a rare and minor deviation; and it would then exploit the resulting opportunities for a presentational account to the fullest possible extent.

Now it could well turn out that the correct handling of the first issue would not leave much opportunity, if any at all, for the development of a presentational account. This is partly because, even in its ordinary forms—the forms with which we are familiar from ordinary observational experience—non-veridicality is a widespread phenomenon. To appreciate its extent, we only have to remind ourselves of such common-place points as the one about acuity already mentioned (that it is often possible to get a more accurate view of the details of the physical scene by taking a literally closer look at it), and the fact that most people could, to some extent, improve their vision by wearing glasses, or a more suitable pair of glasses. But in addition, and more crucially, science seems to show that the real character of the physical world is, through and through, quite unlike how things sensibly appear in the context of ordinary observation. In part, this is just the point, already mentioned, about the status of the secondary qualities—that science seems to show that such qualities as colour, sound, flavour, and odour are nothing more, in the physical items themselves, than powers to affect human sense-experience, together with the primary structures on which these powers are grounded. But, importantly, it also extends to the primary structures themselves. For, even in respect of spatial patterning, how things sensibly appear to the ordinary visual and tactual observer is not, except in broad outline, the same as how things turn out in the light of microscopic and sub-microscopic investigation. The conclusion to be drawn seems to be that our perception of the physical world is non-veridical on a global scale, and so almost entirely beyond the reach of presentationalist treatment.

It might be suggested that we could avoid this conclusion by the device of relativization. Thus, rather than thinking of the common-sense and scientific accounts as in conflict—a conflict which, it seems, could only be rationally decided in favour of science—perhaps we should think of physical reality as having different characters relative to different perceptual and epistemological viewpoints, so that what is correctly described as a smooth and uniformly coloured surface from the viewpoint of ordinary visual observation can also be correctly described as granular and multicoloured from the viewpoint of the microscope, and ultimately described as a scattered array of colourless particles from the viewpoint of physics.[12] But while this suggestion has some plausibility, it would not help to restore the opportunity for a presentational account in the relevant sense. For if veridicality really is under threat from science, and if the relativization device is the only way of preserving it in the face of this threat, then, even if we allow that, from the appropriate viewpoint, we can correctly speak of physical objects as having the character of their ordinary sensible appearance, we must also accept that their having this character, relative to this viewpoint, is, in the final analysis, wholly constituted by their possession of the properties which science ascribes to them, together with the way in which these properties dispose them to affect human sensory experience. And this would mean that, while genuinely characterizing the objects in this relativistic way, this sensible character would not be something available for presentational display *at the level of what is psychologically fundamental*—the only level which is relevant to the pursuit of a presentationalist approach *in the framework of SDR*.

It could well turn out, then, that, by the time we have finished redescribing the physical world in scientific terms, there will not be much, if anything, left in ordinary perception which is a candidate for presentational treatment. And, in fact, I am inclined to think that this is so. Moreover, we have to bear in mind that even a partial vindication of the scientific case against veridicality is, in its implications for a presentationalist approach, liable to have a knock-on effect, simply because of the ways in which qualities in one category would not be presentationally separable from those in some other. For example, once we have come to accept the Lockean view of physical colour, ruling out a presentational account of our perception of it, it surely becomes equally impossible to give a presentational account of our perception of its spatial arrangement. For even if our ways of perceiving such arrangement are (typically) veridical, it surely makes no sense to suppose that a quality of arrangement is presented *on its own*, without the presentation of whatever it is, in reality, that is thus arranged.

However, even if we set aside the challenge of science, and assume, quite generally, that, with well-endowed percipients in favourable conditions,

---

[12] This seems to be P. F. Strawson's approach in 'Perception and its objects', in G. Macdonald (ed.), *Perception and Identity* (London: Macmillan, 1979), reprinted in J. Dancy (ed.), *Perceptual Knowledge*.

things are, typically, as they sensibly appear, there is a quite different reason why the modified presentational view is not viable. The reason is simply that its mixing of the different approaches—its adoption of a presentational account for some cases and a non-presentational account for others—is unacceptable *in principle*. We can best bring this out by initially focusing on a specially designed example—one in which it is made absolutely clear that the veridical and non-veridical perceptions involved have to be treated in the same general way.

Suppose we have ten lenses, which can be arranged in a series, the first being simply a piece of plain, flat glass, of the sort one would find in an ordinary window, and the others being curved in a way which, for someone looking through them, distorts the sensible appearance of shape in a systematic fashion, the amount of the distortion being very slight initially, but steadily increasing as we move through the series. And let us assume three things about the relationship between the relevant forms of curvature and their distorting effects. First, let us assume that the different forms of curvature can be represented as different degrees of curvature along some continuous qualitative dimension, with the zero-curvature of the first lens falling at the initial point, and with the curvatures of the subsequent lenses falling at points which match their positions in the series, so that the greater the degree of the curvature involved, the greater its distorting effect. Second, let us assume that the way in which the different degrees of curvature affect the transmission of light, and so generate the phenomenal distortion, is, in its general character, constant through the series, with the effect of the zero-curvature of the first lens being just the limiting case of the effects of the curvatures of the subsequent lenses. And third, let us assume that the connections between curvature and distortion covered by these first two assumptions hold true of the dimension quite generally, or at least of the relevant portion of it, so that they do not just apply to the ten degrees of curvature that feature in our example, but also to all the other degrees that lie in between. In all these respects, of course, what is being envisaged falls securely within the framework of how the world actually works. The curvature of glass *does* distort the appearance of shape in the relevantly systematic way, and it would be a routine matter to construct a series of lenses which met the specified conditions.

Now, given this set-up, suppose we have a circular object O, and we have a subject who views O through each lens in turn in reverse order—each viewing being from a frontal angle. Since the final viewing is through the uncurved lens, we know that the resulting visual perception will be, in respect of O's shape, wholly veridical: the subject will see the object the way it really is—as something circular. But, in the case of the preceding nine viewings, there will be phenomenal distortion, the degree of the distortion being greatest at the start, and gradually decreasing as the viewings continue. Let us assume—and again it would be straightforward to arrange things in this way—that the distortion takes the following specific form. Throughout the first nine viewings, the object is seen, non-veridically, as elliptical, the shape of the ellipse beginning as something which is paradigmatically oval, but becoming steadily less elongated (more squat) as the series progresses, until, at the ninth (the penultimate) viewing, it is scarcely distinguishable from the circular shape which characterizes the appearance of the final perception. So while the first nine perceptions are all non-veridical, the degree of their non-veridicality steadily diminishes through the series, as the shape-appearance moves steadily closer to the appearance of circularity.

This, then, is the example on which I want to focus. And the question we need to consider is: how should we understand the nature of the perceptions which feature in it, and, in particular, how should we view the relationship between the first nine perceptions, which are all, to some degree, non-veridical, and the final perception, in which the shape of the object is seen as it really is? Well, we already know that, where a perception is non-veridical, it is not presentational: it does not, in the relevant respect, draw the qualitative ingredients of its phenomenal content directly from the character of the perceived item. And this is so irrespective of the *degree* of non-veridicality involved. So, in the situation envisaged, only the final—wholly veridical—perception would be a candidate for a presentational account. But we also know that, in respect of both the causation of the perceptions and the factor of veridicality, there are no sharp discontinuities. Thus all the perceptions are brought about in the same general way, the resulting shape-appearance depending, in a constant fashion, on the combination of O's actual shape and the influence of the lens on the transmission of light. And although only one perception is *fully* veridical, the other perceptions have a measure of veridicality which corresponds to their position in the series, so that the penultimate perception is much closer in its degree of veridicality to the final (fully veridical) perception than to those at the start. Moreover, and crucially, even where a perception is non-veridical, it is still perceptive of the object's actual shape, as physically realized—perceptive of the physical instance of circularity which forms the object's actual boundary. Thus just as the final perception involves the fully veridical seeing, or visual registering, of this physical shape, so the other perceptions likewise involve the seeing or registering of this same physical shape—this same physical instance of circularity—though in a less than fully veridical way. In this respect, the case stands in sharp contrast with what would happen if someone were viewing a circular object, but—as a variant of the case of Henry—a device which was attached to his optic nerves eliminated a certain portion of the sensory input, in a way which severed visual contact with the object's boundary and its immediate surroundings, and replaced what was eliminated with neural signals that created the false impression of an elliptical boundary. Here, the element of non-veridicality within the total visual experience would be purely hallucinatory. It would not be a case of the subject's seeing the circular boundary as elliptical, but of his not seeing the boundary at all. But, in the case of the lenses, there is no such element of hallucination. Even where a perception is non-veridical, it is, through and through, perceptive—each portion and aspect of its phenomenal content perceptually covering a real portion or aspect of the physical scene.

In view of all this, it is surely clear that all the perceptions in the series have to be thought of as of the same general kind, with the full veridicality of the final perception being just the limiting case of the increasing partial veridicality of the perceptions which precede it. It would be utterly irrational to suppose that there is a sudden and radical change in the character of the perceiving at the point where we move from the case in which, viewed through glass with only a slight degree of curvature, the object is seen (with a minute degree of inaccuracy) as *almost* circular, to the case in which, viewed through perfectly flat glass, it is seen (wholly accurately) as *exactly* circular. Such a supposition, it is true, is not *logically excluded*; but given the continuities in the character of the causal process and the degree of veridicality, and given that even the non-veridical perceptions are perceptive of the object's actual shape, the rational pressure to apply a uniform account throughout the series is irresistible. But this means that none of the perceptions can be taken as presentational. Even the final perception, which is fully veridical, cannot be thought of as involving the presentational display of the physical shape, since it has to be construed in the same general way as the other perceptions, whose lack of full veridicality automatically excludes a presentational account.

Now this, of course, is just one case. But it is clear that the conclusion drawn, if correct here, will extend to cases of visual perception in general. In the first place, there is obviously no theoretical significance in the fact that the object in the example was *circular*. If we are obliged to reject a presentational account where there is veridical viewing of a *circular* object through plain, undistorting glass, we are equally obliged to reject such an account for the veridical viewing of *any kind* of object or scene through such a medium. Secondly, there is not the slightest reason to doubt that the perceptual relationship involved in seeing something through *plain, undistorting glass* is of the same general character as the relationship which obtains when the only medium is *air*. So if we reject a presentational account for the one type of case, we have to reject it for the other as well. Finally, it is just obvious that if the presentational view fails for the straightforward case of viewing things *through the medium of air*—the case which would surely constitute the presentationalist's best scenario—it must be rejected for visual perception *quite generally*.

This result, admittedly, is still confined to the *visual* realm. But, although I shall not try to argue the point in detail here, similar results can be obtained for all other sense-realms too. For, in the case of each realm, it is possible to devise a similar example, in which a veridical perception is represented as the limiting case of a series of non-veridical perceptions, and in which we encounter the same irresistible pressure to apply a uniform account throughout the series. And the need to accept a non-presentational account for the veridical perception in question would then similarly extend to other veridical perceptions in that realm. In short, if our argument about the lenses has been correct, there is no way of avoiding the quite general conclusion that, in whatever form it comes, perception is never presentational.

In pressing this argument against the presentationalist, I am, admittedly, taking for granted a crucial point, namely that only the *determinate* aspects of the physical world are candidates for presentational display. If this point did not hold—if *determinable* aspects were also available for such display—then the argument would collapse. For it would then become possible to give a presentational account of veridical perception, while preserving its continuity with non-veridical. Thus, in the example of the lenses, the presentationalist could say that where the shape-appearance is (inaccurately) elliptical, there is still an aspect of O's real shape that is both veridically registered and presentationally displayed. For, taking the abstract dimension of elliptical shape, and selecting that range of determinate shapes which runs from the ellipse that characterizes the relevant appearance to the circle that characterizes O itself, he could say that what is both veridically registered and presentationally displayed is O's possession of the determinable shape-attribute which covers this range. This would allow the fully veridical final perception to provide a presentational display of O's fully determinate shape (its circularity), but in a way which gives it the same general character as the other perceptions in the series. For its display of O's circularity would be the limiting case of their display of shape-aspects of steadily increasing specificity—the increasing specificity matching the increasing degree of veridicality. The same account could then be extended to all other cases of this general kind. Thus, quite generally, the presentationalist could say that, where the perceptual registering of the presence of a determinate physical quality Q is veridical to a certain degree, it is also, to that same degree, presentational—presentationally displaying the presence of that determinable of Q which matches the measure of its phenomenal accuracy.

I have taken it for granted that only the determinate aspects of the physical world are candidates for presentational display, and so implicitly excluded this account. And the reason why I have taken this restriction for granted is that the alternative seems to me to be clearly incoherent. On the one hand, it is self-evident that a determinable attribute has no means of realization except in a determinate form. And this does not mean merely that any realization of a determinable attribute is necessarily *accompanied by* a realization of a determinate of it; it means that any realization of a determinable attribute is *itself* (qua concrete event) a realization of a determinate, and only counts as a realization of the determinable by being a realization of this determinate. Thus the only sense in which something can count as a realization of ellipticality is by being a realization of some specific elliptical shape, with precise degrees of elongation and squatness. On the other hand, the presentational display of a physical attribute is, *ex hypothesi*, a display of that attribute *qua physically realized*: the attribute features in the phenomenal content of the perception as an *element of the concrete external situation*, so that its featuring in that content is not something ontologically separate from its occurrence as an attribute of the physical item. In other words, what is on display is not the attribute *in the abstract*, but the relevant physical *instance*. Put together, these two points ensure that the determinable aspects of physical items are not available for presentational display in their determinable form. If they are to be available at all, it can only be as part and parcel of the availability of the determinate forms in which they concretely occur.

It turns out, then, that once the case of non-veridical perception has forced him to abandon the presentational view in its general form, the SDR-theorist is obliged to abandon this view altogether. And this is so, irrespective of how the issue about science is resolved, and, quite generally, irrespective of how broad or narrow we take the domain of veridical perception to be. The point is simply that whatever account we give of veridical perception has to apply to non-veridical perception too, or at least to the kinds of non-veridical perception on which our argument has focused. And there is no disputing that, for cases of non-veridical perception, the presentational view fails.

5 THE INTERNALIST VIEW

I

According to the presentational view, the phenomenal content of perception directly draws its qualitative material from the physical items perceived. A sensible quality is held to feature in the content because perceptual awareness reaches out to the external environment and brings a physical realization of that quality within its scope. The featuring of the quality is not just something which serves to *represent* its external realization: it is that very realization made transparent to the mind—the external qualitative situation made experientially present. Now that this view has been discredited, and discredited in its entirety, the SDR-theorist is forced to think of phenomenal content in a radically different way. He is forced to say that, when a subject S Φ-terminally perceives a physical item x, and x sensibly appears to S as characterized by a certain quality Q, this featuring of Q in the phenomenal content of S's perceiving is ontologically separate from its realization in x (if it is so realized), or in anything else in the physical world—that, whatever it consists in, this phenomenal featuring of Q is not, in itself, the featuring of any physical instance of Q. In other words, although he is committed to taking the perceptual relationship with the external item to be something psychologically fundamental, and although phenomenal content is the manner in which this relationship obtains, he is forced to say that, instead of being drawn from the external environment, the qualitative ingredients of this content are wholly internal to the mind. Let us refer to this new conception of phenomenal content as the *internalist view*. Even if the theorist had been able to retain the presentational view in its modified form, he would, of course, have needed to adopt this internalist view with respect to those qualitative ingredients of content that resisted presentational treatment. But, having abandoned the presentational view in its entirety, he now has to embrace the internalist view in a correspondingly general form—as applying to *all* cases of perception and *all* elements of phenomenal content. So even if Pauline's seeing of L is wholly veridical—even if the way L visually appears to her, in respect of both colour and spatial qualities, exactly matches the way it is—the theorist will now have to say that the featuring of these sensible qualities in the phenomenal content of her seeing is something ontologically separate from their presence in L itself. This does not, of course, preclude him from acknowledging that the two things are causally related—from saying that it is the presence of these qualities in the relevant portion-stage which in some way makes them sensibly apparent to her. And, in acknowledging this causal relation, he could even, given a suitable conception of event-identity, think of the concrete event of phenomenal featuring as *ontologically dependent on* the event of physical realization; for, given the relevant conception, he could insist that the identity of the phenomenal event is partly fixed by, and logically inseparable from, the identity of its physical cause (so that there is no possible world in which that same event occurs without that same cause). But what he cannot say, as an internalist, is that the presence of a quality in this external item is what itself—in its own ontological person—features in the phenomenal content.

The SDR-theorist is forced to adopt the internalist view, and to adopt it for all cases. And there can be no denying that, in doing so, he avoids altogether the objection brought against the presentationalist. For now that the qualitative ingredients of phenomenal content are ontologically separate from their external counterparts, there is no difficulty in accommodating cases of non-veridical perception, in which sensible appearance is at variance with external reality. But this advantage, of course, does not ensure that the approach will prove to be acceptable in other ways. And, in fact, I shall argue that it has to be rejected. Specifically, I shall argue that, by embracing an internalist conception of phenomenal content, the SDR-theorist is left with no coherent account of how content and contact fit together—of how phenomenal content is able to be, what by definition it is required to be, the manner in which perceptual contact is made.

II

The first point we need to note is that, by adopting the internalist view, the SDR-theorist is taking a step in the direction of BRT. BRT claims that, wherever it obtains, the Φ-terminal perceptual relationship breaks down into two components: the realization of a psychological state which is not in itself perceptive of the relevant physical item; and certain additional facts, not involving anything further about the subject's psychological condition at the relevant time. In advancing this decompositional account, BRT is automatically committed to an internalist view of phenomenal content. But what gives it this commitment is that it is committed to an internalist account of the *whole psychological state*. It is committed to thinking of the qualitative ingredients of content as ontologically separate from their external counterparts because it is claiming that the perceptual relationship itself, by which the subject's awareness reaches out to the external reality, disappears at the fundamental level of psychological description. This means that, in adopting the internalist view of content, the SDR-theorist is embracing one aspect of the internalism of BRT, without embracing this internalism in its full-blooded form. He is conceding to the BRT-theorist that the qualitative ingredients of content are ontologically separate from their external counterparts, but still insisting that the perceptual relationship with the external item is a fundamental aspect of the subject's psychological condition. In this way, his position can be seen as falling between the extremes of BRT and the presentational view. BRT, as we have just said, is the position of full-blooded internalism. And, by parity of reasoning, the presentational view (the presentational version of SDR) is the position of full-blooded externalism—insisting that not only the existence of the external item, but also the relevant (sensibly apparent) aspects of its character, or character and location, fundamentally feature in the subject's psychological condition. The internalist version of SDR is a kind of compromise, or hybrid, position between these two extremes, combining the internalist element of one with the externalist element of the other.

Now it is just the fact that SDR-internalism involves this compromise which, as I see it, creates the problem. In the case of each of the extreme positions, whatever other difficulties it may face, we can see how its view about the nature of phenomenal content harmonizes, quite straightforwardly, with its view about the nature of the perceptual relationship. Thus, in the case of BRT, there may be, as we mentioned, a problem in understanding how the kind of relationship it postulates between the subject and the external environment qualifies as genuinely perceptual.[13] But at least the internalist conception of the phenomenal content involved in such a relationship straightforwardly harmonizes with the nature of the relationship itself. Thus the relationship is psychologically mediated by the subject's being in some more fundamental (not in itself physically perceptive) experiential state; and, in being thus mediated, it is automatically endowed with a specific phenomenal content of an internalist kind—a content fixed by the character of the mediating state. Likewise, on the presentational version of SDR, despite the problem over non-veridicality, there is no diffi-

13 Thus see Part Two, Section 1, II.

culty in understanding how phenomenal content and perceptual contact fit together. For the presentation of an external item would automatically involve the displaying of certain aspects of its character (or character and location) in an ontologically immediate way, and, as thus displayed, these aspects would then form, in their own person, the qualitative ingredients of the phenomenal content. But, with the internalist version of SDR, the accounts of content and contact seem, by their contrasting approaches, to pull in opposite directions. Thus if the qualitative ingredients of content are ontologically internal—ontologically separate from their external counterparts—it is hard to see how the perceptual relationship manages to be psychologically fundamental. How does the unmediated perceptual awareness manage to reach its external target if its phenomenal content does not keep (externalistic) pace with it? Conversely, if the awareness does manage to reach its external target without the content keeping pace, it is hard to see how this content can genuinely qualify as the content of the *perceiving*—as the manner in which the *perceptual contact is made.* If its qualitative ingredients stay within the boundaries of the mind—boundaries which ontologically separate the domain of the mental from the external reality—how can this content be anything other than a mere *accompaniment* of the perceptual relationship? In short, whatever the difficulties for the extremes, it is hard to see how there is room for the middle position. Once we adopt an internalist view of content, it is hard to see how we can understand perceptual contact in any but psychologically mediational terms; and once we adopt an SDR-conception of the perceptual relationship, it is hard to see how we can make sense of phenomenal content except as the ontologically immediate imprint of the external situation on the percipient's mind.

Now, at the moment, this only constitutes a *prima facie problem* for the SDR-internalist position, rather than a *conclusive objection.* After all, we have not yet considered, in any detail, what account of phenomenal content the SDR-internalist might want to offer. We know that, whatever that account is , it will have to represent the qualitative ingredients of content as ontologically separate from their external counterparts, and we have noted the apparent tension between this requirement and the acceptance of SDR. But it might be that the tension will disappear once the details of what is envisaged are revealed. So our next task must be to consider what options are available to the SDR-internalist, and whether any of them will serve to eliminate the difficulty which threatens to undermine his position.

One thing is already clear. Although, in adopting an internalist view of phenomenal content, the SDR-theorist is, to that extent, in agreement with

BRT, he cannot just take over one of the possible BRT-accounts of content and conjoin it with his own (SDR) conception of the perceptual relationship. Under BRT, as we have said, the perceptual relationship between a subject and a physical item is psychologically mediated by the subject's being in some more fundamental, not-in-itself-physically-perceptive, psychological state, and the phenomenal content of the perceiving is then directly supplied by the character of this more fundamental state in the context of its mediational role. This means that although, to qualify for its title, phenomenal content is necessarily the content *of perception* (the phenomenal manner in which *perceptual contact is made*), the psychological phenomenon which underlies it is of a type which is not logically tied to the perceptual context: it is of a type which is equally capable of occurrence in perception *and hallucination*. Now it is quite clear that, if he is to have any chance of disposing of the prima facie problem, the SDR-internalist cannot simply take over an account of content of this sort and recombine it with an SDR-conception of the perceiving itself: he cannot call on the services of some category of not-in-themselves-physically-perceptive psychological states, and redeploy them as the suppliers of content for perceptual relationships which are psychologically fundamental. If a psychological state is not in itself (physically) perceptive, the only conceivable way in which it could serve as a supplier of perceptual content would be mediationally—by being a state whose realization constitutively contributed to the securing of perceptual contact in the BRT-way. What the SDR-internalist needs, then, is a form of content which is specifically and distinctively tailored to fit the claims of SDR. And this involves his thinking of it as tied to perception not merely in respect of its *nominal essence* (what is required for it to count as 'phenomenal'), but in its *fundamental psychological nature*. In other words, he has to think of it as something whose psychological character remains that of the content of perception (the manner of physical-item perceiving) at the most fundamental level of description.

The crucial question, then, is whether the theorist can find such an account of content within the constraints of his internalist view. Certainly, all the standard internalist accounts are excluded: they are ones which represent the underlying psychological state as something *not* in itself physically perceptive, and are, in consequence, confined to the framework of BRT. So is there any alternative? Is there any way of representing content in a form which satisfies the dual needs of the SDR-internalist position—a form which ties it to the context of perception at the fundamental level of description, while leaving its qualitative ingredients ontologically internal?

If there is, it will presumably be by an account which, while leaving the qualitative ingredients internal, in some way gives them an irreducible representational concern with the character (character and location) of the relevant (Φ-terminally perceived) physical item.

As far as I can see, there is only one account which might be thought to fit the bill. This account is best seen as a crucially revised version of a theory which forms an important option under BRT. So we need to begin by outlining this BRT-theory, before introducing the changes which would bring it into line with SDR.

III

Faced with the failure of the presentational view, a number of twentieth-century philosophers have suggested that we should think of perception as making contact with the physical world, not presentationally, but by conveying information about it, and that, accordingly, we should think of phenomenal content as what embodies (or embodies the most basic part of) the information, or putative information, thus conveyed.[14] This suggestion can be developed in a number of ways, according to the type of information which is thought to be involved and the supposed nature of its psychological reception. But let us refer to the generic position (however specifically developed) as the *cognitive theory*.

Now, notwithstanding their variation in detail, all the standard ways of developing this theory involve an acceptance of BRT. Thus, in its standard form, the generic cognitive thesis can be formulated like this:

There is a kind K of cognitive seeming, which is not in itself physically perceptive, such that, for any subject S, physical item x, and time t, if S Φ-terminally perceives x at t, then:

(1) it K-seems to S at t that things are currently environmentally a certain way;

(2) S's perceiving of x at t is psychologically mediated by his being in this cognitive state (so that the fact of perceptual contact is constituted by the fact of its K-seeming to him in the relevant way,

[14] The chief exponents of this view are David Armstrong and George Pitcher. Thus see Armstrong's *Perception and the Physical World* (London: Routledge & Kegan Paul, 1961) and *A Materialist Theory of the Mind* (London: Routledge & Kegan Paul, 1968), and Pitcher's *A Theory of Perception* (Princeton: Princeton University Press, 1971).

together with certain additional facts not involving anything further about his psychological condition at t);

and

(3) in the context of this psychological mediation, the content of the
seeming logically determines the phenomenal content of the perceiving.

Thus, in the case of Pauline, the standard cognitivist would see the situation in the following terms. (i) Light from L (the relevant portion-stage of
the apple's surface) enters Pauline's eyes and induces the appropriate firings in her optic nerves. (ii) These firings set up a process in the visual centres of her brain, which issues in the realization of a certain cognitive state
of the relevant kind—an event of its K-seeming to her that there is a hemispherical patch of a certain size and colouring at a certain distance in front
of her. (iii) Her seeing of L at the relevant time t is psychologically mediated by her being in this cognitive state: it is constituted by the combination of its K-seeming to her in the relevant way and certain further facts of
the relevantly restricted kind (in particular, a suitable qualitative relationship between the content of the seeming and the actual character and subject-relative location of L, and a suitable causal role for L in bringing about
this seeming). And (iv) in the context of this mediation, the phenomenal
content of the seeing—L's sensible appearance as a hemispherical patch of
a certain size and colouring and at a certain distance—is logically determined by the informational content of the seeming; in effect, the cognitive
seeming on its own (i.e. without the perceptual contact which it mediates)
covers the strictly mental aspect of how things sensibly appear—an aspect
which is capable of occurring without anything being perceived—and this
then qualifies as the phenomenal manner of the *seeing* (embodying the
sensible appearance of a particular seen item) by virtue of its constitutive
role, in combination with the other relevant factors, in securing contact.

It is clear how, in this standard form, the cognitive theory involves an
acceptance of BRT; and, indeed, it will be as one of the major options under
BRT that we shall be examining it in detail in due course. But what concerns us, at present, is that, by altering this standard version in two crucial
respects, we can adapt the theory to suit the needs of SDR. And it is this
revised version of the theory which might be thought to offer the SDR-
internalist his one chance of success.

The first alteration is concerned with the nature of the environmental information which the theory sees as relevant. In the standard version, as outlined above, the putative information which forms the content of the relevant cognitive seeming is of a purely *general* character: it claims the current instantiation of a certain type of environmental situation, but does not make reference to any particular physical object or event in the subject's actual environment. So, in the case of Pauline, the putative information is merely that there is something of a certain kind and at a certain distance from her—information which makes no reference to the actual physical item seen or to any other physical particular. However, we can at least envisage a way in which the cognitivist could change this aspect of his position. For, instead of taking the relevant information to have this purely general character—claiming that things are currently environmentally thus and so—he could insist that it involves an irreducibly singular reference to the relevant physical item, around which the rest of the informational content is, as it were, ascriptively wrapped. So, in the case of Pauline, instead of saying that the way things K-seem to her is merely that there is a hemispherical patch of a certain size and colouring at a certain distance in front of her, he could say that, *concerning the relevant physical item L* (the particular Φ-terminally seen portion-stage of the apple's surface), the way things K-seem to her is that *it—that particular item*—is currently something with the relevant character and at the relevant distance.[15] And he could insist that there is a similar irreducibly singular reference in the content of the K-seeming in each case of Φ-terminal perception. This, then, would constitute the first of the two relevant alterations to the standard theory. Let us speak of what results as the *de re version* of the cognitive theory, or, for short, the *de re theory*—the title '*de re*' indicating the crucial role of the relevant singular reference.

Now it would be possible for a cognitivist who adopted this new version to confine the revision to that one respect. And, if he did, then the *de re* theory would take its place in an overall account that conformed, in an admittedly eccentric way, to BRT. Thus, despite their irreducible concern with particular physical items, the states of *de re* seeming would be thought of as not, in themselves, physically perceptive, and the perceptual relationship between the subject and the relevant physical item would be thought of as constituted by the cognitive relationship, together with certain further facts. But, while this would be possible, what gives the *de re* theory its

[15] In practice, of course, the total item Φ-terminally seen by Pauline, and hence the total item to which the singular reference will need to be made, will be a larger environmental item, of which L is only one part. Confining our attention to the portion-stage of the apple's surface is purely for the sake of simplicity.

interest is that it provides the opportunity for a quite different approach, involving a further and more far-reaching revision. For, instead of taking the perceptual relationship to be *psychologically mediated* by the cognitive relationship, the *de re* theorist might simply construe the perceptual relationship *as* this cognitive relationship, thus allowing the perceptual relationship to be something psychologically fundamental. Thus, in the case of Pauline, he might say that her Φ-terminal seeing of L under the relevant sensible appearance *consists in* its K-seeming to her that L (that particular item) is of the relevant character and at the relevant distance, and that because the *de re* seeming is something psychologically fundamental, the perceptual relationship (which he equates with it) qualifies as fundamental too. This would yield a position which accords with SDR. Moreover, as well as meeting the requirements of SDR, such a position would also meet the requirements of the internalist view. For, as on any version of the cognitive theory, the featuring of qualities in the relevant cognitive episode would be ontologically quite separate from their featuring (if they do feature) in the external situation. So the *de re* theory seems to offer the opportunity for an account of just the kind that the SDR-internalist needs—an account which combines, and seemingly harmonizes, a fundamentalist conception of the perceptual relationship and an internalist conception of the qualitative ingredients of phenomenal content.

IV

Have we, then, found here a satisfactory SDR-internalist account—an account which eliminates the prima facie problem and allows the theorist to reconcile the two elements of his position? Well, let me start by putting on one side two possible sources of objection.

In the first place, I shall not, in the present context, try to pursue the general issue of *de re* thought. There are those who would insist that the very notion of a subject's standing in an irreducibly singular cognitive relation to an external particular is simply incoherent—that in any case in which a subject stands in a cognitive relation to such an item, we can only make sense of this relational fact by taking it to decompose into the subject's being in a more fundamental cognitive state (not in itself involving such a relationship), together with certain further (non-cognitive) facts. If this claim were correct, then, of course, it would automatically rule out the viability of any *de re* cognitivist account of perception. But, for present purposes, I am happy to leave this challenge on one side, and proceed on the assumption that, whatever the merits or failings of the particular proposal in front of us, its commitment to the existence of *de re* forms of cognitive mentality is not as such objectionable.

Secondly, I shall not try to deal, at this point, with the general issue of the acceptability of the cognitive theory. There are, it must be said, a number of prima facie problems which the theory faces, irrespective of whether it is developed in the standard or *de re* fashion—the most obvious being the difficulty of seeing how a purely cognitive account of phenomenal content could do justice to its phenomenological character, as something quasi-presentational. This, and other general difficulties with the cognitivist approach, are ones which I shall be considering in detail in Part Three, when I focus on the cognitive theory in the framework of BRT. For the time being, I am happy, once again, to put these difficulties on one side, and leave open the possibility that some form of cognitivist account may prove acceptable.

But even when we set aside any general worries about the notion of *de re* thought, and any general difficulties for the cognitive theory as such, there are special reasons why we should not think of the *de re* theory as affording the SDR-internalist an adequate account. The main reason, as we shall see, is that, irrespective of whether it features in the context of SDR-internalism, the theory itself is simply untenable. But before I turn to this point, there is another factor which I want to bring into the picture, not only for its bearing on the particular question before us, but also because it will give us a better understanding of the full extent of the problem which the SDR-internalist faces.

V

In order for a subject to be in Φ-terminal contact with a certain physical item, the phenomenal content involved has to be, to an adequate degree, qualitatively appropriate to that item, relative to the conditions of observation. We can best bring out this point by focusing on a case where all the other conditions associated with perception are present, but the factor of appropriateness is conspicuously absent. Thus suppose that Pauline is sitting at home, with her eyes turned towards the apple on the table, with nothing obstructing her line of vision, and with all the other external factors favouring the achievement of visual contact. And suppose that light reflected from the surface of the apple, and from other things in the vicinity, enters her eyes in the normal way and sets up the appropriate kind of process in her optic nerves, which then transmit the appropriate kinds of signal to the brain. But, at this point, something peculiar happens. The brain responds to the incoming signals in a totally bizarre way, producing a visual experience which is not remotely like the sort of experience which is normal for that kind of photic input. It might be, for example, that the resulting experience is, subjectively, like that of someone viewing a herd of elephants at an African water-hole, or like that of someone seeing the Eiffel Tower in moonlight. Now it is surely clear that, given the extent of the disparity between the real character of the external situation and the content of her experience, we cannot think of Pauline as in visual contact with the apple, or anything else in her environment. It is true that the environment plays a causal role in producing the experience, and with respect to the photic input, its role is of the normal kind for those circumstances. And we can even suppose that, as in the case of normal visual perception, the brain response preserves a kind of causal isomorphism between elements of the resulting experience and elements of the input, so that, relative to a suitably fine-grained division, different elements of the experience can be causally traced back to different elements in the environment. But it would be absurd to suppose that the experience qualifies as an actual seeing of the apple, and that the only way in which its deviant content affects the situation is in making this seeing radically non-veridical. It is just obvious that, in the context of the conditions envisaged, the extent of the non-veridicality precludes visual contact altogether. So here we have a clear illustration of the point at issue, that there can only be Φ-terminal contact where there is a sufficient degree of qualitative appropriateness of phenomenal content to the item perceived, relative to the conditions of observation; and it is easy to think of a host of other examples which would illustrate this point in an analogous way. Strictly speaking, I should speak here not of the qualitative appropriateness of *phenomenal content*, but of the qualitative appropriateness of that experiential content which passes the subjective tests for phenomenality, i.e. that content which is either phenomenal or subjectively poses as such. For since phenomenal content is, by definition, tied to the context of (physical-item) perception, then where the degree of appropriateness fails to meet the perceptual requirements, the content involved does not qualify as genuinely phenomenal. But, having noted this point, we can conveniently continue to use the simpler, if slightly looser, mode of locution without risk of confusion.

Now we already know that, for the purposes of Φ-terminal contact, phenomenal content can have a sufficient degree of appropriateness without being *fully veridical*; that is why we were able to recognize cases of partially non-veridical perception, where the sensible appearance of the perceived item is in certain respects at variance with its actual character, and why, in recognizing such cases, we were obliged to reject the presentational view. But what also needs to be stressed is that the relevant kind of appropriateness is not even entirely a matter of *veridicality*. For it is partly a matter of conformity to whatever mode of sensible appearance is *normal*, or *normative*, for the relevant sort of item, in the relevant sort of conditions. Thus, in the case of the stick in water, there is no denying that its bent appearance is non-veridical: the stick is not in reality as it sensibly appears. But looking bent in those circumstances, where the light involved is subject to the relevant forms of refraction, is the *appropriate* way of looking for the purposes of perception, and it would be someone who *failed* to see it as bent who would need to consult an oculist. Another, and rather more complicated, example is that of colour-perception construed in a Lockean fashion—where physical colour is taken to be a mere power to produce certain kinds of colour-experience in us. For then, presumably, the appropriateness of someone's colour-experience on a given occasion will be partly a matter of conformity to the normal way in which the relevant type of pigment, or light, is disposed to look to that subject, or perhaps to some larger group of subjects to which he belongs (though it may also be thought to depend on the fact that the normal colour-system of this subject or group is sufficiently veridical with respect to degrees of qualitative similarity and difference at the physical level). However, the details of all this need not concern us. All that matters, for present purposes, is that, where there is Φ-terminal perceptual contact, there has to be an adequate degree of qualitative appropriateness, irrespective of how, precisely, such appropriateness is to be construed. Let us speak of this as the *appropriateness-requirement*.

There can be no denying that (in some form) the appropriateness-requirement holds. But the question we need to focus on is: why? How is the requirement to be explained? What is its rationale? After all, even in such an extreme case as that of Pauline above, there is the formal possibility of representing it as a case of perception—representing it as a case of the subject's perceiving something (in Pauline's case, the domestic scene) but under a totally deviant appearance. So exactly what is it that makes such a representation unacceptable?

From the standpoint of BRT, the situation is straightforward. For the appropriateness-requirement is an immediate consequence of the way in which perceiving is construed. Thus Φ-terminal perceptual contact is psychologically mediated by the subject's being in some more fundamental experiential state—the state which logically determines the nature of the phenomenal content—and this state's having a sufficient degree of appropriateness to the external item is a precondition of the contact being (thus mediationally) secured. In the standard version of the cognitive theory, for example, the obtaining of perceptual contact is, in part, constitutively dependent on the fact that the propositional content of the relevant seeming—its K-seeming that things are environmentally thus and so—is appropriately related to the actual environmental situation. Likewise, the requirement would be immediately explicable on the presentational view—though, of course, in a form which is distinctive to that account. For, as we have seen, by insisting that phenomenal content draws its qualitative ingredients from the external situation, the presentational view entails that wherever there is Φ-terminal perceiving, there is full veridicality. And although full veridicality is not what sufficient appropriateness actually demands, it would be what full appropriateness amounted to *from the presentational view's own standpoint.* But what is much more difficult to see is how the appropriateness-requirement could be explained in the framework of SDR-internalism. *Ex hypothesi,* the explanations offered by BRT and the presentational view are not available: the requirement cannot be represented as a consequence of the way in which perceptual contact is mediationally secured, since contact is taken to be psychologically direct; nor can it be attributed to the presentational character of perceptual awareness, since that is excluded by the internalist view of content. The difficulty is in envisaging any alternative. If contact is psychologically direct, but the qualitative ingredients of content are ontologically internal, why *should* there be any limit on how far the content can be out of keeping with the character of the item with which the contact is made?

This difficulty for SDR-internalism is, in a sense, just a special aspect of the general problem already identified—that the SDR-conception of the perceptual relationship and the internalist view of phenomenal content seem to be pulling in opposite directions, thus preventing any coherent account of how contact and content fit together. For obviously a proper understanding of the contact–content relationship would have to include, in particular, an understanding of why content has to reach a certain standard of appropriateness, with respect to the relevant physical item, for contact to obtain. But, while the difficulty is a special aspect of the already familiar general problem, it is not one which explicitly featured in our earlier discussion. Nor, crucially, is it one whose special significance was implicitly taken into account.

What gives this aspect its special significance is the combination of two factors. The first is simply that it presents the general problem in a particularly clear and sharp form. Even in its general form, the problem calls for a response: SDR-internalism will not be acceptable unless it can provide

some account of how its externalist conception of the perceptual relationship and its internalist conception of phenomenal content can be coherently
combined. But, in the specific form concerned with the appropriateness-
requirement, the problem becomes especially acute. For it identifies a quite
specific respect in which we know that contact and content have to har-
monize, and which, on the face of it, SDR-internalism is not equipped to
explain. Within the context of the general challenge to the SDR-internalist
approach, what we find here is a quite clear-cut objection, which the theorist needs to address and eliminate if his position is to survive.

The second factor which gives the difficulty over the appropriateness-
requirement a special significance is that it is not something which the
adoption of the *de re* theory would, in any obvious way, help to overcome.
It is easy enough to see how, assuming it to be acceptable in other respects,
the theory would answer the *general* problem, conceived in purely *general*
terms. For, by construing the perceptual relationship as a *de re* cognitive
relationship, it would precisely show how this relationship can be psychologically fundamental when the qualitative ingredients of its content are
ontologically internal. But what is wholly unclear is how the theory would
deal with the special point about appropriateness. For how would the *de re*
construal of the perceptual relationship help to explain why the phenomenal content—embodied by the relevant putative environmental information—stays within the limits of appropriateness which perception
requires? What in the structure of the envisaged situation would exclude
cases in which—taking into account all the relevant factors—the way
things seem to the subject about the relevant external item is wholly out of
keeping with the character of that item, relative to the conditions of observation? It seems that the only way in which the *de re* theorist could ensure
that the putative information involved stays within the relevant limits
would be by arranging for the content of this information to play a crucial
role in determining that a particular physical item forms its external refer-
ent, so that the information only counts as being about a given item on
condition that the properties of the item are of the relevant—appropriate-
ness-conferring—kind. But no such arrangement can be coherently envisaged. For it is only in so far as its reference to the item is already fixed,
independently of the content of the information, that it is possible for this
information to be *irreducibly* about it; and if the information is not *irreducibly* about it—if it is only about it by virtue of the item's answering to
some specification which the information provides—then we have shifted
from the *de re* version of the cognitive theory to the theory in its standard
form. The basic information will then simply be that there is something of

a certain character which currently stands to the subject in a certain spatial relation—without singular reference to anything other than the subject and the time.[16] Admittedly, there is *one* way in which a *de re* theorist
could make provision for the appropriateness-requirement. For he could
say that, while there is nothing in the structure of the cognitive situation
which prevents the putative information from being wayward, it is only
when it is sufficiently appropriate that the cognitive relationship qualifies
as perceptual. But this, crucially, would be to pursue the *de re* approach in
a *BRT*-fashion. It would amount to saying that perceptual contact is constituted by the combination of the cognitive relationship and those facts—
about the character of the relevant item and the external situation—which,
in relation to the information involved, ensure that appropriateness
obtains. And so this would be of no help to someone defending a version
of SDR.

It seems to me, then, that the SDR-internalist cannot deal with the problem of the appropriateness-requirement by invoking the *de re* theory. Nor,
as far as I can see, can he deal with this problem in any way at all. As I see
it, we have here a decisive objection to the SDR-internalist position, and
one which is additional to the general problem that we had already
encountered.

VI

If I am right, the *de re* theory cannot help the SDR-internalist to deal with
the specific problem of the appropriateness-requirement. And if, as seems
to me, there is no other source of help available, this, on its own, shows his
position to be untenable. But it is not the only respect in which the outcome for his position turns out to be negative. For, on reflection, we can
see that, even with respect to the general problem, the *de re* theory is of no
assistance. And the reason for this is simply that the theory is, in itself, incoherent.

If the putative information supplied by perception is to be irreducibly
de re, the *de re* reference must, as we noted, be fixed independently of the
content of the information. But it is also necessary that the subject have,
independently of his acquisition of the information, a way of *grasping* the
reference: he must have a way of *identifying* the item referred to, a way of

---

[16] From the viewpoint of the one who is receiving the information, these references would,
of course, be demonstrative—the subject being identified as 'I' and the current time as 'now'.

knowing which item the information concerns. After all, he is not just receiving some *symbolic vehicle* of information, where it would be possible to register the presence of the vehicle without registering what it signifies. The information forms the very content of his cognitive state: it is a matter of its (in some way) cognitively seeming to him that things are, with respect to the relevant item, a certain way. And this seeming would not be possible unless the identity of the item which the information is irreducibly about was part of what was cognitively registered.

The underlying point here, of course, is not specifically about *perceptual* information; it applies quite generally. Thus a subject cannot come, *in any way*, to acquire information which is irreducibly about a particular object, unless he has, independently of that information, a way of identifying the object in question. But, in the case of perceptual information—at least the perceptual information directly associated with sensible appearance—the point applies in a distinctive way. Typically, when one acquires information about some particular object, the object is something of which one already has identifying knowledge, and one is able to acquire the new information because one is able to recognize—for example, from the symbolic form in which it is being communicated—that it is *that* object (thus identified) which it is about. One knows already, say, who President Clinton is, and, on opening one's newspaper, learns some new fact (or alleged fact) about him—picking up the reference to the Clinton of one's prior knowledge from the occurrence of his name and title in the journalist's report. Now, in the case of perception, the subject *may* have, prior to the perceptual encounter, identifying knowledge of the item which he comes to perceive, or of the persisting object of which that item is a momentary stage; and, in acquiring perceptual information about it, he may then be able to exploit this knowledge and recognize what he encounters, and gains information about, as, or as a stage of, this already familiar thing. But, crucially, such prior identifying knowledge is not *essential* for perception; and even where it is present, the subject can only make use of it, to achieve a recognition of the identity of the perceptual object, because there is a more basic way in which, quite independently of this knowledge, the object is made available for identification by the perceptual encounter itself. This more basic form of identification is demonstrative. Thus, in order to see the apple, Pauline does not need to know of its existence beforehand. And if she does happen to have this prior knowledge (for example, she may have bought the apple the day before and placed it in its present position), her ability to apply it to the perceptual situation, and identify the item it concerns with the item which she now sees, depends on her ability to identify what she now sees in a demonstrative way, simply through its being a current object of perception.

The significance of this to our present discussion is that it puts an immediate constraint on the kind of identifiability which the *de re* cognitivist has to ascribe to the relevant *res* in the context of the relevant seeming. It means that, in taking Φ-terminal perception to involve a kind of *de re* cognitive seeming—a seeming which is irreducibly concerned with the particular item perceived—he has to say that the way in which the subject must be able to identify the relevant item, in order to be a subject to whom things thus seem, is the demonstrative way made available by the perceiving itself. But we can now see that the *de re* cognitivist is in deep trouble. For it is clear that this demonstrative mode of identification, though perceptually available, is not available independently of the item's sensible appearance. And here the point is not just that it is only available through perception, and that anything perceived is perceived under a sensible appearance. The point is that it is only in so far as an item is perceived under a sensible appearance that it is before the mind in a way which permits the relevant form of identification. Thus it is only in so far as the apple, or its relevant portion-stage, is visible to Pauline as an item of a certain shape and colouring, at a certain distance from her, that she is equipped to identify it as *this* thing, now perceptually before her. It is precisely through its visual appearance that it becomes relevantly identifiable.

The incoherence of the *de re* theory is now clear. The account presupposes that the subject has a way of identifying the item he perceives which is independent of the information which his perceiving supplies about it; while, in actual fact, the only form of identification which is needed in cases of perception—and often the only form which is available—is one which relies on the very phenomenal content which the presence of the information is (from the standpoint of the account) supposed to provide. In short, we can coherently suppose that the information fundamentally supplied by perception is *de re*, so long as we allow that the way in which the relevant item is perceptually identifiable is independent of the acquisition of this information. And likewise, we can coherently suppose that perception itself is to be construed in a cognitivist fashion, so long as we refrain from giving a *de re* account of the kind of information which features in this construal. But what we cannot coherently do is take the fundamental perceptual information to be *de re*, but, by construing perception itself in cognitivist terms, represent the identifiability of the relevant item as depending on the acquisition of the very information—the *de re* information—whose acquisition would only be possible if an independent mode of identification were available. And it is just this incoherence which we find in the *de re* theory.

It turns out, then, that, whatever role the SDR-internalist may have hoped to assign to it, the *de re* theory fails in its own terms.

VII

This completes the demise of SDR-internalism. It was clear from the start that, by combining an SDR-conception of perceptual contact with an internalist conception of phenomenal content, the theory faced a prima facie problem, since these different elements seem to pull in different directions. For a while, it seemed that the theorist might be able to deal with this problem by invoking the *de re* version of the cognitive theory—a version in which the information that determines phenomenal content is irreducibly concerned with a particular physical item. But, on closer examination, it turned out that the *de re* theory was powerless to help with the specific difficulty over the appropriateness-requirement. And it has further turned out that, whatever help it might seem to offer with respect to the general problem, the theory itself is incoherent. The upshot is that, within the framework of SDR-internalism, there is no way of providing a satisfactory account of how contact and content fit together, either in general terms, or in relation to the specific issue of appropriateness. None, at least, that I can see.

6 CONCLUSION

With the discrediting of SDR-internalism, our argument against SDR itself is now complete. For we have considered all the various ways in which SDR can be developed, and shown that none is satisfactory. The whole argument can be summarized thus:

1. SDR takes the Φ-terminal perceptual relationship to be something psychologically fundamental—in particular, something which does not decompose in the way envisaged by BRT.

2. Like any other theory of perception, SDR has to be able to give an adequate account of phenomenal content (the phenomenal manner of perceiving) and the way in which it relates to the obtaining of perceptual contact.

3. One of the uncontroversial points about contact and content is that, given any case of Φ-terminal perceiving, the relevant fact of content involves something genuinely additional to the bare fact of contact, or sense-modally specific contact.

4. This point, together with the claim of SDR itself, limits the possibilities for an SDR-account to two broad approaches. One is the *perceptualist strategy*, which takes the bare fact of contact to be psychologically fundamental, and represents the fact of content as constituted by the combination of the contact-fact and certain other facts. The other is the *integrational strategy*, which takes the facts of contact and content to be different and complementary aspects of a single psychologically fundamental fact—the fact of the subject's perceiving a certain physical item in a certain phenomenal manner.

5. The perceptualist strategy can be quickly dismissed. A little reflection reveals that, in any given case, there is no set of facts which can combine with the fact of contact to yield the fact of content in the right (constitutive) kind of way. So the integrational strategy offers SDR its only chance of success.

6. The integrational strategy itself allows for three options, according to the ontological relationship which is held to obtain between the featuring of a quality in the phenomenal content of a perception (as a quality of how the Φ-terminally perceived item sensibly appears) and its featuring in the external environment (as a quality which the perceived item actually instantiates). First, there is the *presentational view*, which holds that the qualitative ingredients of content are directly drawn from the external environment, so that each phenomenal featuring of a quality is the featuring of that very instance of it which occurs in the physical item perceived (the qualitative elements of the external situation becoming present to the mind in a mode of absolute ontological immediacy). Secondly, there is the *internalist view*, which holds that the qualitative ingredients of content are ontologically separate from their external counterparts, so that a phenomenal featuring of a quality is *not* the featuring of some physical instance of it. Finally, there is the *modified presentational view*, which is a mixture of the other two, holding that the featuring of a quality in phenomenal content is sometimes to be construed in a presentational way, and sometimes in an internalist.

7. The presentational view fails because it does not accommodate cases of non-veridical perception, in which the sensible appearance of the perceived item is, in some respect, at variance with its actual character.

8. The internalist view accommodates cases of non-veridical perception. But, by combining an SDR-conception of perceptual contact with an internalist conception of phenomenal content, it does not permit a coherent account of how contact and content fit together.

9. The modified presentational view fails because of its hybrid character. Once the need for an internalist account is recognized for cases of *non-veridical* perception, there is irresistible pressure to extend the same treatment to *veridical* perception too.

10. So, within the framework of the integrational strategy, there is no satisfactory version of SDR.

11. But, with the exclusion of the perceptualist strategy, this means that there is no satisfactory version of SDR at all.

12. So we are forced to conclude that SDR is false.

There are two final points which we need to note in connection with this outcome.

First, we need to be aware of the full extent of what we have established. SDR itself makes a *general* claim about cases of Φ-terminal perception. It asserts that, *whenever* a subject Φ-terminally perceives a physical item, this perceiving is psychologically direct. So it would suffice for the falsity of SDR if there were one instance of Φ-terminal perceiving that was psychologically mediated. But, in showing that there is no acceptable version of SDR, our argument has shown that the SDR-account fails for *all* cases of Φ-terminal perception. It has shown that there is no instance of Φ-terminal perceiving where there is an acceptable SDR-account of the nature of contact and content, and how they fit together.

Secondly, we need to remind ourselves of the framework in which our examination of SDR has been conducted. At the end of Part One, I indicated that, along with the assumption of physical realism, there was something else that I was provisionally going to take for granted and build into the framework of our discussion. This further assumption was that, whatever the correct account of it, we do have perceptual access to the physical world, and one which allows physical items to become perceptible to us in just those kinds of circumstance, and by the use of those sense-organs, that we ordinarily suppose. Now this assumption has a crucial bearing on what we are entitled to think of our argument as having established. What, in the first instance, the argument shows is that, if we take any supposed type of Φ-terminal perceiving, SDR is not able to offer an adequate account of how the relevant perceptual relationship works. And from this it is natural to conclude, as indeed I concluded above, that SDR is false. But, without the relevant assumption, this conclusion would not strictly follow. For it would still be possible to insist that our ordinary concept of perception is committed to SDR, and that what our argument shows is not that SDR gives the wrong account of perception in the abstract, but that the phenomenon which passes as perception for ordinary purposes does not satisfy the requirements which this concept imposes. It could even be insisted that, by its commitment to SDR, our ordinary concept of perception becomes logically incapable of application at all.

These, indeed, remain—in the long term—options, and ones about which I shall have more to say in due course. But, for the time being, I want to continue to approach the topic of perception from a common-sense standpoint, and look for an account which will not only meet the requirements of our concept, but allow us to retain our ordinary beliefs as to how this concept applies. Since we are also, provisionally, taking for granted the truth of physical realism, this will mean, in the first instance, looking for an account of perception in the framework of BRT.

PART THREE

THE MEDIATING
PSYCHOLOGICAL STATE

1 INTRODUCTION

I

SDR—the strong, full-blooded version of direct realism—has been refuted, and indeed has been shown to fail for all cases of perception. Given this, it is natural to conclude that the correct account, and the correct account for all cases, is that of its realist rival, BRT, which is the broad (flexible) form of the representative theory. Like SDR, BRT accepts the framework of physical realism, which takes the physical world to be something whose existence is logically independent of the human mind, and something which is, in its basic character, metaphysically fundamental. But, in contrast to SDR, it claims that Φ-terminal perceiving is always psychologically mediated. That is, it claims that, for any subject S, physical item x, and time t, if S Φ-terminally perceives x at t, then there is some psychological state Σ, which is not in itself x-perceptive, such that S's perceiving of x at t breaks down into (is constituted by the combination of) two components, one component consisting in S's being in Σ at t, the other comprising certain additional facts, though ones which do not involve anything further about S's psychological condition at t (anything over and above his being in Σ). In claiming that *Φ-terminal* perceiving is always psychologically mediated, BRT is committed to claiming that *all* physical-item perceiving is psychologically mediated, since any psychological mediation which applies at the point of Φ-terminality will automatically carry over to contact with something perceptually more remote—though perhaps with an expanded Σ. Moreover, in stipulating that the Σ involved in the mediation of Φ-terminal perceiving is one which is not in itself perceptive of the *relevant physical item*, BRT is in effect committed to saying that it is not, in itself, physically perceptive *at all.* It is committed to taking it to be a state which it is logically possible for someone to be in without there being anything physical which he perceives.

Given the failure of SDR, it is, as I said, natural to conclude that BRT is correct. What makes this natural is that BRT is the only alternative to SDR within the framework of physical realism, and this framework itself seems, on the face of it, not open to serious challenge. At any rate, let us, for the time being, continue with the assumption of physical realism, and, on this basis, look for an account of perception in accordance with BRT.

Within this framework, there are now two main areas of investigation. In the first place, there is the question of the nature of the mediationally relevant psychological states. BRT stipulates that these states are not, in themselves, perceptive of the relevant physical items, and, as we have just noted, this involves taking them to be states which are not, in themselves, physically perceptive at all. But, beyond this, the theory does not impose any restrictions on their nature; this, of course, is why it received the title of the *broad* (or *flexible*) representative theory, in contrast with the *narrow* (or *restrictive*) version, which requires the psychological states to involve the occurrence of internal objects of awareness. Within the framework of the broad theory, then, one whole area of investigation concerns the nature of the psychological states mediationally involved, and, in particular, whether they have the specific form ascribed to them by the narrow theory.

The other area of investigation concerns the nature and role of the additional facts—the facts which (as the second of the two components) combine with the realization of the psychological state to secure, constitutively, the fact of perceptual contact. BRT stipulates that these facts do not involve anything further about the subject's psychological condition at the relevant time, but otherwise, again, leaves things open. We can already identify, in broad outline, some of the basic factors that will be involved. It is clear that the nature of the perceived physical item, its spatiotemporal relation to the subject, and the conditions of observation will all be relevant, since on these depend the qualitative appropriateness of the psychological state to the item. Nor can there be any doubting the relevance of the causal role of the physical item in bringing about a realization of the psychological state. But we still have to work out the details of how these factors apply and how they manage to combine with the psychological component to create perceptual contact.

In this present phase of our discussion, I shall focus exclusively on the first of these areas of investigation, concerning the nature of the relevant psychological states. The second area, concerning the nature and role of the additional facts, will be considered in Part Four.

There is one point of terminology which I should mention at the outset. I have already made it clear that I am using the term 'state' to mean *type*-state, not *token*-state, so that the very same state can be realized in different objects and on different occasions. What I additionally need to make clear, as we begin this new phase of our discussion, is that when I use the term 'psychological state', I mean this to cover the full range of different kinds of thing which can form ingredients of a subject's psychological condition at a time. So, as well as covering ingredients that would be *standardly* classified as states (things like beliefs and moods, which a subject can remain in over a period of time), I also mean the expression to cover types of mental *occurrence* and mental *act*. Thus in formulating BRT as a thesis of psychological mediation, and in using the term 'state' to signify the kind of thing whose realization plays the psychologically mediating role, I am not intending to impose, in advance, any restrictions on how the theorist might develop his position. I am allowing him to suppose that perceptual contact is mediated by the subject's being in a certain psychological state in the ordinary sense; but I am also allowing him to suppose that the contact is mediated by the subject's undergoing some psychological event or performing some psychological act. This wide use of the term 'state', in the relevant context, is purely for ease of expression: it is convenient to have a single word which will cover the whole range of ways in which, with respect to the psychological aspects of the situation, the mediation thesis might be developed.

II

We are only interested, at this stage, in the psychological mediation of Φ-*terminal* perception, where the relevant physical item is the most immediate among physical items perceived—where the perceiving of the relevant item is not perceptually mediated by the perceiving of a further item which is also physical. In the case of Φ-terminal perception, the psychological states which are mediationally involved are experiential states of a narrowly circumscribed kind. We have already noted the intimate connection between Φ-terminal perception and what I have called 'phenomenal content'. Thus whenever a physical item is Φ-terminally perceived, it is perceived under a certain sensible appearance, and the phenomenal content of the perception is what, on the mental side, embodies this appearance: it is that aspect of the experiential manner of the perceiving which embodies the sensible manner in which the item perceptually appears. Now the psychological states which are capable of playing a mediational role in

Φ-terminal perception exactly correspond to the available forms of phenomenal content. Thus, for each relevant psychological state Σ, there is a
correlated form of phenomenal content F such that (1) wherever a Φ-terminal perceiving is mediated by a realization of Σ, it has, by virtue of this,
a content of form F, this content drawing its whole character from the character of Σ, and (2) wherever a Φ-terminal perceiving has a content of form
F, it has this content by virtue of being psychologically mediated by a realization of Σ. In other words, the psychological states which are mediationally involved in Φ-terminal perception are precisely those experiential
states which, in their mediational role, underlie and qualitatively furnish
the phenomenal content of such perception.

Notice that I do not *identify* the relevant states with the relevant forms
of content: the states and the forms of content are 1–1 correlated, but they
are not the same. This is because the forms of content are, by definition,
forms of *perceptual* content—modes of *physical-item perceiving*—and so
are essentially tied to the context of perception. But the relevant psychological states are, *ex hypothesi*, not essentially physical-item perceptive: they
are equally capable of realization in the contexts of perception and hallucination. The difference is reflected in the different forms of locution that
we need to employ in recording cases of the two types of thing. Thus, in
recording the phenomenal content of Pauline's perception at a particular
time, we would say something along the lines of

   'L visually appears to Pauline as a roughly hemispherical green patch of
   such and such a size and at such and such a distance in front of her'

where L is the momentary item (the particular portion-stage of the surface
of the apple) which she Φ-terminally sees; whereas in recording the realization of the mediationally involved psychological state, we would have to
say something like

   'It is with Pauline visuo-experientially as if there is currently a roughly
   hemispherical green patch of such and such a size, and at such and such
   a distance in front of her',

or perhaps better—to make clear that the 'as if'-clause is intended to characterize how things are *represented to the subject*—

   'It is with Pauline visuo-experientially in a way which makes it seem to
   her as if there is currently a roughly hemispherical green patch of such
   and such a size, and at such and such a distance in front of her'.

Quite generally, in recording the realization of a mediational state, we would need to employ some such mode of locution as

> 'It is with S M-experientially as if (or in a way which makes it seem to S as if) things are currently, environmentally, thus and so',

with S as the subject and M as the sense-modality involved. It is obvious how statements of this form leave it entirely open as to whether the experience involved is physically perceptive or hallucinatory.

Because of their 1–1 correspondence with the forms of phenomenal content, I shall call the relevant psychological states *phenomenal-experiential* states (PE-states), and correspondingly speak of the psychological particulars which form their concrete instances—the instances or episodes of experiential mentality which occur when such states are realized—as *phenomenal experiences*. It is the issue of the nature of these states that we now need to investigate. The mode of locution introduced above, as a model for recording cases of phenomenal experience, is, of course, to be seen as entirely neutral on this issue. It serves to bring out the relationship between phenomenal experience and phenomenal content, but does not commit us to any particular account of how the states are to be ultimately (philosophically) construed. It helps to set up the target for our philosophical investigation, not to indicate its results.

III

Each phenomenal-experiential state (each PE-state) in some way represents a certain type of environmental situation, defined by its sensible-qualitative features and its spatiotemporal relationship to the subject at the relevant time. Thus, in as much as it is with Pauline visuo-experientially as if (in a way which makes it seem to her as if) there is currently an item of the relevant sensible type, at the relevant distance, and in the relevant direction, her PE-state is one which in some way represents that type of environmental situation—the situation of there currently being just such an item at just such a location. Now, for any situation-type represented by a PE-state, there are other ways—not PE-ways—in which this type could be represented. For example, someone could just *think about it*, or *describe it*, or *want it to be realized*, or, in the visual case, *paint it*, and none of these forms of representation would be the same as the *PE*-form. Moreover, there is a multitude of situation-types which are capable of being represented in other (non-PE) ways, but which are not capable of being represented by

PE-states. For PE-states can only represent those types of situation which can feature in the content of sensible appearance—types which are definable by the sensible qualities distinctively associated with the relevant sense-realm, together with spatial and temporal relations. Putting both points together, we can see that the issue over the nature of PE-states becomes, at its core, the issue of the precise character of PE-representation, and of why this distinctive form of representation is restricted in scope to the relevant class of situation-types.

Two things are clear in advance. First, whatever its precise nature, the way in which a PE-state represents a certain type of environmental situation is such as to invite a subject who is in that state to believe that such a situation obtains. Thus in as much as it is with Pauline visuo-experientially as if there is currently an item of a certain sensible character, in a certain location, she is thereby invited to believe that this is how things are; and such an invitation would remain even if her experience were hallucinatory, rather than physically perceptive. Being in receipt of an invitation is not, of course, a guarantee that one accepts it, and, in this respect, the case of the PE-invitation is no different: it can easily happen that a subject judges or suspects that things are not as his experience invites him to believe, and so rejects the invitation. He might, for example, know that he is the victim of hallucination, or that the situation is one (such as the stick in water) in which things are not as they sensibly appear.

Secondly, the way in which a PE-state issues this invitation-to-believe is such as to give the subject the impression—itself a sort of belief-invitation—that he is directly presented with an instance of the relevant situation-type. Thus in as much as it is with Pauline visuo-experientially as if there is currently an item of a certain shape, size, and colour, at a certain location, it is not merely that she is invited to believe that this is how things are. Rather, she is invited to believe that this is how things are *by* being invited to believe that she is directly visually presented with an environmental situation of this type—directly presented with an item of this sensible sort, in such a spatial relationship to her. This, of course, is just a re-applying, to PE-states, of the point that was earlier made about sensible appearance—that its carrying the subjective impression of being presentational is one of the things which distinguishes it from other forms of appearance. We also know, from that earlier discussion, what it is for a relationship between a subject and an environmental situation to qualify as presentational in the relevant sense. Thus the relationship qualifies as presentational if and only if it brings the situation before the subject's mind in a way which (1) makes it available for demonstrative identification, (2) displays the relevant aspects of its character (in a way which makes them immediately available for cognitive scrutiny), and (3) is wholly non-representational (something ontologically immediate, rather than involving concepts, symbols, or images, as a psychological means of registering the presence or character of the situation). So, in receiving the impression that he is directly presented with an instance of the relevant situation-type, the PE-subject is being invited to believe that there is an environmental situation to which he is related in this sort of way. This does not, of course, mean that the subject has to grasp the content of the invitation *in the form* which its analysis brings to light—as an invitation to believe that the bringing-to-mind meets the three conditions specified above. All it means is that what he is invited to believe is something whose truth-conditions can be spelt out in that fashion.

The importance of these two points, for our present discussion, is that they impose requirements—or in effect a single rich requirement—on the adequacy of any account of the nature of PE-states. For any account must be one which explains why these points hold. It must explain why the way in which a PE-state represents a certain type of environmental situation is such as to invite a subject who is in that state to believe that he is directly presented with a situation of this type, and thereby to invite him to believe that a situation of this type obtains. Of course, the simplest way of explaining this would be to suppose that what the subject is invited to believe is true—that his phenomenal experience *does* make him presentationally aware of some aspect of his current environment. But we have already seen that this presentational account is untenable, since it does not accommodate cases of non-veridical perception. And our present framework, which assumes the truth of BRT, and so takes the relevant experiential states to be ones which are not in themselves physically perceptive, does not even allow such an account as an option.

IV

Since PE-states are not in themselves physically perceptive, the way in which each such state represents a certain type of environmental situation is not by putting the subject into a perceptual relationship, nor indeed any other sort of relationship, to an instance of this type. But this leaves open a number of possibilities. In practice, the options which we shall need to consider fall into two general categories. One category comprises those accounts which take a PE-state to include two contrasting elements: a core or basic element, which does not, in itself, involve the employment of concepts, and an additional (superimposed) element, which forms some kind of conceptual interpretation of it. The most familiar position in this category is that of the narrow version of the representative theory (NRT), which takes the non-conceptual element to consist in the occurrence of an internal object of awareness. The other category comprises those accounts which take a PE-state to be conceptual through and through—a state which is wholly defined by the combination of its conceptual content and its psychological character (e.g. as a certain kind of propositional attitude) qua possessor of this content. The most familiar position in this category is the *cognitive theory*. In restricting attention to these two categories, I am not suggesting that, between them, they are formally exhaustive. Clearly they are not. But in so far as there are further possibilities, they are either ones which are manifestly false, and which no one would want to take seriously, or ones which will be automatically ruled out by the conclusions which I shall try to establish.

Of the two general categories, the approach of the second—the *pure conceptualist approach*—is, in the abstract, the simpler, since it does not assign two quite different types of element to the makeup of a PE-state. For this reason, it will be appropriate to start our investigation at this point. And since it is the most familiar instance of this approach, and additionally the most straightforward, I shall begin by considering the cognitive theory.[1] We have already touched on this theory in our earlier discussion. Our interest now, however, will be exclusively in the standard form of the theory, not the *de re* version which we constructed to meet the special needs of SDR.

2 THE COGNITIVE THEORY

I

The claim of the cognitive theory is that PE-states are information-acquisitional states: for someone to be in a PE-state (to undergo a phenomenal experience) is for him to acquire, in a certain way, an item of putative information about the current state of his environment. So, according to the theory, the fact that, on a certain occasion, it is with Pauline visuo-experientially as if (in a way which makes it seem to her as if) there is cur-

---

[1] The main defenders of the cognitive theory are David Armstrong (see especially his *Perception and the Physical World* and *A Materialist Theory of the Mind*, ch. 10) and George Pitcher (see especially his *A Theory of Perception*).

rently a roughly hemispherical green patch of such and such a size, and at such and such a distance in front of her, consists in the fact that, in the relevant fashion, she is putatively informed, on that occasion, that there is currently an item of this sensible type, standing in this spatial relationship to her. And, quite generally, for any subject S, time t, and sense-modality M, its being with S at t M-experientially as if (in a way which makes it seem to S as if) things are currently, environmentally, in a certain way is held to consist in the fact that, in the relevant fashion, S at t is putatively informed that things are currently, environmentally, in that way.

Notice that what the theory takes the PE-subject to acquire is only *putative* information—something which *offers itself* as, or *purports to be*, information, but may not be so. The point of this is to leave room for two types of case where there is phenomenal experience, but the requirements for genuine information are not met. The first is where the phenomenal experience is not wholly veridical, and where the propositional message associated with it is, in consequence, not entirely accurate. So, in the case of the stick in water, what the PE-experience purports to tell the subject does not, in all respects, strictly count as information, because it is not, in respect of the shape of the stick, *true*. Likewise, if we take a Lockean view of colour, so that we exclude the colours which feature in the content of sensible appearance from the physical world, then the environmental message to Pauline will also be, in its colour-ascriptive content, false, and so not information in the strict sense. The second type of case is where the environmental message, even if accurate, is not causally controlled by the situation to which it putatively relates in an epistemically appropriate—knowledge-conferring—way. The obvious example of this is the case of hallucination. Thus if my visual experience, on a particular occasion, is induced by the artificial stimulation of my optic nerves (as in the earlier case of Henry)[2]—and if the state of the environment is causally irrelevant to its character, then its environmental message does not have the epistemic credentials of genuine information, even if it happens to be correct. One way, of course, in which, even in the context of perception, the environmental message is *always* epistemically defective is by purporting to tell the subject how things *currently* stand. For, in reality, the external situation to which it is causally responsive is earlier than the time of its psychological reception. Thus, given the time it takes for light to travel from the surface of the apple to her eyes, and the time it takes for her eyes to send the relevant signals to her brain, Pauline's visual experience at any moment is

---

[2] See Part Two, Section 2.

causally responsive to the state of the apple at a fractionally earlier moment, and so does not provide genuine information (genuine knowledge) about the current situation.[3]

Although it is crucial for the cognitivist that he should be able to accommodate these cases, and so crucial that I should have formulated his thesis in the way I have, I shall often, in what follows, speak of putative information as simply 'information', leaving the relevant qualification to be understood. This is just for ease of expression, and will not, I think, engender any confusion.

The information (putative information) which features in the cognitivist's account—the information which the PE-subject is said, on this account, to acquire—purports to characterize some aspect of the subject's current environment: it is information that things are currently, and in a certain spatial relationship to the subject, thus and so. So, as well as claiming the instantiation of a certain type of physical situation (what features in the 'thus and so'), the information contains singular references to a certain time and a certain subject, relative to which the spatiotemporal location of the relevant instantiation is (though not necessarily very precisely) specified. In the conceptual perspective of the information itself, these references to the relevant time and the relevant subject are, of course, demonstrative: they are explicitly made from the demonstrative viewpoint of the subject who acquires the information at the time of this acquisition. So, if Pauline were to formulate the information she receives, at any time when she is viewing the apple, the result would not be of the form 'there is, at such and such a *descriptively identified* time, an item of a certain sensible type, located in a certain way relative to such and such a *descriptively identified* subject', but rather of the form 'there is *now* an item of a certain sensible type, located in a certain way relative to *me*'. Of course, the PE-subject may also have, independently, descriptive ways of identifying the relevant time and subject: Pauline may know that it is currently four o'clock on 5 November 1998, and that she is the first woman to have travelled in space. But it is only the demonstrative modes of identification that feature in the information supplied by the phenomenal experience itself.

The information contains these anchoring demonstrative references to a certain time and a certain subject. But, apart from this, its propositional content is of a purely general form ('things are environmentally thus and so'), without any singular references to particulars. This is because we are

---

[3] Strictly, of course, there will be a range of earlier moments involved, because of the varying distance of the points on the apple's surface from the visual receptors.

now focusing on the cognitive theory in its *standard* form, rather than in the *de re* version which we considered earlier.[4] In the *de re* version, the relevant information makes reference to an environmental particular—the item Φ-terminally perceived—and what it purports to tell the subject is how things sensibly and locationally are *with respect to that item*. So, in the case of Pauline, there is, at the given moment, the particular portion-stage, L, which she Φ-terminally sees, and the relevant information is then that L (*that particular item*) is currently something with a certain sensible character and at a certain distance in front of her. This version of the cognitive theory was designed exclusively as an account of the *phenomenal content of perception*, not (more broadly) as an account of *phenomenal experience*; and the point of the *de re* reference was to meet the distinctive needs of SDR, in which Φ-terminal perceptual contact is held to be psychologically unmediated. In the present context, where we are taking SDR to be refuted, and provisionally assuming the truth of BRT, it is only the standard form of the theory which is relevant—the form in which the putative information purports to characterize the environmental situation in a purely general way, and is thus equally capable of featuring in the context of perception and hallucination. In any case, of course, we have already established that the *de re* version is incoherent.

At this point, an important question arises, though, curiously, one of which cognitivists themselves seem unaware. Apart from the anchoring references to the time and the subject, the relevant information characterizes the environmental situation in a purely general way. But what kind of concepts feature in this characterization? We know of course, for each sense-realm, what kinds of qualities and relations such characterization has to cover: the qualities and relations which feature in the relevant types of environmental situation are the same as those which occur in the content of the relevant forms of sensible appearance. But what still needs to be investigated is the intentional manner in which, within the content of the PE-information, these qualitative items are conceptually represented. Pauline is putatively informed of the presence of an item of a certain shape, size, and colour, at a certain distance in front of her. But in what form, as they feature in this information, are the relevant spatial and colour qualities conceived?

Despite its importance, I shall leave consideration of this question till later. It is true that, until it is answered, there will be a crucial gap in our understanding of what a cognitivist account of phenomenal experience

---

[4] We considered this in Part Two, Section 5, III.

would involve. But, in the overall dialectics of our discussion, filling this gap will become more relevant in a context where we have already come to recognize the inadequacy of the cognitive theory and are looking for ways of developing an alternative. At this stage, and precisely to bring out that inadequacy, there is a quite different area of investigation which requires attention, and one which we are equipped to pursue without needing to settle the nature of the qualitative concepts that feature in the content of the information.

The claim of the cognitive theory is, as I have said, that PE-states are information-acquisitional states: for a PE-state to be realized (for there to be an occurrence of a phenomenal experience) is for the subject to acquire, in a certain way, an item of putative information about the current state of the environment. But before this can become a definite proposal, the cognitivist needs to specify the relevant *mode of acquisition*. He needs to tell us in what psychological form, or fashion, the PE-information is received. In our earlier discussion, I characterized the type of informational episode involved as 'K-seeming', so that, in the case of Pauline, I spoke of its *K-seeming to her* that there was an item of the relevant sensible character, at a certain distance in front of her.[5] But this was merely to *label* the relevant type of episode, not to reveal its nature. I did not specify what, in fundamental psychological terms, such K-seeming is.

We are owed an account, then, of what the acquisition of the relevant information amounts to. And it is on this issue that we must now focus. It will become, in fact, the critical area of enquiry in our appraisal of the cognitive theory. What will emerge, when we consider the range of options available, is that there is no account which gives the cognitivist what he needs. Indeed, it will emerge that, in this respect, the theory is vulnerable to attack from two quite different directions, revealing contrasting respects in which it is incapable of yielding an acceptable account. I shall set out these two lines of attack in turn.

II

The cognitivist needs to provide a construal of phenomenal experience which is both sufficiently weak and sufficiently strong. In other words, he has to find a type of informational (information-acquisitional) episode, or perhaps a disjunction of types, whose occurrence is both *logically necessary* for the realization of a PE-state and *logically sufficient*. The first line of

---

[5] Part Two, Section 5, III.

attack focuses on the difficulty of providing a construal which is suffi-ciently *weak*—of finding a type of episode, or disjunction, whose occur-rence is *logically necessary*.

The cognitivist's simplest account, and in effect his natural starting point, would be to equate a phenomenal experience with the acquisition of an environmental *belief*. So Pauline's visual experience, as she views the relevant portion-stage of the apple, would be equated with her acquisition of the belief that there is, currently, an item of the relevant sensible type, at the relevant distance in front of her. But we already know that this would make the cognitive requirements for phenomenal experience too strong. For, as we noted, a subject may judge or suspect that his experience is not entirely veridical, and so fail to acquire the relevant belief. Thus someone who is familiar with how partial immersion in water distorts shape-appearance may well refuse to accept that the stick in water is (as it appears) bent, and someone who suspects that his experience is hallucinatory may well reject its message entirely. Contrary to the proverb, seeing is not always believing. And the same holds for other forms of sense-perception, and the kinds of phenomenal experience associated with them. It is here that the difficulty begins.

One way in which the cognitivist could try to make progress would be to say that, where there is no full-blooded belief, the informational episode takes the form of an *inclination to believe*—an inclination which is held in check by other beliefs already in place. So if Pauline has doubts about the veracity of her experience, she will, on this account, at least feel to some degree *inclined* to believe that there is an item of the relevant kind at the relevant location, and the occurrence of this inclination will then be what creates the phenomenal experience. But while this improves the situation, it does not solve the problem entirely. For it still leaves the cognitive requirements for phenomenal experience too strong. Thus while an incli-nation to believe is *sometimes* present in cases of the relevant sort, it is not *always* so: it can easily happen that the subject is *quite sure* that things are not as his experience represents them and has no inclination at all to believe the contrary. This is likely to be so, for example, in the case of the stick, if, as well as being familiar with the distorting effects of immersion, the subject has independent and conclusive evidence that the stick is straight. Given this independent knowledge, why should he harbour the slightest suspicion that the appearance of bentness is veridical?

What the cognitivist *can* properly insist is that, where there is no belief or inclination to believe, the subject must at least be in receipt of an *invi-tation to believe*, though one which he declines. For, as we have already stressed, the presence of such an invitation is one of the points which *any* account of the nature of phenomenal experience has to acknowledge and accommodate. But obviously the cognitivist cannot just settle for the presence of this invitation as the way in which the putative information is received. For the invitation has to be issued in some concrete psychological form: there has to something in the mind which does the inviting. The obvious candidate for what does this inviting is, of course, the phenomenal experience itself: prima facie, what invites Pauline to believe that there is an item of the relevant sort at the relevant location is the visual experience which represents her environmental situation in that way. But if this is what does the inviting, the cognitivist needs to offer some independent account of the nature of the experience. The problem is in seeing what he could offer other than one of the accounts (in terms of the acquisition of belief or an inclination to believe) already rejected.

Acknowledging the point that the subject may not even have an inclination to believe, David Armstrong, a vigorous defender of the cognitive theory, proposed an ingenious solution. For he insisted that, at its weakest, the informational episode could take the form of the acquisition of a merely *potential* belief.[6] Armstrong assumes, quite plausibly, that when a subject has a phenomenal experience, he either acquires the belief that his current environment is relevantly thus and so, or at least comes into a state in which he *would hold* this belief but for the contrary influence of his other beliefs. And his claim is then that, even if it is only this state of potential belief which gets realized, this is still enough for the cognitivist's purposes: it provides an informational episode which can be equated with the occurrence of the experience. So, in the case of the stick, Armstrong would say that, where the subject fails to acquire the belief that the stick is bent, and perhaps even fails to acquire an inclination to hold this belief, it at least becomes true of him that he *would* hold this belief if he were not familiar with the distorting effects of partial immersion and had no independent evidence of the object's straightness; and Armstrong would then insist that even this acquisition of potential belief suffices to create the relevant (bentness-representing) aspect of the phenomenal experience, and can thus serve as the relevant informational episode in the cognitivist account.

This is a clever idea. The only trouble is that it is vulnerable to an obvious objection. For the acquisition of a merely potential belief does not, in itself, furnish the subject with an *experience*, or indeed with any introspectible episode of mentality at all. Thus the state of affairs of someone's

---

[6] *A Materialist Theory of the Mind*, ch.10, sect. IV.

holding a potential belief amounts to nothing more than the truth of a certain counterfactual conditional; it involves nothing more than the abstract fact that the subject would hold a certain belief if circumstances were appropriately different. And the coming to obtain of this abstract fact does not, in itself, involve any concrete mental occurrence. Armstrong, it is true, thinks that, underlying this abstract fact, there is something in the brain which provides the concrete vehicle of the potentiality—some neural process or structure which, given the whole functional organization of the brain, would suffice to put the subject into the relevant belief-state if the inhibiting beliefs (themselves neurally realized) were absent. But even if such a neural item exists, its presence does not help to meet the difficulty. For since its intrinsic properties are exclusively physical, and since its only psychological significance is in terms of its *potential* to yield or form a certain type of belief, this item would still not furnish the subject with an experience, or provide anything else that was accessible to introspection. It would provide something concrete, but not at the level of what occurs or obtains psychologically.

It might be suggested that, to avoid this objection, we should develop Armstrong's idea in a different way. It is true that the acquisition of a merely potential belief does not create an experience or any other introspectible item of mentality. But where a PE-subject does not acquire an actual environmental belief, or inclination to believe, of the relevant kind, perhaps his phenomenal experience, or its relevant aspect, should be equated, not with this mere potentiality, but with his recognition that it obtains—with his acquisition of the actual belief that he would come to hold the relevant environmental belief if it were not for the inhibiting influence of his other beliefs. For this would mean that, even without the environmental belief or inclination, the subject still had something—the acquisition of a different kind of belief—to introspect. So, in the case of the stick, the experiential representation of bentness would be equated, not with the abstract fact that the subject would believe that there was a bent item before him if he did not already believe the various things that count against this, but with the subject's concretely coming to recognize, or believe, that this counterfactual fact obtains; and this concrete cognitive event would be one which the subject himself could introspectively register.

But while this would avoid the objection to the original account, it would also make the proposal unacceptable at another point. For there is simply no guarantee that, in the kinds of case envisaged, subjects *do* have these further, second-order beliefs. Thus, in the case of the stick, it is

perfectly conceivable that someone who knows how appearance gets distorted in these circumstances, and, in consequence, does not believe that
the stick is bent, should be entirely agnostic about what he would believe
if he did not have this knowledge. Perhaps it would be *rational* for him to
expect that, without the knowledge, his judgement would be in line with
the sensible appearance. But this does not mean that such an expectation
is bound to occur. Moreover, it is surely obvious that, in so far as we find it
plausible to suppose that someone in the kind of situation envisaged would
come to hold the second-order belief, this is only because we are thinking
of the subject as having, independently of this belief, the relevant form of
phenomenal experience, and as arriving at the belief by introspectively surveying this experience, noting what it invites him to believe about the current state of his environment, and recognizing that the only thing which
prevents his yielding to this invitation are his independent reasons for
thinking that the experience is non-veridical. So the very attempt to
develop the cognitive theory in this way would involve a tacit admission
that phenomenal experiences cannot be construed in the way that the
theory, thus developed, claims.

In conclusion, it seems to me that the initial difficulty for the cognitive
theory turns out to be insuperable. The cognitivist cannot construe phenomenal experience as the acquisition of the relevant environmental
belief, or inclination to believe, since the PE-subject does not have to
accept, or even have any inclination to accept, the veracity of his experience. Nor, in cases where the belief and inclination are absent, can the cognitivist equate the occurrence of the experience with the acquisition of a
merely *potential* belief, since the latter would not provide any episode of
concrete mentality. Nor again, as a way of securing such an episode, can he
appeal to the fact that, if the PE-subject fails to acquire the environmental
belief, he will at least believe that he would acquire it if the inhibiting beliefs
were absent; for there is no guarantee that this second-order belief will
occur. As far as I can see, there is no further progress that the cognitivist
can make in trying to overcome the basic problem. He cannot find a type
of informational episode, or disjunction of types, whose occurrence would
be logically necessary for the realization of a PE-state; or at least, he cannot
find such a type, or disjunction, except in a form, like the acquisition of a
merely potential belief, which is clearly inadequate in some other way. In
short, the cognitivist cannot find a way of construing phenomenal experience which is sufficiently weak for his purposes. The most that the realization of a PE-state logically requires, in the sphere of cognition, is the issuing
of a doxastic *invitation*—an invitation to acquire the relevant environ-

mental belief. But the only types of informational episode which have any chance of serving the cognitivist's purposes in other respects involve something doxastically stronger—something involving the subject's actual acceptance, or inclination to accept, that the environmental situation is of that kind.

III

The cognitivist cannot find a type of informational episode, or disjunction of types, which is sufficiently weak for his purposes—one whose occurrence is *logically necessary* for the realization of a PE-state. And this is one respect in which his position shows itself to be fundamentally flawed. But his position can also be attacked from the opposite direction. For it can be argued that, as well as being unable to find a type of episode which is sufficiently *weak*, he cannot find one which is sufficiently *strong*—one whose occurrence *logically suffices* for the realization of a PE-state. Given its first point of failure, we are not *obliged* to pursue this further objection in order to be justified in rejecting the cognitive theory. But doing so will be helpful, not only in reinforcing the case against the theory, but also in indicating the sorts of ways in which it would need to be altered before there was any chance of reaching something acceptable.

Let us start with an obvious point. There are various ways in which a subject can acquire putative information about the current state of his environment—and can acquire it in the form of full-blooded beliefs—without receiving this information in the form of a phenomenal experience. For example, I could be sitting in an unfamiliar room blindfolded and be told by someone else, who surveys the scene, how things are colourwise arranged. Or again, I could see an intact orange, and be able to tell, from its being an orange, how it is coloured and structured inside. In both these cases, I acquire the relevant information perceptually, but the acquisition is not integral to the phenomenal experience itself. In the first case, there is no visual experience at all: I merely extract the information about the colour-arrangement from a linguistic input which I receive in an auditory form. In the second case, there is a visual experience, but one which only covers the sensible appearance of the orange's *surface*: I am only able to gauge how things are internally because the surface-appearance enables me to recognize the object as an orange, and because I know, from past experience, what oranges look like when opened up. Since the cognitivist is claiming that phenomenal experience always takes an information-acquisitional form—the acquisition of putative information about the current state of the environment—he has to tell us what it is about the *PE*-acquisition of information which makes it distinctive.

One thing which the cognitivist can say is that if the acquisition of the information is to have the character of a phenomenal experience, then it must be *cognitively direct*: it must be achieved without recourse to further evidence, or inference (explicit or implicit) from other things believed. This is certainly a step in the right direction. As we noted earlier, a phenomenal experience does not simply invite its subject to believe that a certain type of environmental situation obtains; it does this in a subjectively distinctive way—a way which creates the impression that an instance of the relevant type is directly presented. If the cognitive theory is to have any chance of explaining this impression, it must discern a comparable directness in the form in which the relevant items of information are cognitively registered, and this directness would exclude any form of evidential or inferential dependence on a prior source of data. Moreover, by insisting that the acquisition of the information be cognitively direct, the theorist excludes the two cases considered above, and others like them. For, in both these cases, the relevant information is not made available in that direct way. Thus, in reaching my conclusions about how things are arranged in the room, I am relying on my knowledge of what my informant purports to tell me. And, in reaching my conclusions about the internal properties of the orange, I am relying on my knowledge of its external sensible appearance, and of what things with that kind of appearance are like inside. In neither case, of course, need there be any process of conscious reasoning: given my existing knowledge and cognitive dispositions, it is likely that the conclusions will occur immediately and automatically, without my having to reflect on the situation. But that does not undermine the point that these conclusions are rationally grounded on the other things which I know, and this is enough to exclude their cognitive directness in the relevant sense.

Insisting that the PE-acquisition of information be cognitively direct is a step in the right direction, but it does not give the cognitivist all that he needs. For we can still envisage cases in which the environmental information is received in a relevantly direct way, but without yielding a phenomenal experience. One such case is that where a verbal message is passed to the subject's cognitive centres *subliminally*, so that he acquires the putative information which the message carries—he is caused to believe that things are, environmentally, as the message represents them—but does not experientially register the input of the message through his eyes or ears. For example, it might be that the subject is watching television, and the message is momentarily flashed on the screen—just long enough for it to be physically registered by his visual receptors, but not long enough to be perceptually detected. Because the message is not perceptually detected, the subject's acquisition of the relevant information is cognitively direct; in particular, it is not based on the recognition that he has received a message and that this message tells him that things are a certain way. But the acquisition does not take the form of a phenomenal experience; indeed, it does not have an experiential character at all. Another type of case would be if the subject was under a general anaesthetic and the environmental information was directly fed into his cognitive centres by some kind of surgical intervention. Again, the acquisition of the information would be cognitively direct—achieved without recourse to evidence or inference—but the person would not be the subject of any experiences at all at the times when it occurred.

To deal with these cases, and others like them, the cognitivist would have to add a further requirement. He would have to say that, in order for the acquisition of information to form a phenomenal experience, it must be not only cognitively direct, but also *conscious*: it must be something which is either introspectively registered, or at least subjectively present in a way which permits such registering. This additional requirement, of course, would be just a particular application of a quite general requirement of consciousness on anything which is to qualify as experiential; and indeed, it was this general requirement which lay behind our earlier definition of the notion of the *experiential content* of perception.[7] Its relevance here is that it enables the cognitivist to exclude the sorts of case envisaged. For these cases were precisely designed to be ones in which it was the absence of consciousness which revealed the absence of phenomenal experience. Thus it was because the input of the verbal message was stipulated to be subliminal (and so below the threshold of consciousness), and because the surgical intervention was stipulated to be during a period of general anaesthesia (and hence during a period of total unconsciousness), that we could present the cases as ones in which the acquisition of the information was cognitively direct, but manifestly failed to meet the conditions for phenomenal experience. By adding the requirement of consciousness—of introspective accessibility—the cognitivist ensures that these cases do not qualify as counter-examples to his thesis.

However, even with this additional requirement, we can still envisage cases which meet the cognitivist's conditions as so far elaborated, but do not involve phenomenal experience. The most obvious case is that of

---

[7] In Part Two, Section 3, I.

clairvoyance, or what might pass as such. Thus suppose that, even when I am blindfolded, I only have to focus my investigative attention in a certain direction to acquire, in a cognitively direct way, the same putative information, with the same conceptual content, as I would acquire if the blindfold were removed and the relevant portion of the environment became visible. And suppose that this acquisition is something of which I am conscious: I know when I am exercising my clairvoyant faculty, and have introspective access to the informational episodes it yields. These informational episodes will then meet the twin requirements of cognitive directness and consciousness. But we can easily suppose that they do not qualify as phenomenal experiences. We can suppose that, when I am exercising my clairvoyant powers, or what I take to be such, I do not *see* the relevant portion of my environment; nor do I have any visual experiences which might give me the impression that I see it. My acquisition of the relevant information, or putative information, is purely intellectual, and this is exactly how it subjectively seems to me. So if there is an apple on the table in front of me, and, with the blindfold in place, I focus my attention in that direction, I find myself seeming to know, without evidence or inference, that there is an item of the relevant sensible type at the relevant place. But it is only when the blindfold is removed that I come to have genuine visual experiences; and the difference between the two types of case is introspectively manifest to me. Analogous examples, of course, could be devised for the other sense-realms. Thus we can envisage a subject who, without having any genuine auditory experiences, is able to tell, directly and consciously, what sounds, if any, are occurring in his neighbourhood, or one who, without tactual experience, is able to detect, directly and consciously, the qualities of hardness and temperature characterizing nearby material surfaces. Or, at least, we can envisage cases in which such clairvoyant capacities *seem*, both to the subjects themselves and to others who investigate them, to be in play.

What is it, then, that the clairvoyant episodes lack that is present in phenomenal experience? When I seem to be clairvoyantly aware of some portion of the colour-arrangement in my environment, how do my experiences differ in character from the visual experiences which occur when I use my eyes? The answer is that, in the clairvoyant cases, as envisaged, there is no provision for the *presentational feel* of phenomenal experience—for the subjective impression that an instance of the relevant type of environmental situation is directly presented. It is true that the factors of cognitive directness and consciousness move things in the right direction: directness of cognitive registering is at least akin to directness of presentation; and presentation has to be accessible to introspection, and so conscious in the relevant sense. But these factors, on their own, are not enough. For the clairvoyant acquires his information (or putative information) in a form which is both cognitively direct and introspectively accessible, but without there being anything to make the acquisitional events seem to him to be anything other than what they are—the purely intellectual acquisition of information. There is nothing to conceal the purely cognitive character of what is taking place and create the illusion that the environmental situation is before the mind in a non-conceptual and ontologically immediate form. When, blindfolded, I focus my investigative attention in a certain direction, I find myself seeming to know, directly, how things are in that direction; but this consciousness of my direct knowledge, or putative knowledge, is precisely a consciousness of *that*—of something transparently cognitive, not of something which poses as presentational.

It follows that, if the cognitivist is to find a type of informational episode which is logically sufficient for the occurrence of phenomenal experience, he has to find some further factor which he can ascribe to the relevant sorts of case, and which would suffice, in conjunction with the factors of cognitive directness and consciousness, to create the requisite presentational feel. But it is here that his position seems to be bankrupt. For, with the factors of directness and consciousness in place, there seems to be nothing left to which he can appeal. The clairvoyant episodes seem to be precisely what—if they were possible—the cognitive versions of phenomenal experience would have to be like, and, as we have noted, these do not subjectively pose as anything other than the cognitive episodes they are.

In fact, the only way in which the cognitivist could now try to make provision for the presentational feel of phenomenal experience would be by altering his theory in a crucial respect. As we have so far represented it, the theory claims that for someone to have a phenomenal experience is for him to acquire an item of putative information about the current state of his environment; and we have been assuming that the subject-matter of this information is *purely* environmental—purely to the effect that things are environmentally thus and so. In this framework, any attempt by the cognitivist to cover the presentational feel of phenomenal experience—in a way which sufficed to distinguish such experience from mere clairvoyance— would have to be in terms of the psychological form in which the information was acquired; and it is surely now clear that nothing along these lines would be successful. But a quite different way in which the cognitivist could try to deal with the problem would be by incorporating a claim of presentational awareness into the content of the information itself, so that what it purports to tell the subject is not merely that the current environmental situation is thus and so, but that he is presentationally aware of a current situation which is thus and so. So, in the case of Pauline, he could say that what the relevant information purports to tell her is not merely that there is, currently, an item of a certain shape, size, and colouring, at a certain distance in front of her, but that she is visually presented with such an item in such a locational perspective. This, in a quite direct way, would cover the presentational feel; for if his putative information characterizes his relationship with the environment as presentational, then the subject is, in that respect, given the impression that such a relationship obtains. It is not that the psychological episode would contain any genuine presentational element, or even something which posed as such. But, by its very content, the information itself would invite him to believe that a presentation was occurring.

This is the cognitivist's only remaining option. But it only takes a moment's reflection to see that it is untenable. The problem is in understanding *how*, in the circumstances envisaged, the putative information could come to be acquired. For, unless there was some presentational or quasi-presentational element in the psychological episode, the subject would only need to be introspectively conscious of the nature of his mental condition to see that the proposition of whose truth he is supposed to be putatively informed is false. It is not, of course, that such putative information is *not*, in reality, acquired: on the contrary, the whole assumption of our discussion is that phenomenal experience *does* have a presentational feel and thereby invites the subject to believe that the external situation is directly presented. The difficulty is in seeing how it could be acquired in a form in which its falsity was introspectively manifest; and its falsity would, surely, be introspectively manifest if there were no other psychological factor to make a presentationalist construal tempting. I suppose the cognitivist might say that the acquisition itself is a kind of introspective illusion: not something which runs contrary to how things are introspectively represented, but something which, as itself the work of introspection, puts the truth beyond the reach of introspective detection. But we cannot make sense of there being this sort of illusion without supposing the subject to be deranged. It would be analogous to envisaging someone who, though not in pain, introspectively seems to himself to be so, or someone who, though having a taste-experience, introspects it as an auditory one. Maybe such things can happen to a madman. But we can hardly take them to be a systematic feature of the everyday perceptual life of the rational subject.

There is no way in which the presentational feel of phenomenal experience can be captured in purely cognitive terms. And, consequently, there is no type of informational episode whose occurrence is logically sufficient for the occurrence of such an experience. On this score too, then, we are forced to conclude that the cognitive theory is fundamentally flawed. Just as the cognitivist cannot find a type of informational episode which is sufficiently *weak* for his purposes—one whose occurrence is logically *necessary* for the realization of a PE-state—so also he cannot find one which is sufficiently *strong*—one whose occurrence logically *suffices* for such a realization.

3 THE IMAGIST PROPOSAL

I

The cognitive theory has been shown to fail in two respects. Its first failing is that it cannot find a suitable type of informational episode which is sufficiently weak for its purposes. What is needed, to coincide with the cognitive implications of phenomenal experience, is something which merely embodies an *invitation* to believe that things are thus and so. But any episode of a purely cognitive character, if it takes the form of an introspectible item of mentality at all, would have to involve some stronger form of cognitive commitment—something which responds to the invitation by some measure of belief or inclination to believe. Its second failing is that it cannot find a type of informational episode which embodies the *presentational feel* of phenomenal experience—a type which provides the subjective impression that the environmental situation is directly presented. The closest that the theory can come to capturing this feel is by insisting that the acquisition of the relevant information, or putative information, be both cognitively direct and conscious. But this, as the case of clairvoyance shows, is not sufficient. A clairvoyant episode can have the requisite directness and consciousness without carrying the impression of being anything other than purely cognitive.

Given the failure of the cognitive theory, we need to look for a new account of the nature of phenomenal experience; and, in particular, we need to look for an account which is successful at the two points where cognitivism showed itself inadequate. The cognitive theory is a version—the most familiar and straightforward version—of what I have labelled the *pure conceptualist approach*. On this approach, we take a PE-state to be something which is conceptual through and through—a state which is wholly defined by the combination of its conceptual content and its psychological character qua possessor of this content. It contrasts, as we saw, with an alternative approach, in which a PE-state is held to include two quite different kinds of component, one of which is entirely non-conceptual, and the other of which is an element of interpretation. So, in looking for a new account, we have to begin by deciding whether we are going to continue with the conceptualist approach, or switch to the radical alternative.

Given the particular failings of the cognitivist account, the attractions of this radical alternative are not hard to discern. As we noted, the most familiar version of this approach is the narrow version of the representative theory (NRT), which takes the non-conceptual element to consist in the occurrence of an internal object of awareness. Its basic idea is this. When a subject has a phenomenal experience, he is not in presentational contact with any *external* item (anything in his physical environment). But there is, nonetheless, an *internal* item which is directly presented to him—an item which has no existence separate from its being thus presented—and, by occurring in combination with the relevant forms of interpretation, this internal item poses to the subject as (carries the impression of being) an aspect of his current environment. What makes this account attractive is that it offers a straightforward way of dealing with the two factors which created the problem for the cognitivist. The presentational feel of phenomenal experience is covered by the fact that the internal item is both presented to the subject and interpreted as external; and the acquisition of the environmental information occurs in a suitably weak form, whereby the impression of presentational contact issues an invitation to hold the relevant belief, without compelling acceptance. All this is something which I shall elaborate in detail later, when this NRT-account becomes the focus of our discussion.

Despite the attractions of this alternative, I want, for the time being, to continue to explore the pure conceptualist approach, to see whether there may be resources here too for achieving a satisfactory account. The direction in which we might look for such an account is not, at the moment, clear. But there is, I think, one option available, and this will come to the surface if we pause to examine a preliminary issue. It is an issue to which I drew attention earlier—in the course of our discussion of the cognitive theory—but put on one side.

II

It is uncontroversial that, in some fashion, phenomenal experience purports to inform its subject (invites him to believe) that things are currently, environmentally, a certain way. And, for each sense-realm, we know what kinds of qualities and relations feature in the types of environmental situation involved. But, as we noted in our earlier discussion, what still has to be determined is the manner in which, within the content of the information, these qualitative items are conceptually represented.[8] So far, whenever I have had occasion to formulate the information involved in a particular case, I have relied on the descriptive resources of ordinary language. Thus, in the case of Pauline, I have spoken of her as being informed of the presence of a *roughly hemispherical green patch at a certain distance in front of her*—using such ordinary terms as 'hemispherical', 'green', and 'in front of' to signify the relevant qualities and relations. But, in employing these ordinary modes of description, I was not trying to settle the issue of conceptual content. I was not intending to indicate that the terms I used succeed in capturing the conceptual perspective of the information itself—that, as well as serving to identify the relevant qualitative items, they express the intentional manner in which, as recipient of the information, the PE-subject conceives of them. And, in fact, a little reflection reveals that they do not—that, to express the intentional manner of the conceiving, we need to formulate the information in a quite different way.

To get a clear view of the situation, it will help if, for a moment, we switch our attention from the visual to the auditory realm. Suppose we have two subjects: James, who is a musical expert, and John, who is a musical ignoramus. On a certain occasion, both subjects, who happen to be in the same vicinity, hear a certain snatch of tune played on a flute; and let us assume that the physical sounds and their temporal structure have exactly the same sensible appearance for them, so that their auditory phenomenal experiences are of exactly the same kind. Being a musical expert, and additionally (let us suppose) enjoying perfect pitch, James is able to identify the character of the tune in musical terms: he recognizes it as, say, *a tune in 3/4-time and in the key of F major, starting with a minim of F on the first beat of the bar, followed by a crotchet of G a tone above it, followed by . . .* and so on. John, in contrast, is not able to identify the character of the tune in these terms, or anything approaching them. For, being a musical ignoramus, he has no grasp of the notions of time, key, quantity, and pitch which feature in James's analysis, and so has no idea that what he hears is structured in that sort of way. And this, it must be stressed, is not just a matter of his lacking the musical *terminology*—of his not understanding such terms as '3/4-time', 'key', 'crotchet'. It is a matter of his not having the *concepts* which this

---

[8] See Part Three, Section 2, I.

terminology expresses. Nonetheless, John does hear the tune clearly, and, as we have stipulated, has exactly the same kind of phenomenal experience as James. And we can suppose that, just through having this experience, he succeeds, in his own way, in cognitively registering the character of the tune and preserving this information in his memory, with the result that he has no difficulty in either recalling how it went or recognizing it when he encounters it again. The question now is: what form does this item of auditorily conveyed information take—the information he receives and retains from his phenomenal experience? Well, it is clear that this information, in the form in which he acquires and retains it, is not something which can be expressed in descriptive terms at all. After all, the only descriptive terms which could be relevant would be the musical ones already excluded, or others along the same lines. Rather, the way in which John identifies the character of the tune, both in the original cognitive intake and in his subsequent retention of the information thus acquired, is simply as—if I may put it schematically—'di-da-di-da'. It is a form of identification which we can only express by means of a *quotational designator*—a designator which denotes the relevant tune-type by displaying an instance of it for auditory sampling. This is because the form of identification is itself *in auditory perspective*—the perspective of someone who *hears* such a tune. It is a form of identifying conception such that, if the subject wanted to make it consciously explicit—to spell out, to consciously to express, to himself his possession of it—he would need to rehearse the character of the tune in his auditory imagination, framing in his 'mind's ear' a mental image of the relevant pattern of sounds, or a series of images of the successive sounds and silences that compose it.

The same form of identification is, of course, available in the case of other sense-realms too. Thus, just as it is possible to identify a type of sound, or sequence of sounds, in *auditory* perspective, so also it is possible to identify a type of scene in *visual* perspective, and identify a type of odour in *olfactory* perspective; and in these cases too, the subject could only make the mode of identification consciously explicit (spell out, consciously express, to himself his possession of it) by framing the relevant kind of visual or olfactory image. Quite generally, for any sense-realm R, and any situation-type S represented by a PE-state associated with R, there is this same distinctive way of identifying S and its qualitative ingredients—a way which embodies the perspective of R-perceptual experience, and which the conceiver could only make consciously explicit by framing the relevant kind of R-image or image-sequence. I shall speak of this form of identification, or identifying conception, as *imagistic*.

In the case of John, then, we can say that, in so far as his phenomenal experience supplies information to him, it supplies it in this imagistic form. It invites him to believe that there currently is, and indeed that he presentationally hears, an instance of a certain type of tune, and the way it identifies this tune-type, in the context of this invitation, is simply as 'di-da-di-da'—or whatever would qualify as an accurate quotational designation of the type in question.[9] What John does not acquire, as a result of his experience, is a knowledge of the character of the tune in *musical terms*—in terms of such things as key, time, pitch, and length, descriptively conceived—and in this he contrasts with James, the musical expert. But what must now be stressed is that, even though James acquires a knowledge of the character of the tune in musical terms, and in this way differs from John, this difference does not relate to the nature of the information supplied by his phenomenal experience *as such*. For where James differs from John is not in respect of the nature of his phenomenal experience (the content of how things sensibly appear to him), nor in what this experience, in itself, purports to tell him, but in the further analysis which he is able to apply to the information thus acquired. So we must suppose that, for James too, the information supplied by the phenomenal experience itself—the information implicit in how things sensibly appear—is imagistic. James too, in being in the relevant PE-state, or sequence of states, is invited to believe that he confronts an instance of 'di-da-di-da'. It is just that, fed into the framework of his musical expertise, this basic imagistic information comes to elicit a further and conceptually more sophisticated response.

But now it is clear that this conclusion must extend to phenomenal experience in general. It is clear that, for any phenomenal experience, in any sense-realm, the basic putative information it supplies—what, simply qua phenomenal experience, it invites the subject to believe about his environmental situation—is of this imagistic kind. So, in the case of Pauline, the relevant information, expressed in the form in which she receives it, would be not that there is currently a roughly hemispherical green patch of such and such a size, at such and such a distance in front of her, but rather that there is currently an instance of:

'   '

where we slot into the blank (between the quotation-marks) a picture of

---

[9] Strictly, I would need to insert, in place of 'di-da-di-da', a device which the reader could press to obtain an accurate rendering of the tune.

the relevant type of scene in the perspective of Pauline's apparent view of it. The reason why I chose to switch our focus to the auditory realm in order to make the initial point was simply that the facts of the situation stand out more clearly in the auditory case. This is because, in the auditory case, the typical subject is already close to that of the musical ignoramus, while, in the visual case, most people have a reasonable competence with the descriptive conceptual scheme for colour and spatial arrangement.

The conclusion which we have reached is clearly an important one. And, in particular, it reveals a further strong requirement which a satisfactory account of phenomenal experience has to meet. For it now turns out that, as well as doing justice to the presentational feel of such experience, and allowing the information it supplies to be received in a suitably weak (merely belief-invitational) form, an acceptable account has to explain why the content of this information is imagistic. Once again, it is not difficult to see how such a requirement would be met by NRT, which postulates an internal object of presentational awareness. For the presentational nature of this awareness would explain the imagistic nature of the information supplied. But what is of particular interest, in the present context, is that the recognition of this further requirement also gives us our first real clue as to the direction in which we should look for a new *conceptualist* account.

III

When I speak of imagistic *information*, I mean information (putative information) which contains an imagistic *identification* (identifying conception); and when, in this context, I speak of an *identification* (identifying conception) as imagistic, I mean that it is one which is imagist in its *content*: it identifies the relevant sensible universal (the relevant type of sensibly characterized item or situation) under an imagistic concept, for example as '   ' (where we slot in an appropriate picture) or as 'di-da-di-da'. Identification which is imagistic in this sense is not tied to any special kind of psychological state: it can feature in the full range of states which take propositional content, or any form of conceptual content rich enough to include entity-identification. So one can believe that one has seen an instance of '   ', hope that one will see an instance of '   ', recognize something as an instance of '   ', and so on. However, there is one form of psychological activity which is imagistic in a special sense. It is a form which *has to be* imagistic in its content and which necessarily makes the imagist nature of its content *consciously explicit*. I am thinking, of course, of that form of conceiving in which a sensible universal is brought before the mind by the framing or occurrence of an actual mental image, for example a visual image in one's mind's eye or an auditory image in one's mind's ear. So I am thinking of the sort of conceiving that would occur if John were to rehearse the character of the tune in his auditory imagination, or if I were now to visualize the scene of the Grand Canal, as I recently saw it from the Rialto Bridge. Let us call such conceiving *explicit imagistic conceiving* (EI-conceiving).

It is the availability of EI-conceiving which provides the opportunity for a new conceptualist account. There can be no denying that, in its undisputed forms, like that of John's auditory rehearsal of the tune, or my visualization of the scene of the Grand Canal, EI-conceiving has a definite *subjective resemblance* to phenomenal experience. In particular, it brings the relevant sensible universal before the subject's mind with a transparency and seeming immediacy which echo the quasi-presentational character of such experience. The option which now becomes available is to say that phenomenal experience *is itself a form of* EI-conceiving—that when someone has a phenomenal experience as of encountering a certain type of environmental situation, the way in which this situation-type is brought before his mind does not merely *subjectively resemble,* but is of the *same basic kind as* the way in which it is brought before the mind by the appropriate form of imaginative (image-framing) act. It is to say that, in both cases, the situation-type is brought before the mind by, or by something involving as its core, the occurrence of a mental image.

Such an option, of course, will only be available in the framework of the conceptualist approach if EI-conceiving itself is something purely conceptual. And already there is here a point of controversy. For some of those who adopt an NRT-account of phenomenal experience—taking it to involve the occurrence of an internal object of presentational awareness—would favour a similar account for EI-conceiving. They would say that when someone visualizes a certain type of scene, or imaginatively rehearses a certain tune, the imaginative activity is indeed a form of conceiving, but one which contains within it an element of non-conceptual presentation. This view of EI-conceiving is, I think, mistaken, though the issue is not one which I am in a position to address at this stage. In the present context, I shall simply *assume* that EI-conceiving is conceptual through and through, so that the new proposal becomes one which the conceptualist can at least entertain. Since I shall be arguing *against* the proposal, I cannot, in making this assumption, be accused of begging the question. I am simply giving my opponent the benefit of the doubt.

The proposal is, then, that, within the framework of this assumption, we should construe phenomenal experience as a form of EI-conceiving. But before we can begin to consider this suggestion we need to make it more specific. What form of EI-conceiving is envisaged? And how is it supposed that it could possess the characteristics needed for phenomenal experience? To help answer these questions, we must begin by taking note of a crucial distinction.

Even within the class of undisputed cases, EI-conceiving comes in two quite different forms, according to whether the subject is involved in an active or a passive way. Thus, on the one hand, such conceiving can occur as something which a subject *does*—as an event of subject-agency. For example, given his imagistic knowledge of the character of the tune, John might, on a particular occasion, deliberately run through it in his mind— actively framing the auditory images of the sounds and silences. Or again an architect, in trying to decide how to design a house, might (with a view to comparing their aesthetic merits) actively visualize—frame visual images of—various forms of house-appearance. On the other hand, EI-conceiving can also occur as something which *happens* to the subject, where the subject is a passive recipient of the images rather than their active framer. The obvious example is that of quasi-perceptual recall. Thus, in the case of the Rialto Bridge, we can envisage the following episode: I actively direct my recollective attention on to the relevant place and time (when I was standing on the bridge looking in a certain direction), and then, with my attention rightly focused (the video tape, as it were, rewound to the right point), the image of the view just imposes itself on my mind, giving me the impression that I am in some way seeing again the original scene, and indeed in some way having again the original experience. Or again, we can envisage an episode in which John directs his mind back to the occasion when he first heard the snatch of tune—perhaps the event was for some reason memorable—and finds images of the sounds imposing themselves on his consciousness, making it seem to him as if he is in some way re-hearing, and indeed reliving the experience of hearing, the original playing. There is, of course, a subtle but crucial distinction here between this type of quasi-perceptual recall, where it seems to the subject that he is having a second encounter with the original instance of the sensible universal in question (imagistically seeing again the original Venetian scene, imagistically hearing again the original playing of the tune), and the sort of case in which, possessing imagistic knowledge about some past perceptual encounter (knowing that he saw '   ' or heard 'di-da-di-da'), the subject consciously rehearses that knowledge by the active framing of the appropriate image, or images.

Now if phenomenal experience is to be identified with a form of EI-conceiving at all, the form involved must be, like that of quasi-perceptual recall, passive. A subject can be active in choosing his environment, and thereby the possibilities of sensory input; and he can, in certain ways, be active in choosing whether to allow these possibilities to be actualized—for example, in choosing whether to open his eyes, and in selecting the direction in which he looks. But, having exercised his choice on these matters, any phenomenal experience which the subject then has, he has as a passive recipient: the experience is something which *happens* to him, rather than something which he *does*. So when it is suggested that we should construe phenomenal experience as a form of EI-conceiving, the passivity of this form must be envisaged as an essential factor. Moreover, such passivity would be needed to give the relevant conceiving the requisite presentational feel—to enable it to carry the subjective impression of being a presentation of an instance of the situation-type on to which it is directed. It is true, as we noted, that, just through the way in which it brings the situation-type before the mind, EI-conceiving *as such*, whether active or passive, echoes the quasi-presentational character of phenomenal experience. But, when the conceiving is active, this echo does not create an actual impression of presentational perception. Thus if I actively frame an image of a type of scene in my mind's eye, it does not feel to me—I do not find myself invited to believe—that I am in presentational contact with some actual instance of that type. In contrast, in the case of quasi-perceptual recall, where the EI-conceiving is passive, there *is* this feeling of presentational contact. Thus, in the example of the Rialto Bridge, it is not just that, once I have directed my recollective attention on to the right place and time, a visual image of the relevant type of scene impresses itself on my mind. It is that, in impressing itself on my mind in that way, the image poses as (purports to be) a sort of re-seeing of the relevant instance of that type—the instance originally seen on the relevant earlier occasion—and, in thus posing, it shares the presentational feel of seeing itself. Obviously, if phenomenal experience is a form of EI-conceiving, the passivity of this form would, in a similar way, be crucial to its capacity to pose as presentational. In effect, its capacity for this presentational pose would, at least largely, stem from the combination of this passivity and the general phenomenological character of EI-conceiving as such.

Assuming we can endow the relevant form of EI-conceiving with the right presentational feel, the meeting of the other requirements which we have specified for phenomenal experience will follow as a matter of course. The impression that one is in presentational contact with an instance of the

relevant situation-type will convey the relevant environmental information in a suitably weak form: it will issue an invitation to believe that things
are currently, environmentally, thus and so, but without requiring any particular doxastic response. And, since what supplies it is a form of EI-conceiving, this information will be imagistic in content—the relevant
situation-type being identified in the intentional manner in which the EI-
conceiving brings it before the mind. In all this, there is a close parallel
between the EI-conceiving to be identified with phenomenal experience
and that involved in quasi-perceptual recall. The most conspicuous difference is that, in the case of phenomenal experience, the impression is given
that one is presentationally aware of a *current* instance of the situation-
type, while, in the case of recall, the impression is concerned with the *past*.
But this too is easily explained. *Any* impression of presentational awareness
would, without some additional factor, give rise to the impression that the
putative object is *current*, simply because it represents this object as what
is *currently presented*. What gives rise to the impression of pastness in the
case of recall is simply that the image imposes itself on the subject's consciousness in an explicitly recollective context—the context of his trying to
recall, or taking himself to be recalling, something already witnessed.

The proposal before us, then, is that we should construe phenomenal
experience as a special form of EI-conceiving—a form which is stipulated
to be passive, and which, by this passivity, carries the requisite presentational feel. And, for the sake of argument, we are assuming that EI-conceiving is conceptual through and through, so that the proposal is available
as an option on the pure conceptualist approach. Let us speak of this
option as the *imagist proposal*. The question we must now consider is
whether this proposal is correct. If we can set things up in the way we are
envisaging, the proposal meets the requirements we have so far specified:
as well as providing for the presentational feel of phenomenal experience,
it both ensures the requisite cognitive weakness in the way in which the
environmental information is received and gives this information an imagistic content. In all these respects, at least, it seems to be moving things in
the right direction. But what we still need to consider is whether the proposal is satisfactory in other ways. And in fact, on closer scrutiny, it soon
becomes apparent that it is fundamentally misconceived.

IV

Perhaps the most obvious prima facie problem for the imagist proposal
concerns its capacity to deal adequately with the phenomenological aspects

of the situation. By assigning a presentational feel to phenomenal experience, it comes much closer than the cognitive theory to capturing the subjective character of such experience. But, on the face of it, it still fails to do
justice to this character in its entirety. This is because, notwithstanding the
subjective resemblance, introspection also seems to reveal a crucial intrinsic difference between the kind of sensible awareness involved in the undisputed cases of EI-conceiving (the manner in which a sensible universal is
before the mind when it is EI-conceived in the context of something like
imagination or recall) and the kind of sensible awareness involved in phenomenal experience (the manner in which a sensible universal is before the
mind when it is PE-represented). Thus when I visualize a certain type of
scene in my mind's eye or rehearse a familiar tune in my mind's ear, the sort
of sensible awareness involved (of the type of environmental array, or of
the type of sequence of sounds) introspectively strikes me as crucially different from the sort of visual or auditory awareness which occurs when I
am in the corresponding PE-states—for example in the context of actually
seeing such a scene or hearing such a tune. It was to this manifest subjective difference that Hume was responding when he drew his famous distinction between *impressions* and *ideas*, the former (corresponding to what
I have called *phenomenal experiences*) being defined as awareness-episodes
of a relatively 'forceful and lively' sort, and the latter (corresponding to the
undisputed cases of EI-conceiving) being defined as awareness-episodes
which, while involving the same types of sensible content, are 'fainter and
duller'.[10] Hume's terminology may not succeed in making the nature of the
distinction clear. But that there is a real subjective distinction, and indeed
one which we might initially think of describing in terms of a difference in
'force and liveliness', cannot be denied.

Now the problem for the imagist proposal is that it does not seem to
have the resources to account for this distinction. For if the sensible awareness in both cases is that of EI-conceiving, it is hard to see how there could
be this striking difference in the way things introspectively appear. It is no
good the theorist appealing to the *passivity* of the EI-conceiving involved
in phenomenal experience, together with the *presentational feel* that this
gives rise to, since these are also features of the EI-conceiving involved in
quasi-perceptual recall; and, of course, the subjective distinction holds as

---

[10] D. Hume, *Treatise of Human Nature*, ed. L. Selby-Bigge, 2nd edn. revised P. Nidditch
(Oxford: Oxford University Press, 1978), Bk. 1, Pt. 1, sect. 1, and *Enquiry Concerning Human
Understanding*, ed. L. Selby-Bigge, 3rd edn. revised P. Nidditch (Oxford: Oxford University Press,
1975), sect. II. Hume, of course, referred to awareness-episodes as 'perceptions'.

much between phenomenal experience and such recall, as between phenomenal experience and active imagination. Nor is it any use pointing out that in phenomenal experience, unlike recall, the presentational feel relates to the *present*—that the subject feels himself to be in presentational contact with a *current* instance of the relevant sensible universal rather than with a *previous* instance. For that, in itself, would not explain why the sensible awareness involved (the manner in which the sensible universal is before the mind) seems to be of a different kind. Nor again would it help to appeal to the fact that the sensible content of phenomenal experience tends to be richer and more detailed than that in recall. This may be true as a *tendency*, particularly in the case of the visual realm. But at best it is *only* a tendency, not a universally applicable distinction. The content of phenomenal experience is sometimes very simple, as in the case of someone just hearing the single note of a flute; and the images involved in quasi-perceptual recall are sometimes rich and intricate.

Perhaps the imagist will say that what accounts for the subjective difference between the EI-conceiving of phenomenal experience and that of quasi-perceptual recall is that the PE-form of the conceiving is passive *in a stronger sense*. Thus, in the case of recall, although the mental image is not fashioned by the subject, it is still, in a sense, only there by his permission, since he has the power to eliminate it by focusing his mind on something else, or to modify its details by active interference. But, in the PE-case, the experience is wholly beyond the subject's control except in so far as he can control the physical circumstances which cause it. And whereas the EI-conceiving involved in recall competes with active imagination for the same mental space (so that the recall cannot be sustained if the active imagination takes the focus of the mind elsewhere), phenomenal experience has a mental space of its own, and permits additional episodes of active EI-conceiving, or indeed of quasi-perceptual recall, to go on, without obstructive contact, alongside it. However, while phenomenal experience is indeed distinctively passive in this way, and while this distinctive passivity is no doubt associated with its distinctive introspective appearance, it is hardly a point which lends support to the imagist's account. What it suggests, rather, is that, in the case of phenomenal experience, the presence of the sensible universal before the mind is not a form of EI-conceiving at all—that it is something of a quite different kind, which can *only* occur in this more strongly passive form. It suggests that, if there is a sort of imaging involved in phenomenal experience, it is not the imaging of conceiving, but an imaging which provides a pre-conceptual given, and that it is because it is thus pre-conceptual that it does not compete for mental space with the

EI-conceiving of active imagination and quasi-perceptual recall. This suggestion, indeed, is one that I shall take up and pursue in detail in due course, when I come to advance my positive account.

As far as I can see, the imagist proposal does not allow for any adequate explanation of the difference in subjective character between the undisputed cases of EI-conceiving and phenomenal experience. And so, on these grounds alone, I think that the proposal fails. However, the proposal is also vulnerable to a more fundamental objection, and it is on this that I now want to focus. The objection is not unrelated to the problem we have been considering. Indeed, in a sense, it serves to reinforce it; for it brings to light the factors which create the subjective difference that the imagist proposal cannot explain. But the new objection undermines the proposal at a more basic level. It shows it to be guilty not merely of phenomenological inadequacy, but of positive incoherence.

V

We need to begin by noting that there is a close parallel between imagistic conception and something else.

Let us return to the case of John, and let us suppose that, as well as his auditory encounter with the snatch of tune, John experiences, a little later, a sharp stab of pain in his back. In the original example, we envisaged him as acquiring and retaining a knowledge of the character of the tune in imagist terms—a knowledge which identifies it not descriptively (using the concepts available to a musician), but simply, and more vividly, as 'di-da-di-da'. And, given his possession of this knowledge, we were able to envisage him as making it consciously explicit, on particular occasions, by acts of EI-conceiving, in which he rehearsed the character of the tune in his auditory imagination—framing the appropriate type of image or sequence of images in his mind's ear. Now, in a similar way, we can envisage John as acquiring and retaining a knowledge of the character of his pain in terms which are distinctively vivid and non-descriptive. For we can envisage him as acquiring and retaining a knowledge which identifies this character *introspectively*—in terms of what it is like, subjectively, to have an experience of that sort. And we can correspondingly envisage him as able to give conscious expression to this knowledge, on particular occasions, by something closely analogous to the framing of a mental image, namely by consciously rehearsing the character of the pain-experience in his introspective imagination—consciously focusing, in first-person (from-the-inside) perspective, on what it feels like to have such a pain. Any such rehearsal, of course, like the analogous rehearsal of the tune, would be a form of *active* conceiving—something which the subject *does* as a way of deliberately expressing (making consciously explicit) the relevant introspective knowledge. But we can also envisage episodes of introspective recall—parallel with episodes of quasi-perceptual recall—which involve the same intrinsic type of conceiving, but in a passive form. So just as John may sometimes have, passively, an imagistic experience in which he seems to re-hear the original instance of the tune, so he may sometimes have, similarly passively, an introspective experience in which he seems to relive the original experience of the pain. Moreover, there is another point of similarity that now stands out. For just as there is a striking subjective difference between the EI-conceiving of the tune-type, in rehearsal or recall, and the original auditory experience (the phenomenal experience), so there is an analogous subjective difference between the conscious introspective conceiving of the pain-type, in rehearsal or recall, and the original pain-experience. And, indeed, it is hard to avoid concluding that the subjective relationship of the imagistic conceiving to the auditory experience and that of the introspective conceiving to the pain-experience are not just analogous, but exactly the same. Finally, to complete the picture, we can see that, to provide a linguistic expression for the content of the introspective conception, we would need to devise something analogous to the quotational designation we have envisaged for the imagistic conception. So, in specifying what John knows, in knowing that his experience was of the relevant type, we would have to arrange for something like the following: we provide an inscription of the uncompleted sentence 'John knows that he had an experience of type . . .', such that, when the reader's visual focus reaches the blank (having passed through the sentence up to that point), it triggers a device which stimulates the relevant part of his brain in the appropriate way, to produce a token of the type of experience in question. This would be just like displaying a token of a sensible type in quotational designation—such as when we say that John knows that he heard an instance of 'di-da-di-da'.

The parallel between John's imagistic conception of the tune-type and his introspective conception of the pain-type is clear, both with respect to the acquisition and retention of knowledge and with respect to the conscious episodes of conceiving. But what is also clear, on a moment's reflection, is the reason for this parallel. The situation revealed in the pain case is, of course, just one instance of something quite general. Thus, for any type of experience, there is an introspective way of conceptually focusing on that type—identifying its subjective character in the perspective (first-person, from-the-inside, perspective) of one who is having such an experience. And this introspective mode of identification can characterize both the content of propositional attitudes (for example, believing that one has had such an experience) and the activity of someone who is consciously thinking about such experience or recalling a particular episode of it. Now what is clear is that the imagistic identification of the tune-type is itself just a special case of this general phenomenon. Thus, in retaining the imagistic knowledge that the tune was of the 'di-da-di-da'-type, John is retaining the knowledge of what it would be like, subjectively, to encounter this tune-type in auditory experience. And, in consciously rehearsing the character of the tune in his mind's ear, he is consciously rehearsing what it would be like, subjectively, to have such an experience. In short, the imagistic conception of the tune-type *just is* the introspective conception of the experiential type, but with a narrower point of focus—a focus not on the experiential type as such, but on the sensible type which features in its content and whose nature this featuring reveals. So the reason for the parallel between the cases of the tune and the pain is that they are, in different ways, versions of the same generic phenomenon, of which the second case is, as it were, the more explicit example. In introspectively focusing on the pain-type, the subject directly focuses on how things are, subjectively, when such a pain-experience occurs. In imagistically focusing on the tune-type, he focuses on it in the perspective of his introspective grasp of the type of auditory experience in whose content it features. Moreover, it is clear that what holds for the case of the tune-type holds for imagistic conception quite generally. With whatever sense-realm it is associated, and in whatever form it occurs, imagistic conception is just a special—a specially focused— form of introspective conception. It is to conceive of a type of sensible item or situation in terms of what it is like, subjectively, to encounter it in the content of a certain type of experience. It is to conceive introspectively of this type of experience, but with the spotlight on the sensible universal which features in its content.

It does not take long to see how this reveals the imagist proposal to be incoherent. According to the proposal, phenomenal experience is a form of EI-conceiving—an EI-conceiving of the type of sensible item or situation which the experience represents. But it has now turned out that any imagistic conceiving of a sensible universal is (in a slightly re-focused form) an introspective conceiving of a certain type of experience, and the experiential type on to which it is directed is precisely that PE-type (i.e. PE-state) which represents the sensible universal in question. Thus the imagistic conceiving of a type of environmental colour-array is the introspective conceiving of the corresponding visual PE-state (that state in which it is with the subject, visuo-experientially, as if his current environment is thus arrayed), and the imagistic conceiving of a type of physical sound-pattern is the introspective conceiving of the corresponding auditory PE-state (that state in which it is with the subject, audio-experientially, as if his current environment is thus sounding). But, as a matter of logic, a PE-state cannot be construed as a type of introspective conceiving of itself. So, whatever its nature, the one thing that phenomenal experience cannot be is what the imagist proposal claims it to be—a form of EI-conceiving. To suppose that it is, is comparable to supposing that genuine pain is just some kind of introspective conceiving of pain, or genuine anger some kind of introspective conceiving of anger.

There is something else which now falls into place. For, in identifying this incoherence in the imagist proposal, we have also discovered what creates the subjective difference between the sensible awareness involved in phenomenal experience and that involved in EI-conceiving. This difference is simply the difference between what it is subjectively like to have a certain kind of experience and what it is subjectively like to conceptually focus on this kind of experience in a distinctively vivid—introspective— way. It is exactly the same as the subjective difference between being in pain and imagining oneself as in pain, or between being in pain and introspectively recalling the pain one experienced on some previous occasion.

4 THE NATURE OF THE SECONDARY QUALITIES

I

The cognitive theory failed because it did not do justice to the presentational feel of phenomenal experience and because it could not provide for the reception of the PE-information in a sufficiently weak (merely invitational) form. By construing phenomenal experience as a passive form of EI-conceiving, the imagist proposal remedied these failings. But it still failed to do full justice to the subjective character of phenomenal experience, being unable to account for the subjective difference between the sensible awareness involved in the undisputed cases of EI-conceiving and that involved in phenomenal experience. And, more fundamentally, by correcting the failings of cognitivism in that way, it became vulnerable to a charge of incoherence, since the imagistic conceiving of a type of sensible

item or situation is just (in a slightly refocused form) the introspective conceiving of the corresponding PE-state. This, I think, is the end of the road
for the pure conceptualist approach. I cannot see how, except by moving to
the imagist proposal, the conceptualist could hope to correct the failings of
cognitivism. But equally, I cannot see how, except by returning to the aus-
terity of the cognitivist account, he could avoid the incoherence of the
imagist proposal.

We are now almost ready to take our first steps in the development of
the correct account of phenomenal experience. But to give us a clear view
of the direction in which we must move, there is one further piece of the
jigsaw which we need to put in place. Putting this in place will, in fact, serve
a dual purpose. For, as well as indicating the radically new direction in
which we must look for the correct account, it will serve to reinforce our
rejection of the conceptualist approach. For, without reference to any particular versions of this approach (like the cognitivist and imagist versions
which we have examined and found wanting), it will provide a purely general reason why no conceptualist account could be successful.

This new phase of our discussion is concerned with the nature of a certain group of sensible qualities, namely those which, as attributes of physical objects, Locke described as 'secondary'.[11] The group comprises such
qualities as colours, flavours, odours, qualities of sound, qualities of sensible temperature, and certain aspects of tangible texture. These qualities
qualify as *sensible*, in that they feature, or are capable of featuring, in the
content of sensible appearance; in other words, they form ingredients of
the situation-types represented by PE-states. And they are distinguished
from other sensible qualities by the fact that, rather than being modes of
spatial or temporal arrangement, they are the forms of qualitative content
which such modes of arrangement structure, and the fact that each quality is tied, in its PE-occurrence, to a single sense-realm. (These qualities, of
course, form the second group of qualities that we referred to earlier, when
we first focused on the question of the nature of the qualities which are
capable of featuring in the content of sensible appearance.)[12]

In describing these qualities as 'secondary', Locke meant that, as
attributes of physical objects, they are nothing but powers of these objects
to produce certain kinds of sensory experience in us. Thus Locke held that
the only sense in which a physical object possesses a colour is that it is disposed to produce a certain kind of colour-experience in (to look colourwise

---

[11] Locke, *An Essay Concerning Human Understanding*, Bk. 2, ch. 8.
[12] See Part Two, Section 3, II.

a certain way to) the normal subject who observes it in standard conditions, and that the only sense in which a physical object possesses a flavour is that it is disposed to produce a certain kind of gustatory experience in (to taste a certain way to) the normal subject who orally samples it. Of course, Locke did not think that the colours which feature in the content of visual experience (which characterize visual appearance) or the flavours which feature in the content of gustatory experience (which characterize taste) are themselves powers: he recognized that, as they feature in the content of phenomenal experience (characterize sensible appearance), these qualities—the sensible qualities themselves—are intrinsic, not dispositional. They are qualities such that, if anything did genuinely possess them, it would possess them as aspects of its intrinsic character—of what it was like in itself. But he thought that, in this respect, our ways of perceiving the external objects are systematically non-veridical: in so far as physical objects can be said to possess the relevant qualities, they possess them, not by being in reality as they appear, but merely by being disposed to have these forms of appearance. His point could be expressed with less risk of confusion if we employed (as he failed to do) different labels to signify the qualities which feature in experience and their physical counterparts. Thus let us speak of the first—the sensible qualities themselves—as *experiential* secondary qualities (ES-qualities), and the second—the qualities which are genuinely physically instantiated—as *physical* secondary qualities (PS-qualities). Locke's claim is then that, while ES-qualities are intrinsic and non-dispositional, the PS-qualities, though commonly signified by the same names, are merely powers of the objects to produce experiences in whose content the corresponding ES-qualities relevantly feature—dispositions to appear ES-wise in the relevant ways.

Needless to say, Locke's position is not the view of 'common sense'—the view which we hold prior to philosophical reflection. For, prior to reflection, we tend, not surprisingly, to endorse the way that sense-experience itself represents things, thus crediting physical items with the ES-qualities which characterize their sensible appearance. What seems to count strongly in favour of Locke's position are the findings of science. For science shows, or seems to show, that the sensible appearance of physical objects has nothing to do with their actual possession of ES-qualities, but is entirely the result of factors of a quite different kind. Thus, in the case of colour, it seems to show that an object's appearance (for example, the fact that in standard conditions of observation, grass looks ES-green and ripe tomatoes look ES-red) is entirely due to the arrangement and physico-chemical properties of its surface particles, and the way that, by affecting the reflection and absorption of light, this arrangement and these properties affect our eyes and nervous system. But since our only reason for ascribing ES-qualities to physical objects is as an endorsement of their sensible appearance, these scientific findings seem to leave such ascriptions without any justification at all. For how can there be any grounds for crediting physical objects with the qualities of their sensible appearance, if this appearance is to be accounted for in terms of factors of a quite different kind? Moreover, the scientific findings seem to show that, even if, perchance, physical objects do happen to posses such qualities, their possession of them is not something which we ever perceptually register. For we can hardly be said to perceptually register something which makes no causal contribution to how things sensibly appear, or to any other aspect of our perceptual experience.

All this provides, I think, a very strong empirical case in favour of the Lockean view. And it may well have been on this case, or something like it, that Locke himself was primarily relying. However, there is also an argument of a quite different kind that can be brought in support of the view—an argument which only relies on what we can derive from our ordinary understanding of the nature of the ES-qualities, and does not appeal to any special scientific evidence. It is this argument that I now want to develop; for it is this argument, not the scientific one, which is relevant to our present concerns. It is from this argument that we shall obtain both the reinforcement of our rejection of the pure conceptualist approach, and a clear indication of the new direction in which the correct account of phenomenal experience must be sought.

II

We must begin by drawing a distinction. Let us say that a conception of a quality is *transparent* if it reveals the identity of the quality—reveals what quality it is—and *opaque* if it does not. So the conception of triangularity *as triangularity* (or as the quality of being a plane rectilinear figure with three sides and three angles) qualifies as transparent, while the conception of it as that quality (whatever it happens to be) whose geometrical properties are specified in a certain chapter of a book, or as that quality (whatever it happens to be) which is instantiated by the figures drawn on a certain page, is opaque. Just as we can distinguish between the transparent and opaque conception of a *quality*, so, of course, we can draw the same distinction with respect to the conception of other forms of qualitative item—states, kinds, natures, relations, and so on. In each case, there is the difference between a transparent conception, which reveals the identity of the relevant item, and an opaque conception, which does not.

It should not be supposed that transparency of conception has to be philosophically penetrating. To be transparent, a conception has to reveal the identity of the qualitative item in question, but it is not required to reveal how, in the final philosophical analysis, this item is to be understood. Thus suppose someone accepts a functionalist account of the mind, holding that psychological states are to be ultimately construed as functional states. Whatever the merits of this view, it should not lead him to conclude that when we conceive of a psychological state in ordinary psychological terms, with no recognition of the correctness of the functionalist account, the conception is only opaque. If I know that my wife has a headache, or that my pupil has an ambition to become a philosopher, I have identified their psychological states transparently, even if it happens that functionalism is true, but entirely alien to the perspective of my own thoughts.

At the same time, there is also a point to be acknowledged in the other direction. For many of the conceptions which pass as transparent at the level of our ordinary thinking are in fact opaque—not because they fail to impart a philosophically ultimate understanding of the nature of the qualitative items they concern, but because they fail to identify these items at all in the relevantly revealing way. An example is that of natural kinds. At the level of our ordinary thinking, our conception of (say) *water* passes as transparent—we seem to know, from ordinary observation, what, as a type of substance, water is. But, on reflection, we can see that this is not so. Our ordinary conception identifies water as that type of substance (whatever it is) which satisfies certain observational criteria—as that type which has certain kinds of sensible appearance, which we encounter in certain kinds of circumstance, and which has certain kinds of causal power and sensitivity. But it does not reveal what this type is in itself: it leaves this as something to be uncovered (if at all) by science—by an investigation into the chemical, or physico-chemical, composition of the substance in question.[13]

Now our present concern is with the topic of the ES-qualities. And the reason why I have drawn attention to the distinction between transparency and opacity is that I want to focus on a crucial restriction to which the transparent conception of such qualities is subject. The restriction is this: that, for each ES-quality Q, associated with a sense-realm R, it is only by

---

[13] Thus see Hilary Putnam, 'The meaning of "meaning"', in his *Mind, Language, and Reality* (Cambridge: Cambridge University Press, 1975).

knowing what it is like, subjectively, to encounter Q in the content of R-sensory experience, that we are able to achieve a transparent conception of it. Thus, for an ES-colour C, it is only by knowing what it is subjectively like to encounter C visually—in the content of colour-experience—that we can achieve a proper grasp of the identity of C (of what quality C is); and, for an ES-flavour F, it is only by knowing what it is subjectively like to encounter F gustatorily—in the content of taste-experience—that we can achieve a proper grasp of the identity of F (of what quality F is). When I say 'only *by* knowing what it is subjectively like . . .', I am not thinking of mere *causal* dependence. The point is not that a subject needs to have relevant items of subjective knowledge in place before he is causally equipped to achieve—as something further and distinct—the relevant form of transparent conception. The point is rather that any transparent conception must be, explicitly or implicitly, *in terms of* the relevant subjective fact: it must *incorporate* the knowledge of what it is subjectively like to encounter the quality in the content of the relevant form of sensory experience, and must achieve its conceptual transparency *in that way*. In other words, it must be, in the sense explained earlier, an *imagistic* conception: it must be a conception *in the perspective* of the relevant kind of sensory encounter— the sort of conception which the subject could make consciously explicit (consciously express to himself) by framing an actual image of the quality, or some qualitative complex of which it is an element, in his mind's eye, on his mind's palate, or whatever.

A transparent conception of an ES-quality has to involve a knowledge of what it is like, subjectively, to encounter that quality in the content of sensory experience. But we should not take this to imply that someone can only have such a conception if he has at some time *had* such an experience. Thus someone who is sighted, and experientially familiar with a representative range of ES-colours, may well be able to achieve a transparent conception of various colours which he has not yet experienced—for example, by first identifying the points in the colour-spectrum where the colours would fall (something which his familiarity with colours in general would make possible), and then using his powers of imagination to work out what the colours would have to be like, as visually experienced, to fall at these points. (This, of course, was a point which even Hume was prepared to concede as an exception to his principle that simple ideas are always copies of previous impressions.)[14] Nor, a priori, can we even exclude the possibility of someone managing to achieve a transparent conception of an

---

[14] *Treatise*, Bk. 1, Pt. 1, sect. 1.

ES-quality when he has had *no* experience of qualities in the relevant category. For there is no *logical incoherence* in suggesting that someone knows
what it is like (what it *would be* like), subjectively, to have a certain type of
experience, but has not drawn that knowledge from his own past history.
At the same time, there is an understandable expectation that those who
are totally deprived of a capacity for a whole category of sensory experience—for example, someone congenitally blind or deaf—would not, *in
practice*, have any way of knowing what such experience was like, and so
would not be able to achieve a transparent conception of the ES-qualities
involved. And indeed, focusing on such examples can be a helpful way of
bringing out the basic point, that, without a knowledge of the subjective
character of the relevant form of sensory experience, the transparent,
identity-revealing conception of an ES-quality is logically impossible.

   This basic point is, in itself, clear. What we still have to determine is why
it holds—why it is that the transparent conception of ES-qualities is constrained in this way. After all, it is not true of qualities, or qualitative items,
in general that we can only achieve a transparent conception of them in
terms of what it is like to encounter them in sensory experience. Indeed,
on certain commonly held assumptions, it does not even seem to be true
of all *sensible* qualities. Thus it is commonly held that the same qualities of
shape feature in the content of both visual and tactual experience—the difference between the two cases being merely a matter of the different forms
of qualitative content which the shape-qualities serve to structure. And, on
this assumption, it becomes plausible to think of these qualities as capable
of being transparently grasped in a purely abstract, geometrical way, there
not seeming to be anything over and above what an abstract conception
could capture which is also common to the featuring of the qualities in the
two sense-realms. But if the transparent conception of qualities is not *in
general* tied to the perspective of sensory experience, and, arguably, is not
even so tied in the case of certain sensible qualities, what explains this tie
in the particular case of the ES-qualities? Presumably, the restriction must
stem from some way in which, not just in conception, but in their very
nature, these qualities incorporate the perspective of the relevant modes of
experience. But if they do, then how?

   Well, before we try to answer this question, I think it will be helpful to
take note of another factor which calls for explanation and which seems to
be pointing in the same direction—a further respect in which the ES-qualities have an intimate link with the perspective of sensory experience. In
this new case, the link is not in respect of the requirements for a transpar-

ent conception of the qualities, but one which characterizes our ordinary
understanding of what their physical realization involves.

III

There is no denying that we ordinarily think of physical objects as genuinely possessing ES-qualities, and that this ordinary view is in sharp contrast with the philosophical position of Locke, who takes the PS-qualities
(those qualities of colour, flavour, odour, and so on, which the physical
objects actually possess) to be mere powers of objects to affect human
experience. But it is also true that, in ascribing ES-qualities to physical
objects, we think of their physical realization as taking the form of, or as
essentially linked with, certain modes of sensible appearance. Thus, when
we ascribe ES-redness to a ripe tomato, we think of this redness not just as
a quality which we visually detect, but as a quality whose possession by the
tomato consists in, or is essentially linked with, how that object looks. And
when we ascribe ES-sweetness to a lump of sugar, we think of this sweetness not just as a quality which we gustatorily detect, but as a quality whose
possession by the sugar consists in, or is essentially linked with, how that
object tastes. We think of the redness of the tomato not just as a *visible* quality, but as a *visual* quality (a quality of visual appearance), and we think of
the sweetness of the sugar not just as a *tasteable* quality, but as a *taste*-qual-
ity (a quality of gustatory appearance). And likewise for all ES-qualities.
For each such quality, there is a unique sense-realm such that we ordinarily think of the physical realization of that quality as consisting in, or as
essentially linked with, a mode of sensible appearance in that realm. This
does not mean that, in the ordinary course of life, we do not acknowledge
cases in which the actual ES-quality of an object differs from how that
object currently appears, in the relevant respect, to a particular subject.
Obviously we accept that, owing to some distorting factor in the subject's
constitution or in the conditions of observation, something which is really
red may look grey, and something which is really sweet may taste bitter.
But, crucially, even in these cases, where we recognize the perception as
non-veridical, we still feel that what the subject fails to perceive is the true
look of the object or its true *taste*. We feel that when, to a particular subject
on a particular occasion, a red thing looks grey or a sweet thing tastes bitter, then it does not look or taste to that subject, on that occasion, as it *objectively* looks or tastes *in the abstract*. In respect of the ES-qualities, we think
of the veridical perception of an object as subjectively preserving its objec-

tive sensible appearance, and we think of a non-veridical perception as subjectively distorting that appearance.

It is undeniable that this way of thinking is a conspicuous part of our ordinary conception of the physical realization of the ES-qualities, even though we would not ordinarily articulate it in quite that way. At the same time, it is prima facie very puzzling that it should be. For consider what could be meant by the notion of an *objective appearance*. It is surely clear that, in its conceptually basic form, the notion of how an object sensibly appears is the notion of how it *subjectively* sensibly appears—of how it sensibly appears *to a given subject on a particular occasion*. So any elucidation of the notion of an *objective* sensible appearance (of sensible appearance *in the abstract*) will presumably have to relate it, in some way, to this more basic notion. But now there seem to be only two possibilities. On the one hand, we might understand the objective appearance of an object, in respect of a sense-realm R, to be the way in which this object *subjectively* appears to any R-percipient who perceives it *veridically*. Thus to say that something has a certain objective colour-appearance or a certain objective flavour-appearance would be to say that that is how the object has to look or taste to a percipient, if it is to look or taste the way it is. If this is what is meant, it is not difficult to see why we should take the ES-qualities of a physical object to be, or to be essentially linked with, its objective appearance, since to say that an object *objectively appears* F is merely an alternative and long-winded way of saying that it *is* F. But just because of this, the connection between the possession of a quality and an objective appearance would be utterly trivial, and would hardly be something which receives a special emphasis in our ordinary view. It would be wholly idle to think of the possession of a certain quality as consisting in, or as essentially linked with, a certain mode of appearance if, by that mode of appearance, we merely meant, in so many words, the possession of that quality. On the other hand, we might understand the objective appearance of an object, in respect of a sense-realm R, to be the way in which this object *subjectively* appears to any *normal* R-percipient in *standard* conditions. Then, to say that something has a certain objective colour-appearance would be to say that it is disposed to look that way to the normally sighted subject who views it in daylight, and to say that something has a certain objective flavour-appearance would be to say that it is disposed to taste that way to the normally palated subject who orally samples it. If this is the relevant interpretation, then certainly the putative connection between an object's possession of an ES-quality and its objective appearance would be far from trivial. But, at the same time, it is difficult to see how such a connection could be envisaged without undermining the view that the qualities are ones which the physical objects genuinely possess. For, on the face of it, the only way of making sense of the connection would be by construing the claim that a physical object possesses such qualities as reducible to the claim that the object has the power to produce certain kinds of experience in us. And this would make our ordinary, pre-philosophically-reflective, view collapse into the position of Locke, and thus become something which no longer accepts that ES-qualities are genuinely physically instantiated.

It seems, then, that our ordinary view of how the ES-qualities relate to the physical world is incoherent. It contains two components which, on the face of it, can only be reconciled by depriving one or other of them of its prima facie significance within that view. In the first place, it contains the naive, common-sense assumption that the ES-qualities—the intrinsic secondary qualities which feature in the PE-content of sense-experience— genuinely characterize objects in the physical world. Secondly, it involves, in addition, the thought that, as possessed by physical objects, these qualities are, or are essentially linked with, certain modes of objective appearance. On the face of it, these two components are irreconcilable unless we dilute one or other of them to a point where it no longer contributes anything to the overall view. Thus if we retain, without qualification, the assumption that ES-qualities are genuinely qualities of physical objects, it seems that we can only retain their essential connection with modes of objective appearance by making the notion of objective appearance redundant, i.e. by reducing the notion of the objective appearance of an object to the notion of what qualities it possesses. Conversely, if we retain this notion in some significant form—a form in which its phenomenal aspect is not analysed away—then it seems that we can only retain the essential link between the possession of ES-qualities and objective appearance by construing such possession in terms of Lockean powers, so that the claim that an object possesses an ES-quality amounts to no more than the claim that the object has the power to produce the appropriate kinds of ES-experience in us. What, it seems, we cannot have, in combination, are both the genuine realization of ES-qualities in the physical world and some non-vacuous way in which such realization is essentially linked with how the physical objects involved appear.

But if our ordinary view is incoherent, what leads us to adopt it? In other areas, we operate with a sharp conceptual distinction between appearance and reality—between what it is for things *to appear to be* thus and so and what it is for them *to be* thus and so. We have no hesitation in acknowledging this distinction even in cases where we tend to work on the assumption that appearance and reality agree. So why should this intuitive distinction get blurred in our ordinary view about the ES-qualities? Why, in this particular case, do we find it so natural to construe an object's possession of a quality as consisting in, or as essentially linked with, its appearance? And there is a further twist to the puzzle here. For so long as we retain the view that ES-qualities are genuinely physically realized, the seeming incoherence is something which, even on reflection, it seems impossible to avoid. For it just seems self-evident that we cannot do justice to our basic conception of the qualities in question if we regard the association between their physical realization and the relevant modes of appearance as merely contingent. We only need to focus our minds on the qualities themselves—as they are transparently revealed to us in experience—to find ourselves compelled to think of them as inseparably linked with certain forms of sensible appearance.

What is going on here? Well, it seems almost inevitable that the answer, whatever it is, will be closely bound up with the answer to the other question we have raised, of why the transparent conception of an ES-quality has to be imagistic—a conception in terms of what it is like to encounter the quality in sensory experience. When I raised that earlier question, I noted that the answer would presumably involve pointing out some way in which ES-qualities incorporate the perspective of such experiential encounter in their very natures. And, with respect to the present question, it equally seems that the answer must lie in the same direction—that the reason why we ordinarily think of the physical realization of the qualities as essentially linked with modes of appearance, and why, despite its seeming incoherence, we cannot, even on reflection, escape from this way of thinking, is that the experiential perspective is in some way built into the nature of qualities of this kind. Our next step is now, I think, determined. There is, as far as I can see, only one approach which will deliver what is needed—only one approach which will allow the questions we have posed to be answered.

IV

What we are forced to say, it seems to me, is that ES-qualities are, by nature, ones whose realization is achieved in, and necessarily confined to, the content of sensory experience. More precisely, we have to accept the following thesis:

For any category C of ES-qualities, associated with a sense-realm R, there is an M mode of occurrence, such that, for any C-quality Q:

(1) it is logically possible for Q to M-occur in the content of R-experience,

(2) the M-occurrence of Q in the content of R-experience logically suffices for the realization of Q (for the occurrence of a concrete instance of Q),

and

(3) it is logically impossible for Q to be realized in any other way (i.e. M-occurrence in the content of R-experience is necessarily its only mode of realization).

Let us call this the *experiential realization thesis* (ERT). So, in the case of ES-colours, ERT would commit us to saying that there is a mode of occurrence M such that each such colour is capable of being realized, and is only capable of being realized, by M-occurrence in the content of visual experience; and in the case of ES-flavours, it would commit us to saying that there is a mode of occurrence M such that each such flavour is capable of being realized, and is only capable of being realized, by M-occurrence in the content of taste-experience. Quite generally, for each ES-category, ERT would commit us to saying that its qualities achieve their realization by, and exclusively by, occurring, in the relevant way, in the content of sensory experience in the associated sense-realm. It might be wondered why, in formulating the thesis, I have included the reference to a *mode of occurrence*; for would not the relevant mode of occurrence be already covered by the nature of the sense-realm and the nature of the quality? Well, the reason for this will emerge presently—when we come to distinguish the 'sensory' and 'interpretative' components of phenomenal experience— though it will do no harm if, in the context of our present discussion, the reference is simply ignored.

My claim, then, is that it is only by accepting ERT that we are able to give satisfactory answers to the two questions before us—to provide satisfactory explanations of both the constraint on transparent conception and the nature of our ordinary thought. ERT itself, it must be stressed, does not provide these answers (explanations) *in full detail*. Before we can provide the answers in detail, we have to work out *in exactly what way* ES-qualities achieve their experiential realization, and, as we shall see, there are some crucially different options here. But we do not need to have all the details in place to be able to see, in general outline, how an acceptance of ERT makes provision for a satisfactory account. Let us look at the two questions in turn.

The first question concerns the constraint on transparent conception: why is it that, in the case of ES-qualities, such conception has to be in experiential perspective—in terms of what it is like to encounter such qualities in the relevant forms of sensory experience? It is not difficult to see how, in general outline, ERT would provide a straightforward answer to this.

As we have noted, transparency of conception does not have to be philosophically penetrating. And, in particular, we must allow for cases in which someone has a transparent (identity-revealing) conception of a quality without thereby discerning its true mode of realization. Even so, it is only to be expected that, where the conception of a quality is transparent, the true mode of realization will be, in some way, indicated by, or reflected in, its content. It would be strange if a conception made clear the identity of the quality without in some way signalling the nature of the conditions which are required for there to be a concrete instance of it. It is hardly surprising, then, that, if ERT is true, a transparent conception of an ES-quality has to be in experiential perspective—in terms of what it is like to encounter it in the content of sensory experience. For it is precisely by identifying the quality in that perspective that the conception exhibits it in its realization-conferring setting. In effect, with the truth of ERT, the situation here would become just a special (though less immediately apparent) case of something which holds quite generally, namely that one can only have a transparent conception of an experiential state by knowing what it is like (or would be like) to be in it. A transparent conception of an ES-quality has to be in terms of what it is subjectively like to encounter it in sensory experience because it is only by occurring in the content of such experience that the quality is realized, and because there is no transparent grasp of the character of an experience without a knowledge of what such an experience is introspectively like to the subject who has it.

ERT provides, then, in a general way, an immediate and straightforward answer to the first question, concerning the constraint on transparent conception. What, then of the second question—of why we ordinarily think of the physical realization of the ES-qualities as consisting in, or essentially linked with, certain modes of appearance, and why, even on reflection, we find it impossible to avoid this way of thinking, despite its seeming incoherence? Well, here too, ERT makes provision for an answer, though the way this works out is a little more complicated.

The first thing that needs to be stressed is that, if ERT is true, then our ordinary ways of thinking are incoherent at a more basic point. For if, by their very nature, ES-qualities can only be realized experientially, then our very ascription of these qualities to external, mind-independent objects is already incoherent, quite apart from any essential link with modes of appearance that we may additionally see as involved. At least, it is incoherent if we accept, as I am assuming, that we intend this ascription to be taken at face value and not reductively construed as the ascription of Lockean powers. This means, of course, that, as well as the issue over modes of appearance, there is a further puzzle. For if it is incoherent to suppose that ES-qualities have an external realization, how do we come to make this mistake? It is not as if the relevant factors in the situation are hidden from view: we have access to the qualities in the relevant experiential perspective, and this perspective exhibits the qualities in their realization-conferring setting. So how do we come to misunderstand the significance of this perspective and think of the qualities as realized externally? Well, this is an issue which, even in broad outline, we cannot hope to deal with at present; before we can address it, we need to turn ERT into a definite theory—a theory which specifies the *manner* in which ES-qualities are experientially realized. But, in any case, the relevance of this topic to our present discussion lies at a different point.

This point concerns a respect in which, even in its own terms, the extent of the further puzzle—the amount, as it were, of what it presents to be explained—is not as great as might seem. For although we manage to misunderstand the significance of the experiential perspective, this misunderstanding is, in a sense, only partial: even in ascribing the qualities to physical objects, we show a kind of confused recognition of their real nature, and of the way this nature confines their scope for realization to the content of experience. What I have in mind, here, is precisely the phenomenon which forms the focus of our second question—the fact that in ascribing the qualities to physical objects, we think of their physical realization as consisting in, or as essentially linked with, certain modes of objective appearance. This phenomenon seemed puzzling: there seemed to be no coherent way of understanding the thinking involved, and it was not clear why we found it compelling. But, in the framework of ERT, the phenomenon can be understood as the way in which the essentially experiential nature of the qualities continues to make itself felt in the system of our ordinary beliefs. The supposed essential link with modes of objective appearance is what the real experiential nature of the qualities gives rise to (in effect, turns into) when the externalist character of our ordinary beliefs (the fact that they ascribe the qualities to external objects) prevents its explicit recognition. The link is, if you like, the closest that our ordinary beliefs can come to reflecting the real nature of the qualities, given the strategic externalist error to which they are committed. It might still be wondered how the real nature of the qualities manages to exert this influence on our thinking. After all, the *abstract fact* that the qualities are of this sort can hardly be in itself what exerts the influence. But the point must be that, although this fact is rejected by our ordinary beliefs, its acceptance is at least implicit in our basic understanding of the qualities, and it is as thus implicitly registered, and hence psychologically immanent, that the real nature of the qualities exerts its influence. It is as if, beneath the surface of our ordinary system of beliefs, there is an underlying manifestation of the true situation which gets distorted, but not obliterated, by what overlays it. And this, of course, would explain not just the relevant aspect of our ordinary thinking, but also why we find it impossible to free ourselves from it on subsequent reflection.

So ERT allows us to explain the phenomenon at issue in our second question. And, as well as yielding this explanation, it puts the phenomenon itself in a quite different perspective. Initially, it had seemed that the inclusion of the mode-of-appearance element in our ordinary thinking was responsible for rendering that thinking incoherent. For there seemed to be no way of understanding how an object's possession of an ES-quality could be essentially linked to an objective mode of appearance which would not involve either construing the mode of appearance as the mere possession of the quality (thus eliminating the link in any significant form), or construing the possession of the quality as a mere disposition to appear a certain way (thus eliminating the physical realization of the quality in any significant form). But if the envisaged explanation is right, we can now see that the incoherence in our ordinary view stems from its acceptance of the external realization of the qualities, rather than from the link with appearance which it attaches to this. The attachment of this link is simply the extent to which a truth whose recognition is implicit in our basic understanding of the nature of the qualities is able to preserve its influence in a framework of belief which denies it. So when we find ourselves, on reflection, unable to free ourselves from this way of thinking, this is, in effect, the influence of an underlying insight, rather than an irrational compulsion— even though it is an insight which can only express itself, in those circumstances, in a compromised form.

ERT, then, allows us to answer the two questions we raised: it enables us to account for the constraint on transparent conception (to explain why a

transparent conception of an ES-quality has to be in terms of what it is subjectively like to encounter it in sense-experience), and it enables us to
account for the mode-of-appearance factor in our ordinary thinking (to
explain why we think of the physical realization of an ES-quality as consisting in, or essentially linked with, an objective mode of sensible appearance). Moreover, it seems to me that ERT is the *only* position which allows
an answer to these questions. It is true that I have not *proved* that this is so;
I have merely shown how answers are forthcoming under ERT. But I simply cannot think of a way in which they would be forthcoming on any alternative approach—including those approaches which we have already
considered and rejected on independent grounds.

Because it explains (or makes provision for the explanation of) the two
points that need to be explained, and because, as far as I can see, there is no
other position which would do this, I am going to proceed on the assumption that ERT is correct, and consider how we might turn it into a fully
fledged theory—a theory which offers a definite account of the manner in
which ES-qualities are experientially realized. If our quest for a satisfactory
ERT-theory fails—if we cannot find a theory which is not vulnerable to
some objection—then no doubt the status of the thesis itself will have to
be reconsidered. But this is not a possibility that we need to concern ourselves with unless it arises.

V

Before we turn to this new phase of our investigation, I want to round off
our present discussion by getting ERT itself into clearer perspective, and
seeing how it bears on our overall project.

Although I have formulated ERT as a single thesis, it can be represented
as the conjunction of two independent claims. First, there is the claim that
ES-qualities achieve a genuine realization whenever they occur in the content of sensory experience in the relevant way—that experiential occurrence of the relevant form *suffices to confer realization*. Let us speak of this
as the *realization-conferment claim* (RC-claim). Second, there is the claim
that ES-qualities are not able to achieve realization in any other way—that
any form of realization, apart from the experiential, is *excluded*. Let us
speak of this as the *realization-exclusion claim* (RE-claim). Taken together,
these two claims add up to the claim of ERT, that the mode of realization
for ES-qualities is, and is exclusively, experiential.

Combining these claims to form a single thesis was not arbitrary: both
claims had to be included to equip the thesis to play the explanatory role

assigned to it—to deal adequately with the points about transparent conception and modes of objective appearance; and so both had to be included for the thesis to commend itself to us in the way that it did. But what we also need to see is that, in so far as we are now working *on the basis* of the thesis, rather than seeking to *validate* it, the claims have significance in quite different areas of philosophical enquiry. The issue to which the RC-claim has relevance concerns the nature of sensory experience. Thus, by insisting that the ES-qualities *achieve* realization by occurring in the content of sensory experience, the claim obliges us to seek for an account of such experience which reveals it as realization-conferring in that way. In contrast, the issue to which the RE-claim has relevance concerns the nature of the physical world. For, by insisting that ES-qualities *only* have an experiential mode of realization, it rules out any genuine ascription of these qualities to external objects. In other words, it provides an a priori basis for an acceptance of a Lockean view of the secondary qualities—a basis which is independent of any appeal to the scientific, or any other form of empirical, evidence.

Now, of these two components in ERT, it is only the first—the RC-claim—which has an immediate bearing on our present enquiry. It is not that the RE-claim is entirely irrelevant to the topic of perception. For since perceiving is a relationship between the subject and the physical world, any account of how things stand on the physical side is liable to set constraints on the form which the relationship can take. And, indeed, we have already encountered a specific point where the question of the Lockean view becomes relevant. For, as we saw in our discussion of SDR, if the ES-qualities are excluded from the physical world, then our perceptual awareness of the world cannot be directly presentational. But, in the context of our present discussion, where we are taking the demise of SDR for granted, and seeking an account of the psychological states which feature in the mediation of perceptual contact, it is the RC-claim which is important. And it is important in two ways. For it both reinforces the conclusion to which we were brought by our earlier discussion, and, still more crucially, reveals the general direction in which we must now move.

The conclusion which it reinforces is the unacceptability of the pure conceptualist approach. On this approach, PE-states are taken to be conceptual through and through—states wholly defined by their conceptual content and their psychological character qua possessors of this content. The reason why we rejected this approach was that we were unable to find a satisfactory version of it: we could not see how to turn it into a definite theory without making it vulnerable to some clear-cut objection. The need to abandon pure conceptualism now gets confirmed by our establishing of the RC-claim. For clearly this claim and the conceptualist approach are in direct conflict. If the conceptualist approach is right, the sensible qualities which feature in the content of sensory experience do so by forming elements of the types of environmental situation which the relevant PE-states conceptually represent, and this conceptual representation does not, when the PE-states get realized, confer any realization on the qualities themselves. So, in embracing the RC-claim—in insisting that ES-qualities achieve realization by relevantly featuring in sensory experience—we equip ourselves with a further basis for rejecting the conceptualist approach, without having to consider the various forms in which it might be developed.

But the most crucial aspect of the RC-claim is that, in providing this new objection to conceptualism, it brings with it a clear indication of where the correct theory lies. For if the objection is sound, it identifies the respect in which conceptualism has gone astray and the general lines on which a new account must be sought. It tells us that, whatever its details, the new account must be one which makes provision for the relevant form of experiential realization; and this is a very severe constraint on the form which the new account has to take.

5 THE SENSE-DATUM THEORY

I

We are looking for an account of phenomenal experience which accommodates the RC-claim. And there is an obvious place to begin. For the most *familiar* account of such experience is precisely of that sort—an account which represents ES-qualities as achieving realization whenever they feature in the content of phenomenal experience in the appropriate way. What I have in mind is the account offered by the narrow version of the representative theory (NRT)—that version which not only takes our perceptual contact with the physical world to be psychologically mediated, but takes this psychological mediation to be a form of *perceptual* mediation, involving the occurrence of internal objects of awareness. It is the account that has been endorsed by the mainstream tradition of British empiricist philosophy—the tradition of Locke, Berkeley, Hume, Mill, Russell, and Ayer. I should stress that, while this empiricist account of phenomenal experience is an essential component of NRT, the acceptance of NRT is not essential to the acceptance of the account. For it is possible to accept the account, but reject a realist conception of the physical world, and so reject the representative theory in any form. And, indeed, this was the position of Berkeley, Mill, and (at one time) Ayer, who, while accepting this view of phenomenal experience, combined it with either an idealist or a phenomenalist view of the physical world.[15] In the present context, of course, we are still assuming the correctness of physical realism, and, in the framework of this assumption, the relevant account of phenomenal experience and the narrow version of the representative theory are indeed inseparably linked.

The internal objects postulated by the account have, at different times, and in the writings of different philosophers, gone under a variety of names. For Locke and Berkeley, they were sensory 'ideas'; for Hume, sensory 'impressions'; for Mill, 'sensations'; for Broad, 'sensa'. In most recent philosophy—indeed, in most philosophy in the twentieth century—they have been known as 'sense-data', and the account in which they feature has been known as the 'sense-datum theory'. I shall adopt this modern terminology here. Let me begin, then, by setting out what the sense-datum theory claims, or more precisely—since it can vary in detail from one expositor to another—what I shall take it to claim for the purposes of our discussion.

II

According to the sense-datum theory (SDT), the core of a phenomenal experience consists in an episode of sensory awareness. The awareness in question is directly presentational in the sense already explained: it brings its object—the sense-datum—before the mind in a way which satisfies the specified three conditions. In other words, it brings it before the mind in a way which: (1) makes it available for demonstrative identification; (2) displays, and so makes available for cognitive scrutiny, certain aspects of its character; and (3) is ontologically immediate and non-representational—not involving the use of concepts, images, or symbols as a means of registering the presence of the object or the relevant aspects of its character. We

---

[15] Berkeley's idealist account is presented in his *A Treatise Concerning the Principles of Human Knowledge*, in his *Philosophical Works*, ed. M. Ayers (London: Dent, 1975); Mill's phenomenalistic account is found in his *An Examination of Sir William Hamilton's Philosophy* (London: Longmans Green, 1867); and Ayer's phenomenalistic account comes in his *Language, Truth, and Logic*, 2nd edn. (London: Gollancz, 1946).

have already encountered, in the form of the *presentational view*, a theory which takes perception to involve a form of presentational awareness in this sense. But whereas, on this earlier view, the object supposedly presented was something external to the mind, it is here taken to be something internal to the presentational awareness directed on to it—something which has, and can have, no existence outside the context of that awareness. As well as confining its existence to a single presentational context, this internality of the sensory object sets a severe restriction on its *character*. Thus, by being internal to an episode of sensory awareness, each sense-datum is exclusively characterized by sensible qualities associated with the relevant sense-realm (the relevant modality of the sensory awareness), so that, in the visual case, it is just a spatial, or spatiotemporal, array of colour, in the auditory case, it is just a temporal pattern of sounds, in the tactual case, just a felt pattern of textures and temperatures. Moreover, as internal objects of awareness, sense-data cannot possess qualities (even of the relevant sensible type) which are not presentationally registered: all their qualities must be, in the relevant sense, on display, and hence—assuming that the subject has the appropriate conceptual resources—available for cognitive scrutiny. With sense-data, one might say, all the qualitative goods are in the shop window.

On this last point, however, it is important that the nature of the cognitive availability should not be misunderstood. The fact that the character of the sense-datum is fully displayed, and so open to cognitive scrutiny, does not mean that the subject can automatically gain a knowledge of any aspect of it by simply targeting his introspective attention in the right way. It does not mean, for instance, that if someone is looking at a speckled hen, so that his visual sense-datum includes an array of sensory speckles (corresponding to the array of physical speckles on the visible portion of the hen), then he is bound to be able to tell, just by focusing a global attention on this array, exactly how many items it contains. Clearly, if the number of sensory speckles is large, and he is someone of normal cognitive capacities, he will only be able to work out this number, if at all, by *counting*. Likewise, the cognitive availability does not mean that if two components of a sense-datum are characterized by different values along some qualitative dimension, the subject will always be able to detect the difference by direct comparison. For if the difference is very slight, it may fall below the threshold of what that subject, with his particular powers of discrimination, can directly discern: it may be that, to distinguish the two sensory qualities involved, he has to compare each with some third quality, which he can directly distinguish from the one, but not from the other—the difference in the one case being just above the relevant threshold, and in the other case just below.

Nor, of course, is there any guarantee that, when a subject is prepared to make introspective judgements about the character of his current sense-data, his judgements are always correct. Thus if someone is unable to detect the difference between two shades of sensory red which are currently displayed, he is liable to jump to the mistaken conclusion that they are the same. Or again, if someone is presented with three shades of sensory red, R_1, R_2, and R_3, and finds no difficulty in distinguishing any two of them on direct comparison, he may still, just because he is not good at gauging that sort of thing, have an erroneous opinion of their similarity-relations; for instance, he may take R_1 to fall between R_2 and R_3 in the colour-spectrum, when, in reality, it is R_2 which holds the middle position. In fact, the strongest claim that could be sensibly entertained, concerning the subject's capacity to monitor the sensory facts, is that, because a sense-datum is immediately before the mind, and because it has no qualities apart from what are thus presentationally registered, it must be possible for the subject, by focusing his attention on it in the right way, to achieve an *imagistic* knowledge of its full character, whatever difficulties he may have in moving from such knowledge to a non-imagistic (descriptively expressible) recognition of the various facts it implicitly covers. Even this claim, though on the right lines, would, I suspect, need to be modified. It is true that, to gain such imagistic knowledge, the subject only needs to take, as it were, a conceptual impression of what is before his mind, and it might seem that, to achieve this, he would only have to attend to the sense-datum in an appropriately receptive way—allowing it to imprint itself on his cognitive consciousness. But, even so, it would hardly be surprising if the subject's capacity for receiving such impressions was less than perfect, with some limit on the degree of sensory complexity and fineness of qualitative differences that it could reliably handle.

One reason why it is particularly important to get clear about these matters is that, if the form of the cognitive availability is misunderstood—in particular, if the extent of the subject's cognitive powers is exaggerated—the sense-datum theorist can seem, at the outset, to be committed to various forms of incoherence. It might seem, for example, that, when the subject is not able to tell the exact number of shapes of a certain sort that are currently presented to him, the theorist is committed to saying, incoherently, that there is *no* exact number—that the sense-datum is intrinsically indeterminate in its nature. Or again, it might seem that where the subject cannot, on direct comparison, detect a difference between two sensory colours, then the theorist has to say that the colours are truly the same—a claim which becomes paradoxical when it turns out that there is some third colour which the subject can directly distinguish from the one, but not from the other. And, indeed, objections to SDT have been made precisely on these grounds—that the need to acknowledge the cognitive transparency of sense-data in a strong sense forces the theorist to positions which are incoherent.[16] But, in fact, these objections are just the product of a mistaken view of what the theorist has to acknowledge. Certainly, the theorist does have to acknowledge that the character of a sense-datum is, in a certain sense, fully available for scrutiny by the subject to whom it is presented. But the sense is simply that, because the sense-datum has no qualities beyond what are presentationally registered, there is nothing in its character that is cognitively concealed from the subject by its failing to be in presentational view. It does not mean that the answers to all the questions that the subject may raise about this character are immediately forthcoming.

III

SDT takes the episode of sensory awareness—the presentation of the sense-datum—to form the *core* of the phenomenal experience, but it does not, at least on any plausible version, take it to be the *only* component. The PE-state, after all, represents a certain type of environmental situation: it embodies the way things sensibly appear to the subject with respect to his current environment. If the state is to play this representational role, it needs some additional component which, added to the sensory awareness, enables this awareness to point beyond itself. To provide this further component, the theory, when properly developed, recognizes an element of conceptual interpretation, which is directed on to the sense-datum, and which represents it as environmentally located in the requisite way; and it then takes the phenomenal experience to consist, not in the occurrence of the sense-datum on its own, but in the occurrence of the sense-datum as thus interpreted. The basic form of the interpretation is to locate the sense-datum and the subject in a common three-dimensional space, and to do this in a way which, with varying degrees of specificity, purports to characterize the spatial relationship between them from the subject's

---

[16] For example, David Armstrong puts weight on these objections in both his *Perception and the Physical World*, ch. 4, and his *A Materialist Theory of the Mind*, ch. 10. For a fuller discussion of Armstrong's objections see my *Ayer*, Pt. II, sect. 10.

standpoint (in the perspective of his viewpoint). I shall speak of these interpretations as 'externalist'. The point of this label is that, by representing the sense-data as located in the subject's environment, they represent them as existing external to the subject's mind, and indeed external to human mentality altogether. At least they do this if, as in the current framework of our discussion, we exclude any kind of idealist account of the physical world.

We can best see what is involved in this new aspect of SDT by focusing on the visual realm, where the spatial character of the postulated interpretation is a straightforward response to—as it were an externalist rewriting of—the spatial character of the sense-datum itself. Thus take again the case of Pauline. Pauline's phenomenal experience covers how things sensibly appear to her as she Φ-terminally sees the relevant portion-stage of the apple's surface. It represents the environmental situation-type of there being a certain arrangement of colours at various distances and in various (in an integrated field of varying) directions; and, as the particular aspect of this which is involved in her seeing of the apple, it represents the situation-type of there being a certain roughly hemispherical patch of green at a certain distance in front of her. Now SDT, as I am envisaging it developed, will take this experience to be made up of two components. One component is an episode of non-conceptual sensory awareness. This consists in the presentation of a visual sense-datum, which is internal to (ontologically inseparable from) the presentation itself, and which takes the form of a spatial array of colours. This colour-array is, in itself, 'flat'—purely two-dimensional—the position of each point within it being fully fixed by 'vertical' and 'horizontal' coordinates; and, being internal to her awareness, it is not something to which Pauline stands, or could stand, in any spatial relationship. The other component of Pauline's experience is an element of interpretation, directed on to this sensory array and reconstruing it externalistically. This interpretative element represents the array as located and geometrically structured in a three-dimensional space, represents the subject herself as located in this space, and represents the array, in its various parts, as presented to the subject in the perspective of her current spatial position. In other words, it interprets the array as a three-dimensional arrangement of colours, or instances of colour, located at various distances and in various directions from her; and, as part of this, it interprets a particular green patch within the array as a roughly hemispherical item at a certain distance in front of her. In this way, SDT will see these two components (the occurrence of the sense-datum and the externalist interpretation imposed on it) as combining to form the whole experience of how things sensibly appear to Pauline—the experience of its being with her, visuo-experientially, as if her current environment is, relative to her own view-point, thus and so arrayed.

Similar accounts will apply to all other cases of visual experience. And broadly analogous accounts will apply to phenomenal experience in other sense-realms too. Thus, in the case of each sense-realm, the theory will equate a phenomenal experience with the combination of the occurrence of a sense-datum and its externalist interpretation; and the basic form of this interpretation will be, as I indicated, to locate the sense-datum and the subject in a common three-dimensional space, and to provide, however precisely or roughly, a characterization of the spatial relationship between them from the subject's standpoint. Such differences as there are between the accounts applicable to different sense-realms turn mainly on the spatial factors involved—in particular, on the degree to which, if at all, the interpretation of the sense-datum as located in the external space is (as it is *par excellence* in the visual case) directly linked with some spatial or space-like aspect of the sense-datum itself, and on the degree of precision (typically high in the visual case) with which the interpretation positions the externalized sense-datum, or its various parts, in relation to the subject. However, a comparative study of the application of SDT to the different sense-realms is not something which, at present, we need to pursue.

It is crucial that we should have a correct understanding of the *kind* of interpretation that is here being envisaged. Interpretation can often take the form of a *judgement* made about whatever it is that is being interpreted. For example, if a detective sees a footprint on the flowerbed and concludes that it must have been made by the burglar, that is a kind of interpretation of the evidence before him. Or again, if someone hears an unusual sound in the night and, after thinking about it for a while, decides that it was probably the cry of an owl, that too is a kind of interpretation of what he heard. Now the sort of interpretation envisaged by SDT, as an integral component of the phenomenal experience, is not of this judgmental kind. It is not a matter of the subject reaching some conclusion about the sense-datum presented to him—where this reaching of a conclusion is a quite separate psychological episode, and indeed one which is subsequent to the sensory awareness itself. Rather, it is a way in which the sensory awareness forms part of a conceptually enriched awareness, in which the sense-datum is subjectively experienced in the perspective of its interpretation. The situation is not one in which the subject first recognizes the sense-datum in its raw presented form, and then, from things independently known or believed, mistakenly infers that it is a portion or aspect of the external environment. It is one in which the subject only experiences the sense-datum in a form where it poses as an external item in a certain spatial relation to him. The interpretation and the presentation psychologically blend to form a single integrated awareness, and it is this integrated awareness that constitutes the phenomenal experience. One thing which makes this point crucial, of course, is that, as we have already stressed, a subject's judgement about the external situation is not always in line with how things experientially seem, since he may realize or suspect that his experience is non-veridical. It is precisely because the phenomenal interpretation is integral to the way in which the sense-datum is experienced, rather than an extraneous judgement about it, that the subject is able, even at the time of its occurrence, to think it mistaken.

There is a further question which now arises. In contrast with the sensory core, the interpretative component of phenomenal experience is *conceptual*: it is, as we have indicated, a way of enriching the presentation of the sense-datum with a certain conceptual perspective. But what sort of concepts feature in this perspective? When, for example, a colour-spot in the two-dimensional sensory field is experientially interpreted as (seen as) something located at a certain distance, how is this distance conceptually represented in the content of the interpretation? Obviously the concepts involved are not expressible by the descriptive predicates of ordinary language. When the colour-spot is seen as located at a certain distance, this distance is not identified as *so many yards*, or as *roughly the length of a football pitch*, or as *what would take five minutes to walk*, or anything of that sort. But nor can we here, as we did in the case of the information supplied by phenomenal experience, adopt an imagistic account. For, as we have seen, imagistic conception is just a special way of conceptually focusing on the character of phenomenal experience, and so the interpretative element of such experience has to be in place before there is something for imagistic conception to be about. There is not, I think, a great deal which the sense-datum theorist can say by way of positive specification of the nature of the conceptual content involved in the interpretations in question. We know that this content has to be such as to allow the presentational and interpretative components of phenomenal experience to form an integrated awareness—an awareness in which the sensory object is experienced in its conceptually re-characterized form. But, beyond this, all I think that the theorist can do is to invite us to focus on the nature of the content *introspectively*. Thus, in the case of seeing a colour-spot as at a certain distance, all he can say is that, if we want to discern the distinctive intentional manner in which the distance is conceptually represented, we need to focus on that mode of representation in our own experience. I am not suggesting that this limitation should be viewed as problematic.

The notion of an interpretation blending with a presentation to form an integrated, conceptually enriched, episode of awareness may seem rather mysterious. But it is important to realize that, irrespective of our view of SDT, we have to acknowledge the presence of interpretative elements of this general sort in the content of perceptual experience—to acknowledge cases where the interpretation is an integral part of the whole experience, rather than an extraneous judgement about it, or about the object perceived. Some of these cases are very close to what we have envisaged under SDT, in that they are concerned with interpretative contributions to *sensible appearance*. For example, there is a whole range of cases concerned with ways in which drawings give rise to a vivid impression of seeing a three-dimensional scene. The two-dimensional drawing is *seen as* a three-dimensional arrangement, in the perspective of a viewpoint; and this seeing-as is not a *judgement about* the drawing, but integral to the way in which the drawing is visually experienced—a point which is underlined by the fact that the subject's belief that he is looking at a drawing (and so at something two-dimensional) is not affected. The experiential nature of the interpretation in such cases becomes particularly conspicuous, subjectively, when—as for example with the Necker Cube—the two-dimensional figure is amenable to *alternative* three-dimensional interpretations.[17] The subject who is looking at the figure may suddenly experience an interpretational shift, of which he is the passive recipient, in which the figure changes from one three-dimensional appearance to the other. The vividness of the change is so striking that the subject may find it difficult not to believe that there has been an objective change in the drawing itself. All these cases are, as I said, especially close to what we have envisaged under SDT, since the interpretations involved are at the level of sensible appearance. But, in addition to these, there are other types of case, where the subject-matter of the interpretation reaches higher levels of characterization. The most obvious example is that of perceiving a physical item as an object of a specific familiar sort—for instance, *as a house*, or *as a tree*, or *as a dog*. This, in fact, happens nearly all the time in *visual* perception, though usually without announcing itself. Once again, the situation in which it becomes subjectively more conspicuous is where there is a sudden and large-scale shift in interpretation during the observation of a single item—

---

[17] For a psychological discussion of these cases, see G. Fisher, *The Frameworks for Perceptual Localization* (Department of Psychology, University of Newcastle-upon-Tyne, 1968).

for example, when one has not been able to make out what something in the distance is and suddenly recognizes it as (say) the roof of a house. And once again, the presence of the interpretation is not a guarantee of the presence of the corresponding belief; for example, one can see a face in the moon without thinking that it is real.[18]

These various cases of experiential interpretation within the context of ordinary physical-item perception are not just *similar* to what SDT postulates. They are cases which the theory will absorb into its own fully developed account, though with a shift—a pushing back—of the pre-interpretative starting-point. Thus, in all the cases where we would ordinarily speak of the subject perceiving a certain *physical item* in a certain way, the sense-datum theorist will speak of the subject as perceiving the relevant *sense-datum* in this interpretative way. Sometimes this will be simply a matter of replacing the physical item in question by the sense-datum (this will tend to be so in cases where the interpretation does not go beyond the level of sensible appearance). Sometimes it will be a matter of both replacing the physical item by a sense-datum, and adding in a further layer of interpretation to reach the starting-point of the interpretation on the ordinary model (this will be so in cases where the interpretation goes beyond, but presupposes, the registering of sensible appearance). But the details of all this are not, at present, important to us. The crucial point is that, whatever mystery may attach to the relevant notion of experiential interpretation, the sense-datum theorist's use of it is on a par with, and an extension of, the use which we are in any case obliged to make of it in dealing with the ordinary (philosophically neutral) facts of perceptual experience.

As I have already made clear, the fact that the character of a sense-datum is fully displayed, and so, in a sense, fully available for cognitive scrutiny, does not mean that the subject can automatically gain a knowledge of any aspect of it by simply targeting his introspective attention in the right way. Nor does it mean that, if the subject does try to gauge its character introspectively, he is protected from making mistakes. We can now see that, with the presence of the externalist interpretation, there is a further factor which will tend to make an accurate registering of the sensory situation more difficult to achieve. For, as well as misrepresenting the fundamental nature of the sense-datum (by representing it as something external), this interpretation is liable to obscure certain aspects of its sensible character. To be precise, it is liable to obscure those aspects which take on a different sig-

---

[18] Wittgenstein offers some interesting observations about the phenomenon of perceiving-as in *Philosophical Investigations*, trans. G. E. M. Anscombe (Oxford: Blackwell, 1958), II. xi.

nificance in the context of their construal as elements of the external environment. To take the most obvious case—that of visual experience—the presence of the three-dimensional externalist interpretation is bound to make it more difficult for the subject to monitor the spatial patterning of a visual sense-datum in its raw, two-dimensional form. For instance, it will be harder for a subject to gauge the true size-relationships in the sensory field when the items compared are seen as at significantly different distances. This does not mean that, in cases of this sort, a recognition of the genuine features of the sense-datum becomes *impossible*. But such recognition can only be achieved if the subject introspectively focuses on his experience in a special way, such that, under the guidance of the sense-datum account itself, he consciously addresses himself to the question of what is sensory core and what interpretation, and of how things would experientially stand if the externalist interpretation were subtracted.

IV

To complete my exposition of SDT—in the form in which I am here envisaging it—I want to consider an issue which I glossed over in my account above. The issue is not a crucial one: it does not affect the basic character of the theory or the factors which bear on its evaluation. But since I have, in effect, already committed myself to resolving it in a certain way, and since my views here are out of line with those of most modern exponents of the theory, I think I need to say something about this.

In setting out, above, how SDT applies to the visual realm, I took the sense-data themselves to be purely two-dimensional—spatial arrangements of colour in a 'flat', two-dimensional field—and attributed the appearance of spatial depth to the externalist interpretations imposed on them. And, in doing this, I was following the traditional empiricist view, vigorously defended by Berkeley, and subsequently endorsed by Hume.[19] However, in recent years, the predominant tendency among sense-datum theorists has been towards accepting depth as a *sensory* (pre-interpretative) feature. The grounds they invoke for this are phenomenological: the visual awareness of depth seems, subjectively, to have the same presentational

---

[19] Berkeley's main defence comes in his *Essay towards a New Theory of Vision*, in his *Philosophical Works*, ed. M. Ayers (London: Dent, 1975). As he famously summarizes his position in sect. II: 'It is, I think, agreed by all, that *distance* of itself, and immediately, cannot be seen. For *distance* being a line directed end-wise to the eye, it projects only one point in the fund of the eye. Which point remains invariably the same, whether the distance be longer or shorter.' For Hume's endorsement of this view, see his *Treatise*, p. 56 and p. 191.

immediacy as the awareness of qualities, like colour and shape, which are agreed to be sensory. As H. H. Price expressed the point, 'It is a plain phe-nomenological fact that visual fields have the property of depth';[20] and it is clear that he was here taking the visual field to be part of the sensory given. If this is right, then positions in the sensory field will be defined, not by pairs of 'vertical' and 'horizontal' coordinates, but by combinations of distances and directions—directions being what positions in the flat field turn into when depth is added.

Now the reason why I have opted for the traditional version of the theory, in my own exposition, is that the modern approach seems to me to be untenable. One factor here is that I do not see how to reconcile this approach with the logical constraints on the kinds of visual experience that are possible. If depth were an aspect of the geometry of the sensory field, then it should surely be logically possible for someone to have a visual experience in which he was aware of two fully opaque colour-patches, cov-ering exactly the same portion of field-directions, but at different depths (distances). It should be logically possible for him to be visually aware of the one patch as positioned *in front of* the other, but without its seeming to him that (with the nearer one to some degree transparent) the further one was visible *through it.* But it is surely clear that—for visual experience as we understand it—this is *not* a logical possibility. It is not just that, for reasons which stem from the physics and physiology of vision, we do not *in prac-tice* have such experiences. It is that we cannot *make sense* of the suggestion that we could seem to see one fully opaque patch in front of another. And this can only be explained by supposing that our very conception of visual experience requires us to think of the sensory field as two-dimensional, and as thereby not leaving room for positions which have the same verti-cal and horizontal coordinates, but differ in depth.

But there is also a more fundamental reason why I reject the modern view. For it seems to me that the very notion of sensory depth is incoher-ent. It is not that the notion of a three-dimensional sensory field is in itself incoherent: we can certainly conceive of there being a sense-realm with a spatial field (though not a *visual* field as we understand this), where the internal sensory relations between the field-positions require a three-dimensional characterization. But the problem with sensory depth is that it is not, in the first instance, a spatial relationship *within* the sensory field, but a spatial relationship of something in the field *to the subject;* for it is dis-

---

[20] *Perception,* reprint of 2nd edn. (London: Methuen, 1954), Preface, vii–viii.

tance, in perspective, *from him*. And while a sense-datum, or a portion of a sense-datum, may sensibly look to the subject as if it stands in a certain spatial relation to him (and in particular, look as if it stands at a certain distance from him), it cannot *genuinely* stand in such a relation if it is internal to his awareness. So, given the internality of sense-data, the depth-relationship needs to be assigned to the content of the interpretation, rather than to the sense-datum itself. I suppose it might be replied that we should think of sensory depth, not as distance, in perspective, *from a subject*, but as distance, in perspective, *from a point*, and that such depth only gives the impression of being a relationship with the subject because, when it is presentationally displayed, it seems to the subject that he is located at the point in question. But this is clearly not right. For there is no way of making sense of the notion of distance *in perspective* from a point, except in terms of how the situation would sensibly appear to someone who *viewed things* (veridically) from that point. Perspective is not an abstract aspect of geometry: it is a matter of the experiential manner in which the abstract aspects would be veridically registered by a visual subject at a certain viewpoint. So the attempt to divorce the reference point for the perspective from the viewpoint of the subject is wholly misconceived. In short, the only way in which we can think of a visual sense-datum as genuinely structured in depth is by supposing that it exists in an external space, and that its various parts stand, within that space, in certain distance relations to the subject; and this is precisely what is ruled out by the fact that the sense-datum is internal to the subject's awareness. (For a *dualist*, of course, such a supposition would also raise problems over the spatial location of the *subject*. But this is not a matter which we need to pursue here.)

This still leaves the question of the phenomenological evidence. The reason why so many sense-datum theorists take depth to be a genuine feature of sense-data is that the experience of depth carries the subjective impression of being directly presentational, rather than interpretative, just like the experience of colour and shape. Well, I certainly do not want to deny this phenomenological point: depth is an aspect of sensible appearance (an element in the content of phenomenal experience), and, as I have constantly stressed, it is a distinctive feature of such appearance (such experience) to have a presentational feel. But what I would claim is that the presence of this feel is perfectly explicable in terms of the account I have envisaged. For it can be understood as the inevitable outcome of combining the actual presentation of the sense-data and the experiential nature of their three-dimensional interpretation. A two-dimensional sense-datum is what is presented. But it is only experienced in the perspective of its externalist interpretation, and, experienced in this perspective, it takes on the false appearance of being structured in depth.

Before I leave the topic of the structure of the visual field, there is one further issue which I want to deal with, though very briefly. A phenomenologically conspicuous feature of the visual field is that the quality of the spatial patterning that occurs in it is not uniform over its different regions. Thus there is a small central area where the pattern presents itself as maximally sharp and detailed, and then a steady increase in what seems like fuzziness and coarseness as we move outwards towards the periphery. The question which now arises is: how is this variation in the quality of the pattern to be explained in the framework of SDT? One thing which the sense-datum theorist cannot say, of course, is that the sensory patterns in the more peripheral regions are intrinsically *less determinate*. Since the theorist regards these patterns as ingredients of reality—not just as before the mind conceptually—they have to be fully determinate in nature.

Now I do not have space here to discuss this issue in detail. But, having considered the various options, it seems to me that the theorist's right response would be to attribute the variation in the quality of the spatial patterning over the visual field to a variation in the fineness of the field's positional grain. The theorist will presumably already accept that our sensory qualitative repertoires are finitely composed in all areas of experience—that, for a given subject at a given time, there are only finitely many sensory colours that can feature in his visual experience, only finitely many sensory pitches that can feature in his auditory experience, only finitely many sensory flavours that can feature in his olfactory experience, and so on. And so he will presumably already accept that, for a given subject at a given time, there are only finitely many sensory positions in his visual field. All that the theorist now needs to do, it seems to me, to explain the variation in the quality of the patterning, is to suppose that this finite array of positions varies in density (in the ratio of the number of positions to area covered) across the field, and more specifically, that this density decreases as we move from the centre to the periphery. Such a variation in density would, I think, exactly account for what is introspectively apparent; and, of course, it would do so without representing the peripheral patterns as less determinate in their own terms.

V

Given the form in which I have envisaged the sense-datum theory, how should we evaluate it? Have we, at last, found the right account of the nature of phenomenal experience, and thus made good the first stage in the provision of an account of the nature of perception? Well, there is no denying that, in relation to the points that have come to light in our previous discussion, the theory has a number of attractive features, and we should start by setting these out.

To begin with, we were looking for a theory which would accommodate the RC-claim—the claim that the ES-qualities achieve realization by occurring in the appropriate way in the content of sensory experience. Clearly, SDT succeeds on this count. For if SDT is true, then one way in which ES-qualities are assured of achieving realization is by characterizing sense-data, and sense-data are internal to the subject's sensory awareness. In addition to accommodating the RC-claim, the theory also, of course, allows for the accommodation of the whole thesis (ERT) of which this claim is one component. It permits the theorist to say that the ES-qualities are not only *assured* of achieving realization by characterizing sense-data, but can *only* achieve realization in this way. And if the theorist accepts this further claim (the RE-claim), as I think he should, it allows him, along the lines already indicated, to explain the two points which called for explanation, and which formed the basis of my argument for ERT. Thus, on the one hand, he can straightforwardly explain why a transparent conception of an ES-quality has to be imagistic—a conception in terms of what it is like to encounter the quality in the content of sensory experience. This will simply be a consequence of the fact that ES-qualities can only be realized as attributes of sense-data, and that any conception which reveals what qualities they are has to represent them in that sensory perspective. On the other hand, he can equally explain why, in our ordinary attribution of ES-qualities to external objects, we think of their external realization as consisting in, or essentially linked with, a mode of sensible appearance. For if the qualities can only be realized as attributes of sense-data, then their realization is essentially tied to their being presentationally displayed, and it is just this tie that is being recognized, albeit in a distorted form, by our ordinary thought. In these ways, SDT supplies the specific content to the general lines of explanation that flow from ERT.

Another good feature of SDT is that it accounts, in a straightforward way, for the *presentational feel* of phenomenal experience. It does this, in effect, in two stages—each dealing with a different aspect of what has to be explained. Thus, in the first place, it explains why, when we have a phenomenal experience, there is the subjective impression of there being a sensible object directly presented. The explanation here is simply that the impression is *correct*: there *is* such an object presented, namely the sense-datum. Then, in addition, it explains why we have the impression that what is presented is *external*—that it is a portion or aspect of the physical environment itself, presented to us in the perspective of our viewpoint. It accounts for this impression by appealing to the element of interpretation directed on to the sense-datum. This interpretation, after all, is precisely an externalistic one, representing the sense-datum as something located in an external three-dimensional space; and by forming an integral part of the whole perceptual experience, it is precisely equipped to give rise to the impression of being itself presentational. Thus, as we have stressed, this type of interpretation is not something psychologically separate from the sensory awareness; rather, it is something which blends with this awareness to form a single, conceptually enriched awareness—an awareness which brings the sense-datum before the mind in the perspective of its interpretation. The result is that, although the sense-datum is, in reality, internal to the subject's awareness, it manages, in the context of the whole experience, to subjectively pose as something located in the external environment, and as directly presented to the subject from that location. (We have already noted how this result enables us to deny that depth is a genuine feature of visual sense-data, while accommodating the phenomenological factors which have misled certain philosophers into thinking that it is.)

This would still leave the question of *why* our experiences interpret the presented items in this externalist way. How do we come to acquire a system of perceptual experience which so misrepresents its own nature? But here too the sense-datum theorist has, in broad outline, a straightforward answer. The sense-data are internal. But they occur in sequences and patterns which suggest that they are elements of an external three-dimensional arrangement. They collectively exhibit themes and regularities which make them conspicuously amenable to the externalist interpretation which our experiences put on them. So the theorist can plausibly think of the prevalence of this form of interpretation, in the experiential life of the normal and mature subject, as a natural response to the character of the sensory facts. The interpretations are incorrect; indeed, they radically misrepresent the true situation. But they accurately reflect and implicitly register the principles on which the course of sensory experience is organized. There is an echo here of Hume's account in the *Treatise*, when he describes the way in which the imagination responds to the sensory factors of 'constancy' and 'coherence'.[21] The crucial difference is that Hume himself was

---

[21] *Treatise*, Bk. 1, Pt. 4, sect. 2.

concerned to explain the origin of our *belief* in an external world, rather than of the interpretative content of our experiences. Indeed, he gave no indication of having recognized the presence of such content.

A further way in which the theory commends itself is that, by explaining the presentational feel of phenomenal experience, it explains why such experience conveys putative information about the current state of the environment. For obviously, if this experience is such as to give the subject the impression that he is presentationally perceiving a current environmental situation, then *eo ipso* it gives him the impression of *there being* such a situation, and in that way purports to inform him—invites him to believe—that such a situation obtains. Moreover, in explaining the presence of the putative information, the theory meets our requirements in two other respects. First, it explains the putative information in a way which does not require the subject who receives it to make a doxastic response—whether the response of full-blooded belief or just of an inclination to believe. It has no problem in recognizing cases in which someone has a phenomenal experience, but rejects the invitation which it issues. And secondly, it explains why the putative information has to be, in the first instance, imagistic. For the imagistic character of the information, or, more precisely, of the way it conceptually identifies the relevant situation-type, will just be a direct reflection, and an immediate consequence, of the distinctive way in which that type is represented by the experience itself. In effect, the information has to be imagistic because it is in that form that it registers what the sense-datum itself displays, or seems to display, in the perspective of its externalist interpretation.

In all these ways, then, SDT presents itself as an attractive option, and one which avoids the range of problems that beset the pure conceptualist approach, or the specific versions of it that we considered. Moreover, in the form in which we have developed and explained it, the theory immediately avoids many of the objections that are commonly brought against it. We have already disposed of certain objections which arise from a misunderstanding of the sense in which the character of a sense-datum has to be available for cognitive scrutiny. Thus, as we noted, there is no problem, as there is often held to be, in accepting that the subject may not be equipped to gauge the exact complexity and fine differences characterizing what is on display. And by recognizing the element of externalist interpretation, as an integral part of the total perceptual experience, we have implicitly disposed of some other familiar objections. In particular, with the externalist interpretation in place, the sense-datum theorist is not, as he is standardly thought to be, committed to the implausible view that our acquisition of perceptual information about the physical environment is implicitly *inferential*, based on a prior knowledge of facts about sense-data.[22] The theorist can insist that the basic information, or putative information, available to the subject is afforded by the sense-datum as *experientially interpreted*, and is, in consequence, *directly* about how things are externally.

However, even in the form in which we have envisaged it, the theory still encounters a major problem. The theory takes the core of phenomenal experience to consist in the presentation of a sense-datum, and it takes the sense-datum to be internal to the awareness directed on to it. The problem is in seeing how we can make sense of there being things which are internal to awareness in the relevant way. It is to this fundamental issue that we must now turn.

VI

In speaking of sense-data as internal objects of awareness, we mean, as I indicated, that each sense-datum has, and can have, no existence outside the context of the episode of awareness directed on to it—that it exists, and necessarily exists, purely as an object of that awareness. In other words, we mean that, for each sense-datum x, there is an episode of presentational awareness y, such that x is the object of y, and the fact of x's being the object of y fully covers, and necessarily covers, all that is involved in the occurrence of x as a concrete ingredient of reality. Amongst other things, this will mean that a sense-datum cannot occur as the object of more than one episode of presentational awareness (it cannot be presented to different subjects or on different occasions), and that it cannot occur as an ingredient of the physical (mind-independent) world.

Now the claim of internality, thus explained, is clear enough; and it is also clear why the theorist wants to make it. But it immediately raises a crucial question. The internality of sense-data to the episodes of awareness directed on to them cannot be just a brute fact. There clearly has to be something further, about the ontological nature of sense-data, which *accounts for* this internality—something which explains why each sense-datum is confined, in existence, in the way envisaged. So the crucial question is: what is this further explanatory fact? How are we to conceive of the

---

[22] Among the many philosophers who have criticized the theory on these grounds are Anthony Quinton ('The problem of perception', *Mind*, 64 (1955), 28–51), J. L. Austin (*Sense and Sensibilia* (Oxford: Oxford University Press, 1962)), and David Armstrong (*A Materialist Theory of the Mind*, ch. 10).

ontological nature of sense-data, in relation to the awareness-relationships in which they feature, which will make the reasons for their internality clear?

Before we consider this question, there is a preliminary point that needs to be stressed. There is already a familiar range of cases where, at the level of our ordinary thinking, we seem to recognize the existence of things that are internal objects of mental activity—the activities in question involving some form of conceiving. Suppose, for example, that someone asks you to imagine a dog, but not one which you already know of. He might go on to ask you questions about what you have imagined: 'How big is the dog?'; 'What is its colour?'; 'What is its breed?'; and so on. And you might reply in kind: 'Large'; 'Brown'; 'Alsatian'. These questions and answers ostensibly imply that there is an actual dog which is the object of your imagining—a dog which, despite its imaginary status, can be referred to and described. And if there is such an entity, it will clearly have to be an internal object of your imagination in the relevant sense—something with no capacity for existence outside this imaginative context. Obviously, there is a whole range of cases of this general kind, where we seem to recognize the existence of things that are internal to someone's conceiving. Philosophers speak of these putative internal objects as 'intentional' objects.

Now what needs to be stressed is that, to have any chance of providing a satisfactory account of the kind of internality that features in his own theory, the sense-datum theorist must distance himself from these familiar cases. And this is because it only takes a moment's reflection to see that these supposed internal objects of conceiving are not genuine entities at all, and that our apparent references to such things in the context of ordinary discourse are not to be taken at face value. Thus it is just obvious that there cannot be anything which is both a genuine dog and which only exists as a figment of someone's imagination. And when we say things that seem to imply the recognition of such an entity, this is just a *façon de parler*—a device for talking about the *content* of someone's imagining in a simple and vivid way. When someone imagines a dog—a purely *imaginary* dog—all that is going on, and all that we seriously take to be going on, is that he imaginatively focuses on a *type* of dog (or a type of dog-including situation), and entertains some such thought as 'Suppose there is something like this'.

The sense-datum theorist needs to be able to explain the internality of sense-data. But he needs to be able to do this in a way which—in contrast with the type of case we have just been considering—leaves the relevant objects as genuine entities and the mental activity directed on to them as a genuine relation. For it is the central claim of his theory that the core of phenomenal experience consists in an episode of sensory awareness, and this awareness is to be ultimately understood as the presenting of a sense-datum to a subject. He obviously cannot afford an account which represents the sense-datum terminology as just a convenient device for talking about the content of sensory awareness, so that the ontology of sense-data disappears once the true character of the situation is made clear. It is here, I think, that we begin to see a potential source of tension in the theorist's position. For is it really possible to think of a sense-datum as ontologically confined to a particular episode of presentational awareness, and yet accord it the ontological status required? Is there not a suspicion that, by having its existence so tightly tied to this one episode, the sense-datum will simply vanish into it—that there will be nothing left over from the presentational act to form the presented object?

The suggestion of a possible problem for the theorist is already clear. But to allow us to deal with the issue systematically, we need to identify the various ways in which one could try to explain the internality of sense-data, and consider how things stand in each case. Any such attempt will take the form of a certain account of the ontological nature of sense-data, and an indication of how their internality would follow, as a logical consequence, from that account. As far as I can see, there are just three possibilities.

The first possibility would be to say that sense-data derive their very existence from the presentational relationships in which they feature. Put more precisely, it would be to say that, for any sense-datum x, subject S, and time t, if x is presented to S at t, then the fact of x's existence is *constituted by* the fact of its being presented to S at t, so that the first fact *obtains in virtue of*, and its obtaining is *nothing over and above*, the obtaining of the second. It is obvious how, if this were so, sense-data would be rendered internal objects of awareness in the relevant sense—how each sense-datum would neither have, nor be capable of having, any existence outside the context of the episode of awareness directed on to it. For clearly the sense-datum would not have the opportunity for any ontological life outside that context if its existence were entirely constituted by its occurrence in that context.

This proposal would explain the factor of internality. But it is obvious from the start that it would not do so in a satisfactory way. For the explanation envisaged is manifestly incoherent. It is not that the notion of an ontologically derivative entity is in itself incoherent: it is not difficult to think of cases in which we can plausibly represent something as deriving its existence from facts of a more fundamental kind. For example, the existence of a molecule is presumably constituted by the existence of the atoms which compose it, the relations in which they stand to one another, and the relevant laws of nature. But what we cannot coherently suppose is that something derives its existence from (that its existence is constituted by) a fact or set of facts *about itself*. For in supposing its existence to be *derivative from* these facts, we would be supposing that it was not available for the facts *to be about*. It is just this incoherence that is involved in the case envisaged, where a sense-datum is held to derive its existence from the fact of its own presentation. The claim that the sense-datum is ontologically available to feature in the presentational fact is in direct conflict with the claim that it derives its existence from this fact.

The second possibility would be to say that, for a sense-datum, existence *consists in*, or *takes the form of*, presentation to a subject. In other words, the fact of existence is not *constituted* by the fact of presentation—something which requires the two facts to be distinct. Rather, the existence of a sense-datum and its being presented to a certain subject on a certain occasion are *one and the same*: *esse est praesentari*. The situation, thus envisaged, would be like that, as we ordinarily conceive of it, of physical objects in respect of physical space. Just as, for a physical object, location in physical space—or strictly, in space and time—is the very form of its existence (its mode of being), so, on the account suggested, presentation to a subject is the form of existence (the mode of being) for a sense-datum. The sense-datum exists presentationally, without deriving its existence from its being presented, in the same way that a table or tree exists spatially, without deriving its existence from its being spatially located. Here, again, it is clear how what is envisaged would immediately explain the factor of internality. For if the existence of a sense-datum just consists in the fact that it is presented to a particular subject on a particular occasion, it obviously does not have the opportunity for concrete occurrence outside that context.

This new account explains the internality of sense-data. And it at least avoids the blatant incoherence of claiming that sense-data derive their existence from facts about themselves. But, even so, an apparent incoherence remains. For it is still hard to see how there *could* be something whose existence consisted in (took the form of) its being an object of presentation in that way. On the face of it, given any entity x, subject S, and time t, unless x has a form of existence which is distinct from its being presented to S at t, it will not have the right kind of ontological independence to be able to stand in that relationship—to be something there to be presented. The analogy with the physical realm is of no help here. In the case of a physical object, our very conception of its qualitative nature immediately indicates the spatial form of its existence: its location in space is not so much its standing in a relationship to something else, as its possessing its inherently spatial nature in a locationally specific form. There is nothing like this in the case of the sense-datum. Our ordinary conception of presentation is of a relation between two ontologically separate things, and focusing on the qualitative nature of sense-data does not, in any obvious way, show us how to make sense of anything else. On the face of it, we cannot think of the existence of a sense-datum as wholly consisting in the fact that it forms the object of a certain episode of presentational awareness, without undermining the assumption that it is ontologically available to form such an object—that there is something there on which the awareness can get purchase. If we have to construe the ontological nature of sense-data in the envisaged way, then it really does seem that there will be nothing left over from the presentational acts to form the presented objects—that the putative objects will simply disappear into the episodes of awareness that are supposedly directed on to them.

It is manifestly incoherent to claim that sense-data derive their existence from their being presented, and it is prima facie incoherent to claim that the existence of a sense-datum consists in its being presented. But what could still be insisted is that sense-data derive their existence from facts in which they do not themselves feature. It is this possibility which is exploited by the third and final way in which someone might try to account for the factor of internality. Thus it might be claimed that, for any sense-datum x, subject S, and time t, if x is presented to S at t, there is a psychological state Σ, which does not itself—as intrinsically specified—involve the occurrence of a sense-datum, such that the existence of x and its being presented to S at t are constituted by S's being in Σ at t. If this were so, it would obviously make sense-data internal objects of awareness in the relevant sense. For each sense-datum would be ontologically confined to the context of the more fundamental psychological fact by which its existence was constituted, and thereby confined to the context of the presentational relationship which was constituted with it. In other words, the existence of the sense-datum and the fact of its presentation to a particular subject on a particular occasion would be inseparably linked by their common constitutive origin.

As it stands, of course, this is not so much a definite account of how the internality of sense-data is to be explained, as an indication of certain lines on which such an explanation might be sought. For until we are told the nature of the psychological states which are involved, and offered some rationale for thinking that the realization of these states is able to do the constitutive work assigned to it, we do not have a definite theory to consider. Nor, indeed, do the prospects for finding such a theory seem at all promising. Not only have we been offered no example of a category of psychological states that might be plausibly cast in the relevant role, but we do not, at present, have any reason to think that such an example is available. We simply have no conception of how psychological states which are not themselves presentative of sense-data could, when realized, suffice for the occurrence of such presentation.

However, this is not a point which I need to press. For, whatever the prospects of developing it in a plausible way, there is a quite different reason why the approach envisaged would not be of any interest in the present context. The reason is simple. What is presently at issue is not whether, *in the abstract*, there is a satisfactory way of explaining the internality of sense-data, but whether such an explanation is available *in the framework of SDT*. For it is the status of *SDT* that we are trying to determine. But, whatever opportunities there may be for recognizing a category of sense-data that are ontologically derivative in the envisaged way, it is obvious that nothing along these lines would be compatible with SDT. For SDT is offering itself as the correct *philosophical* account of phenomenal experience— the account of how the psychological nature of such experience is to be *ultimately understood*. And so it is essential to its content that, as well as introducing an ontology of sense-data, it takes their existence and presentational role to be a *fundamental aspect* of the psychological situation. To concede that the psychological states fundamentally involved in phenomenal experience are of a different kind—a kind not involving the occurrence of sense-data—is to concede that the correct philosophical theory is to be found in a different direction.

We have considered three ways in which there could be an attempt to explain the internality of sense-data, each involving a certain account of their ontological nature. In the first account, the existence of a sense-datum was taken to be *constituted by* the fact of its presentation to a particular subject on a particular occasion. In the second, the existence of a sense-datum was taken to *consist in* the fact of its presentation to a particular subject on a particular occasion. In the third, the existence of a sense-datum, and the fact of its presentation to a particular subject on a particular occasion, were taken to be constituted by that subject's being in a *further psychological state* on that occasion—a state not itself involving the occurrence of a sense-datum. As far as I can see, these three accounts are the only ones available. And, in the light of our analysis, it seems to me that none of them is satisfactory. The first is blatantly incoherent, and the third is simply irrelevant to the issue at hand. Only the second account merits any serious consideration. But here too there is a prima facie incoherence, and I cannot myself see how the charge of incoherence can be met. I cannot see how the sensory object can be genuinely there, as something available for presentation to a particular subject on a particular occasion, unless it has a form of existence which transcends its standing in that presentational relationship. I cannot see how the episode of awareness can have something to make contact with (something to be directed on to) if the object's availability for this contact precisely consists in the fact that the contact is made. If I am right, then there is simply no way in which (relevantly to the issue that concerns us) the internality of sense-data can be coherently understood; and, despite its many virtues, the sense-datum theory, in the form in which we have conceived it, has to be rejected.

6 THE ADVERBIALIST ALTERNATIVE

I

STD, as I have developed it, takes phenomenal experience to be the combination of two separate components. One component is a sensory core, which is non-conceptual. It takes the form of the presentation of an object—a sense-datum—which is internal to the presentational awareness and exclusively characterized by sensible qualities associated with the sense-realm in question. The other component takes the form of an element of interpretation, which is directed on to the sense-datum, and which represents it as something external—as something located in an external three-dimensional space, and as spatially related to the subject in a certain way. In construing phenomenal experience in this bipartite fashion, SDT stands in sharp contrast to what we have labelled the pure conceptualist approach, which takes phenomenal experience to be conceptual through and through—to be something whose whole character is covered by the nature of its conceptual content and its psychological character qua possessor of this content.

However, SDT is not the only theory which contrasts with the pure conceptualist approach in this way. For there is an alternative position, which preserves the bipartite structure of SDT, but offers a radically different account of the nature of the sensory core. Thus, like SDT, it takes phenomenal experience to be composed of two components, a sensory (non-conceptual) component and an element of interpretation directed on to it.

But, unlike SDT, it takes the sensory core to be, not an awareness *of an object*, but an awareness, or sensing, *in a certain manner*, so that the sensible qualities which were thought of under SDT as features of the sense-datum now come to be thought of as modes of sensing, and as needing to be expressed by adverbs rather than adjectives—sensing *F-ly*, rather than sensing an *F-item*. Because of this, the position is known as the *adverbial theory*; and, among those philosophers who accept that phenomenal experience has a non-conceptual sensory core, it is this theory which has become, in recent years, the most popular approach.[23] As in the case of SDT, the details of the theory can vary from one exponent to another. I shall here characterize it in a way which best suits the purposes of our discussion—in particular, in a way which takes account of the points already established, and which offers the best prospect of a successful outcome.

The adverbial theory (AT), as I here envisage it, preserves the bipartite structure of SDT, in the form in which I have developed it. It takes phenomenal experience to be composed of a sensory core and an element of interpretation directed on to it. This interpretative element is needed in order to allow the whole experience to represent a certain type of environmental situation; and, as in the case of SDT, we should think of the interpretation not as a judgement about the sensory core, but as something which blends with this core to form a single, conceptually enriched, episode of awareness. Clearly, though, because the account of the sensory core is quite different, the content of the interpretation will have to differ in a corresponding way. In the case of SDT, the interpretation is directed on to the sense-datum, and represents it as something external. In the case of AT, it is directed on to the sensing, and represents it as something externalistically perceptive. We can best bring out the relationship between the two approaches by focusing on the case of the visual realm. According to SDT, the sensory core, in this visual case, takes the form of the presentation of a two-dimensional colour-array, internal to the presentational awareness; and the interpretation represents this array as something external and three-dimensional, presented to the subject in the perspective of his

---

[23] Its advocates include C. J. Ducasse (see his 'Moore's refutation of idealism', in P. A. Schilpp (ed.), *The Philosophy of G. E. Moore* (Chicago: Northwestern University Press, 1942)); Roderick Chisholm (see his *Perceiving* (Ithaca, N.Y.: Cornell University Press, 1957), 115–25, and *Person and Object* (La Salle, Ill.: Open Court, 1976), 46–52); Wilfrid Sellars (see his *Science, Perception, and Reality* (London: Routledge & Kegan Paul, 1963), 92–5, and *Science and Metaphysics* (London: Routledge & Kegan Paul, 1968), 9–28); Bruce Aune (see his *Knowledge, Mind, and Nature* (New York: Random House, 1967), 147–8); James Cornman (see his *Materialism and Sensations* (New Haven: Yale University Press, 1971), 178 and 185–90); and Michael Tye (see his 'The adverbial approach to visual experience', *Philosophical Review*, 93 (1984), 195–225).

viewpoint. According to AT, the sensory core takes the form of an episode of sensing in a certain complex manner, where the complexity involved is isomorphic with that of the colour-array postulated by SDT; and, correspondingly, the interpretation represents this sensing as the presentational perceiving, in perspective, of an external three-dimensional colour-array—in a way which matches the externalist interpretation under SDT. In addition to this PE-interpretative component, AT can also, of course, like SDT, recognize further layers of experiential interpretation, which go beyond the level of sensible appearance—for example, the interpretation of what is putatively perceived as a familiar kind of material object. But it is only the nature of sensible appearance—strictly, the nature of phenomenal experience—that presently concerns us.

We have seen how, in the light of the points established by our previous discussion, SDT has a number of attractive features. In particular, it accommodates the RC-claim; it explains the presentational feel of phenomenal experience; and it explains why such experience conveys putative information about the current state of the environment, in imagistic form, and without requiring any kind of positive doxastic response. But we have also noted how SDT encounters a crucial problem. For, if I am right, we cannot make sense of there being internal objects of awareness of the kind it postulates. Now it is in relation to this problem that the adverbialist alternative becomes of interest. On the one hand, by preserving the basic structure of SDT, AT can be represented as having the same virtues. Thus, in the first place, by construing the qualities which feature in the sensory core as modes of sensing, it continues to accommodate the RC-claim, and indeed the whole thesis (ERT) of which this claim is a part: it ensures that, as modes of sensing, all such qualities (including therefore the ES-qualities) are realized, and can only be realized, by featuring in sensory experience. Secondly, by taking phenomenal experience to include the relevant element of interpretation, it explains why such experience has its presentational feel; for the very content of the interpretation is to represent the adverbially qualified sensing as the presentational perceiving of something external. And thirdly, by thus explaining the presentational feel, it explains why the experience conveys the relevant environmental information in the relevant form. In these respects, it seems that AT is able to take over, point by point, the work of SDT. But where it can claim an advantage over SDT is in avoiding the ontological problem. For, by reconstruing the nature of the sensory core—by understanding it in an *adverbial* rather than in a *relational* way—it entirely eliminates the class of sensory objects on which this problem turns.

It is clear, then, that AT is a position which calls for further investigation. We have noted the respects in which it is looking promising. What we must now try to establish is whether it is satisfactory in other ways. Perhaps it will turn out that, by avoiding the problematic ontology of sense-data, the theory becomes vulnerable to objection on other counts.

II

One objection which has been brought against AT is that it does not permit an adequate way of formulating facts of sensible complexity.[24] The area on which the discussion standardly focuses is that of the visual realm. Thus, to take a simple case, suppose a subject S has a visual experience which, in respect of its sensory core, the sense-datum theorist would express as

(1) S senses (is sensorily aware of, is presented with) a red, round sense-datum,

or, put more formally, and taking sensing to be a relation which can only hold between a subject and a sense-datum,

(2) $(\exists x)(x$ is red & x is round & S senses x).

How would this sentence get translated into the adverbial language? Clearly, we cannot translate it as

(3) S senses redly & S senses roundly,

since the latter could be true in virtue of a redly-sensing on one occasion and a roundly-sensing on another. But nor can we translate it, with 't' ranging over times, as

(4) $(\exists t)(S$ senses redly at t & S senses roundly at t);

for this could be true in virtue of the fact that, on a single occasion, S senses redly with respect to a square item in *one* portion of his visual field (as the sense-datum theorist would put it), and senses roundly with respect to a green item in *another*. It seems, then, that to translate the original sentence

---

[24] Thus see Frank Jackson, *Perception* (Cambridge: Cambridge University Press, 1977), ch. 3.

into his own system, the adverbialist will have to introduce a new adverb 'red-roundly', to ensure that the two qualitative factors combine in the requisite way. That is, he will have to offer as the translation of (1):

(5) S senses red-roundly,

where the use of the single (hyphenated) adverb ensures that the separate elements of colour and shape unite to form a single mode of sensing.

But now, it seems, two problems arise. First, there is the prospect of the adverbial language becoming lexically unmanageable. For the adverbialist will need to introduce a new hyphenated adverb to deal with each distinct form of sensible complexity. Thus, as well as 'red-roundly', he will need to introduce such adverbs as '[(red-round)-immediately-to-the-left-of-(green-square)]-ly', '{[(red-round)-enclosed-in-otherwise-(green-square)]-enclosed-in-otherwise-[orange-triangular]}-ly', and a host of others of the same ilk. Indeed, since there is no theoretical limit on the degree of complexity of a visual pattern, there is no theoretical limit on the range of such adverbs that he may need.[25] Secondly, and this is more crucial, by employing these portmanteau adverbs, the adverbialist fails to represent the sensible complexity *as complexity*. For, although these adverbs are *morphologically complex*, they are, as merely constructed by hyphenation, *syntactically simple*. Thus, in saying 'S senses *red-roundly*', the adverbialist is doing no more to represent this mode of sensing as something with both a colour-aspect and a shape-aspect than if he had simply said (making up a completely new word) 'S senses rendly', in which even the semblance of adverbial complexity has disappeared. One consequence of this is that certain forms of inference which the sense-datum theorist can represent as *formally* valid, and which, on the face of it, should be regarded as such, forfeit such validity in the adverbialist's system. Thus while 'S senses something which is both red and round' formally entails both 'S senses something which is red' and 'S senses something which is round', 'S senses red-roundly' does not formally entail 'S senses redly' or 'S senses roundly'. The entailments here are merely *analytical*, depending on the special meaning assigned to the hyphenated adverb.

Even if this analysis of the linguistic situation is accepted, it might be wondered whether it undermines AT itself, as an account of the nature of

---

[25] Thus even granted that both the visual field and the sensory colour-spectrum of any given subject at any time are finitely grained, there is no theoretical limit on the fineness of the grain that could be involved.

sensory experience. For perhaps the adverbialist can afford to concede that the ontology of sense-data is needed for a descriptively adequate language, but still insist that this ontology is not to be treated as *metaphysically basic*—that the adverbial account of sensory experience is the one which specifies the fundamental nature of the psychological situation. After all, this sort of distinction—between what is needed for the practical purposes of formulating the facts and what is needed for the purposes of the final metaphysical perspective—is often pressed in other areas. Thus it is often said that, although mathematics is needed for a description of the physical world (and most especially in physics), its distinctive ontology is not, in the last metaphysical analysis, to be taken seriously: numbers and sets are not to be thought of as real entities, existing in the same sense as the physical objects whose properties and behaviour mathematics is employed to describe.

Such an approach to the metaphysics of ontology is, of course, controversial: if there are those who think that we can metaphysically disown the ontological commitments which are unavoidable at the level of factual description, there are also those who would regard the requirements of such description as metaphysically definitive, as well as still others who would simply reject the notion of there being a *metaphysical* question here altogether. It would be awkward for the adverbialist if he had to rely on a particular resolution of this delicate issue in order to justify his own position. But, as it turns out, he can afford to put this issue on one side. For a little reflection reveals that he is, after all, able to provide, in his own terms, a suitable way of formulating the facts of sensible complexity—a way which does not involve introducing a new portmanteau adverb to signify each complex mode of sensing.

We should begin by noting that, although the adverbialist may be banned from employing an ontology of sensory *objects*, there is nothing to prevent him from recognizing an ontology of *episodes of sensing*—an ontology of sensory *acts*. So, as well as being able to speak of a subject as *sensing redly* or *sensing red-roundly*, he can, if he wishes, make reference to the relevant *acts* of sensing redly and sensing red-roundly. In calling the sensory episodes sensory 'acts', I am here (as indeed at certain points in my earlier discussion) simply following the terminology of the familiar *act–object* distinction. I am not implying that the episodes are things which the subject, in a distinctively active sense, *does*, in contrast with things which just (passively) *happen to him*. Obviously, in terms of the latter distinction, sensory episodes, and indeed the phenomenal experiences of which they are elements, are paradigm cases of mental episodes which just *happen to* the subject—episodes with respect to which he is *passive*. This, indeed, is something which we have already stressed in our discussion of the imagist proposal.[26]

Now, with the ontology of sensory acts in place, the problem of complexity admits of a straightforward solution. For the adverbialist can confine his primitive sensory adverbs to ones which signify *simple* modes of sensing, and handle sensible complexity in terms of relations between sensory acts. Thus let us stipulate that, for any colour C, *sensing C-ly* is to be understood as *sensing **homogeneously** C-ly*. (So, in a case where, in the sense-datum terminology, something is just an act of sensing a homogeneous red patch, this will count as an act of sensing redly, but where something is an act of sensing a patch which is partly red and partly green, it will not.) Likewise, let us stipulate that, for any shape H, *sensing H-ly* is to be understood as *sensing **in overall outline** H-ly*. (So, in a case where, in the sense-datum terminology, something is just an act of sensing a round patch, this will count as an act of sensing roundly, but where something is an act of sensing a round patch within a square patch, it will not.) Then, in place of (5) above ('S senses red-roundly'), the adverbialist can say

(6) (∃x)(x is an act of sensing redly & x is an act of sensing roundly & x belongs to S),

where the elements of colour and shape are integrated by their assignment to the same sensory act. And obviously he can employ the same method for other cases of this kind—sensing green-squarely, sensing red-triangularly, and so on. Moreover, for any predicate which the sense-datum theorist employs to characterize the positions and relations of colour-patches in the visual field, the adverbialist can introduce a corresponding predicate, which is applicable to sensory acts, and has the same descriptive force. So, to represent the case in which, as the sense-datum theorist would put it, the subject senses a red round patch immediately to the left of a green square patch, he can replace the unrevealing

(7) S senses [(red-round)-immediately-to-the-left-of-(green-square)]-ly

by the complexity-revealing

---

[26] See Part Three, Section 3, III. For a fuller discussion of this *active–passive* distinction, see my *The Immaterial Self*, ch. 8, sect. 4, where I use the distinction to try to make sense of the notion of free will.

(8) $(\exists x)(\exists y)(x$ is an act of sensing redly & x is an act of sensing roundly & y is an act of sensing greenly & y is an act of sensing squarely & x belongs to S & y belongs to S & $L(x, y))$,

where the two-place predicate 'L', assigned to the relevant sensory acts, carries the same descriptive implications as the predicate 'immediately to the left of' assigned to the corresponding sensory objects. It is not difficult to see how, by introducing predicates of this sort, and, where necessary, making use of the additional resources of mathematics and set theory, the adverbialist would be in a position to deal with sensory complexity of any kind.

There might seem to be something rather contrived about the procedure envisaged. In effect, the ontology of sensory acts is being employed to achieve a point-by-point transference of the descriptive resources of the sense-datum language to the language of the adverbialist. But, in so far as the challenge to the adverbialist was an essentially *technical* one—a matter of whether he could provide adequate formulations of complexity in his own system—this point is not, in itself, troublesome. It would only become so if it could be shown that the descriptions assigned to the sensory acts do not just mirror the descriptions which the sense-datum theorist assigns to the sensory objects, but have to be construed in terms of them. For that would mean that the supposedly adverbialist formulations of complexity were merely sense-datum formulations in notational disguise. But nothing has yet emerged to show that such a construal is necessary. As things presently stand, the adverbialist can claim to be able to understand the relevant predicates of sensory acts in a distinctively adverbial way. Thus, in the example above, he can claim to be able to understand 'L' as that predicate which applies to an ordered pair $\langle x, y \rangle$ of sensory acts just in case there is a more complex act which includes x and y, and which additionally involves the subject's sensing (immediately-to-the-left-of)-ly with respect to $\langle x, y \rangle$. This is an understanding which appeals to a special mode of field-positional sensing, rather than to a field-positional relation between sensory objects.[27]

[27] In his article 'The adverbial approach to visual experience', Michael Tye has suggested a different way in which the adverbialist could deal with sensible complexity. It involves treating sensory adverbs as operators, which form more complex predicates (or open sentences) from simpler predicates (or open sentences). But although Tye's method is able to handle certain relatively straightforward forms of complexity, it cannot, with a finite stock of operators, handle *all*. In particular, with respect to complex *numerical* facts about the structure of sensory content, it cannot match the descriptive power of a language which applies the resources of mathematics and set theory to an ontology of sensory items (whether objects or acts).

Before we leave the topic of the adverbial language, there is one final point that needs to be stressed. In introducing such terms as 'redly', 'roundly', and '(immediately-to-the-left-of)-ly' to signify the simple modes of sensing, the adverbialist is giving expression to his view that sensory awareness has to be ultimately understood in an adverbial rather than an act-object way. But he is not suggesting—what is clearly not the case—that the concepts these terms express are more basic in our conceptual scheme than the concepts expressed by the ordinary-language predicates ('red', 'round', 'immediately to the left of' . . .) from which they are formed. He would obviously accept, what cannot be sensibly denied, that, in each case, the new concept of *sensing F-ly* is to be explicated, in some way, in terms of the familiar concept of *F*. Presumably, this would be by means of some schema which identifies the relevant mode of sensing in terms of the perceiving of a physical instance, or putative instance, of the corresponding quality or relation—in other words, some such schema as

> Sensing F-ly is sensing in that sensible manner (whatever it is) which is realized whenever a normal subject perceptually encounters a physical instance of F, or what would ordinarily pass as an instance, in such and such conditions.

What is crucial to the adverbialist is not that the terms in his adverbial vocabulary should be conceptually primitive, but that the modes of sensing which they are used to express should be fundamental aspects of the experiential states themselves.

III

By introducing an ontology of sensory acts, the adverbialist can deal with the phenomenon of sensible complexity. Nonetheless, his position seems to me to be vulnerable at two other, and more fundamental, points— points which concern the substance of its philosophical claims, rather than the descriptive adequacy of the associated language. I shall focus on these points in turn.

As we have just noted, the adverbialist is not claiming that the concepts expressed by the terms in his adverbial vocabulary—terms like 'redly' and 'roundly' by which he signifies the simple modes of sensing—are more basic in our conceptual scheme than the concepts expressed by the corresponding ordinary-language predicates. On the contrary, he accepts that the lines of explication run in the other direction—the concept of *sensing*

F-ly being understood in terms of the concept of *F*. But, just for this reason, it would not be by means of such concepts as *sensing redly* and *sensing roundly* that we could achieve a transparent conception of the modes of sensing themselves. A grasp of those concepts might reveal to us, say, that the relevant modes were those involved in the perception of certain kinds of physical item, but we would then, in each case, need to focus on the character of the sensing itself, in introspective perspective, to discern the identity of the mode itself. But it is just in this area that AT runs into its most obvious problem. For what the theory takes to be the true character of our experiential situation is at variance with what an introspective analysis seems to disclose.

Put simply, the problem is that, when we focus on the character of our experiences introspectively, we do not become aware of the supposed adverbial nature of their sensory core. If we accept the distinction between the sensory and interpretative components of phenomenal experience—a distinction recognized by both the SDT and AT accounts—and if we introspectively focus on the character of our experiences in the light of that distinction, we can, indeed, come to identify what (in that framework) qualifies as the sensory core. And, by becoming aware of this core, we become aware of the sensible qualities which feature in its content. But we are always aware of this core as the sensing, or sensory awareness, *of some item* (for example, a colour-array, a felt patch of texture, a sequence of sounds), and are aware of the sensible qualities involved as aspects or elements of this item. We never manage to achieve, introspectively, an explicitly adverbial view, where we are aware of the sensory episode as merely a sensing in a certain manner (a manner not defined by the character of an *object* of sensory awareness), and are aware of the sensible qualities as the modes of sensing which compose this manner. But why not, if an adverbial view would be correct?

Now it might seem, at first, that the adverbialist has a simple way of dealing with this point. It is an essential aspect of AT, as we are envisaging it, that, in the context of a phenomenal experience, a sensing does not occur in psychological isolation. It forms a component of a richer, integrated experience which also includes an element of interpretation, and this interpretation precisely represents (*mis*represents) the sensing as presentationally perceptive of an external item. So the adverbialist could say that the reason why we do not become aware of the adverbial nature of the sensing—why the sensing introspectively appears to us to be a sensing *of an object* rather than a sensing *in a manner*—is simply that, where it occurs as an element of a phenomenal experience, we cannot focus on it in its neat form, abstracted from the distortion of the perceptualist interpretation imposed on it. Nor, of course, can we just arrange, for example by adopting the right sort of mental set, to have such sensings on their own, without the interpretative additions. For, in the case of a normal and mature percipient, these interpretations happen automatically, and outside the scope of conscious control.

This point is well taken. But it does not, to my mind, get to the heart of the problem. For it is hard to see why the presence of the interpretative element should be a barrier to our discerning the truth of the situation *if we approach things in the right way.* It is true that we could not hope to discern the adverbial nature of *particular episodes* of sensing *at the time of* their interpretative misrepresentation; for, in such a context, we could not introspectively distance ourselves from the perspective which the interpretation itself imposes. But there seems to be no reason why the interpretation should prevent a veridical discernment if we either focus on a particular experience through introspective recall, or just focus on a *type* of experience through introspective imagination. After all, even if the interpretation *misrepresents* the nature of the sensing, it does not *alter* it (that, of course, is why it is a *mis*representation): the sensing would remain, in nature, a sensing in a certain manner, without the presence of any sensory object. If the sensing is present in the relevant experience, or experience-type, in that adverbial form, it should surely be possible for us, from the detached viewpoint of introspective recall or introspective imagination, and with a theoretical knowledge of the sort of thing which we are looking for, to deconstruct the complex and become aware of the sensing for what it is— even though, in doing this, we would precisely have to detach ourselves from the subjective feel of the sensing at the time of its occurrence. But the supposed adverbial character of the sensing remains stubbornly hidden. At least, this is what I find in my own case.

I suppose the adverbialist might say that, even though, in the circumstances envisaged, the presence of the interpretative element would not, as such, be an obstacle to deconstructive discernment, we are so conditioned to thinking of experiences as externalistically perceptive—in line with how they interpret themselves—that we are not, in practice, able to make an accurate judgement. We get the impression that we have succeeded in deconstructing the complex, but our failure to discern the adverbial nature of the sensory core shows that the distorting influence of our ordinary (perceptualist) mode of thinking remains. Even from the relevantly detached standpoint, it seems to us that the sensing is a sensing *of some-*

thing, because that way of construing the situation is what predominates in the course of everyday life.

But the suggestion that we cannot avoid this distorting influence, however determined we are to consider the situation dispassionately, and to take account of the factors which might tend to mislead us, is one which it is very difficult to take seriously. It is true that, even in our introspective judgements, we are not infallible. But to suggest that, in the case of sensory experience, we simply have no procedure for getting a correct introspective view of the basics of the situation, even though we focus on the nature of our experience in the relevantly detached way, know exactly what we are looking for, and are fully aware of all that might mislead—this seems to have no rationale other than that of preserving, at all costs, the adverbialist's position. We cannot prevent the adverbialist from digging his heels in in this way, but it is hard to see such a defence as anything other than a case of special pleading.

I think we must conclude that the introspective situation shows the adverbial theory to be highly implausible, even if it does not refute it absolutely.

IV

But the difficulties for the theory do not stop here. AT, as we have stressed, preserves the bipartite structure of SDT. It takes phenomenal experience to be made up of two integrated components: a sensory core, which is non-conceptual, and which takes the form of a sensing in a certain manner; and an element of interpretation, which represents this adverbially characterized sensing as the presentational awareness of an external sensible item. Thus, in the case of visual experience, it takes the sensory core to consist in some act of sensing in a complex manner (a manner whose complexity is isomorphic with the complexity of the internal colour-array that would be postulated by SDT); and it takes the additional component to consist in the interpretation (experiential interpretation) of this sensing as the visual presentation of an external colour-array, three-dimensionally structured and displayed to the subject in the perspective of his viewpoint. The inclusion of this interpretative element is, of course, crucial to the theory's purposes: it is, as I have said, what enables the whole experience to represent a certain type of environmental situation, and to do so in a way which, as the adverbialist would see it, provides the requisite presentational feel. But, although thus crucial, the presence of this element is also, as we shall now see, deeply problematic.

   The problem is that there seems to be no explanation of how this system of interpretation could come about. In the case of SDT, the role of the relevant interpretation is just to relocate, and perhaps to some extent restructure, the sensory objects, so that, for example, a two-dimensional internal colour-array gets interpreted as something three-dimensional and external. And it is not difficult to see how, as an appropriate response to the themes and regularities in the occurrence of the objects, this mode of interpretation should come to prevail. But, in the case of the adverbial theory, the interpretation envisaged involves something much more radical. It involves introducing a completely new ontology of perceived objects, not identified with any ontological ingredients of the experiences; and it involves representing a non-relational sensory state as the relation of presentational perceiving, between the subject and one such object. And it is hard to see how such a radical form of reinterpretation could take effect. It is true, of course, that, given the isomorphism between the adverbialist's modes of sensing and the sensory objects of SDT, the organizational factors which the sense-datum theorist would cite in explaining how our experiences come to embody an externalist interpretation (factors concerning the themes and regularities of sense-data) would also hold for the adverbially qualified sensings, and if the subject were sharp enough to detect them, and clever enough to gauge their significance, he might conceivably, as a way of accounting for them, come to postulate an external reality on the lines of the world whose existence we ordinarily accept. But this would not help to explain why our sensings are experienced (experientially interpreted) as *presentationally perceptive* of an external reality. Indeed, given that the sensings are not themselves presentational, it is hard to see how, in response to the detection of the organizational factors, the subject could come to think of himself as having *perceptual* access to the postulated reality at all.

   One thing which may help to conceal the force of this point, and give the adverbialist hope of a successful outcome, is that the problem does not seem to arise, at least in such an obvious form, if he pursues his approach on a more limited front. Thus if we can take for granted our capacity for visual and tactual perception, and are happy to accept a non-adverbial account of the phenomenal experiences they involve, there is not the same obstacle to developing an adverbial account of other forms of phenomenal experience on this basis. To focus on a particular case, suppose that, for a given subject, it normally happens that, when he sees a certain kind of object at a certain distance—for example, a wild rose close to him—he has an olfactory sensation of a certain sort. Then even if olfactory sensations are to be construed in an adverbial way—as sensings in a certain manner, rather than as sensings of certain types of object—it is not so hard to envisage the subject coming to experience the relevant mode of sensing as the presentational perceiving of an olfactory quality (a certain fragrance) in the object itself. After all, the regular association of the mode of sensing with the visually detected presence of a certain type of object evidentially points to the existence of some factor in the object to which the sensing is responsive; and, given this, it would only be a short step to our supposing that, unconsciously conditioned by this evidence, it comes to seem to the subject (though wrongly) that the mode of sensing is really a mode of sensible appearing, which reveals the nature of the factor involved. It is as if the correlation between the mode of sensing and the presence of the relevant type of object puts pressure on the mind to construe the sensing as perceptive, and as if, in response to this pressure, the mind somehow 'fabricates' a sensible quality to fit what a perceptive construal requires—thus giving itself the impression (illusory impression) that the olfactory encounter with the object affords a transparent conception of the quality in question. The process involved could be thought of as a special form of *projection*—of the mind's 'spreading itself on external objects', to use Hume's memorable phrase.[28] And, indeed, it is a form which is familiar enough from a variety of other cases. For example, many philosophers insist that there is no objective quality of beauty, and that the only reason why we ordinarily think of ourselves as encountering one, when, say, we contemplate a work of art or listen to music, is that we project our aesthetic feelings on to the relevant object, thus creating the illusion of a quality which is externally realized and which these feelings display. Or again, Hume himself, who held that events were not subject to any form of objective necessary connection, argued that the reason why we ordinarily think that we sometimes discern such a connection in the events we observe is that we project our habits of inference on to them, so that, where the observation of one type of event habitually prompts us to infer the occurrence of another, we have the illusion of there being, between the types of events themselves, a real connection of occurrence which this inferential connection reflects.[29] It is this sort of projective process, or mechanism, which we

[28] Hume, *Treatise*, p. 167.

[29] *Treatise*, Bk. 1, Pt. 3, sect. 14. In representing Hume as denying the existence of objective necessary connection, I am following the *traditional* (and I am still inclined to think correct) interpretation of his position. This interpretation has recently been challenged by Galen Strawson in his book *The Secret Connexion* (Oxford: Oxford University Press, 1989).

would need to invoke in pursuing the adverbial account above. We can speak of it as *fabricative* projection, to indicate that what the mind assigns to the external items involved is not a genuine quality or relation, but a fictitious item of its own making. It would thus be distinguished from the more straightforward case of what we might call *replicative* projection, where something real, but internal, gets relocated in the external reality. This latter form of projection is, of course, what the sense-datum theorist would invoke in explaining the externalist interpretations which feature in his own account.

By invoking the mechanism of fabricative projection, we can see how it might be possible to develop an adverbial account in this limited area—dealing with a particular type of olfactory experience. And, if it works in this area, it is not difficult to see how the same approach could be extended to a range of further cases. In the first place, and obviously, it could be extended to cover the whole range of olfactory experience—partly because we could directly appeal to other examples of the same sort, and partly because, once the mind had developed dispositions for perceptualist interpretation with respect to a sufficient number of modes of olfactory sensing, we could think of it as acquiring a general disposition for such interpretation in this whole realm. And secondly, given that the account works for the olfactory realm, we can envisage it working for at least certain other sense-realms in just the same way. Thus there is nothing to prevent the development of an exactly analogous account of fabricative projection for auditory and gustatory experience—invoking the same kind of example as we used in the olfactory case. All this might encourage the adverbialist to think that he could adopt this approach quite generally. It is true that there would still be the first problem to contend with—the fact that an adverbial account of sensing seems to be at variance with what introspection reveals—and this problem applies, I think, across the whole range of sensory experience. But, setting this problem aside, it might seem that, given the adverbial sensings, there is the prospect of a general account of how, by the process of fabricative projection, the system of perceptualist interpretation comes about.

But this would just be an illusion. For the only reason why we were able to envisage the limited adverbial programme was that it *was limited*. It was developed within the framework of the assumption that a capacity for visual and tactual perception was already in place and afforded our basic access to the external reality. And without this basic access—to be accounted for in some non-adverbial way—the envisaged mechanism of fabricative projection would have had nothing to operate on; for there would have been no perceptually identifiable objects to form its external targets. Thus, in our example, it was only because the subject could already perceive and identify the relevant type of object, whose presence was correlated with the particular mode of sensing, that there were things in the external reality on to which this mode of sensing could be projectively directed—things which could become the recipients of the fictitious olfactory quality which the mind was taken to fabricate. This is not an aspect of the approach which could be dropped without forfeiting all plausibility. Without independently perceptible external targets, it would be wholly mysterious how the modes of sensing, which would have to seem like modes of sensing if introspected in their neat form, could come to be experienced (experientially interpreted) as anything else.

I think we cannot escape the conclusion that if the sensory core of a phenomenal experience were as the adverbialist claims—the mere sensing in a certain manner, without any sensory object—there would be no way of understanding how it comes to seem to us that we are presentational percipients of an external reality, or indeed, percipients of such a reality at all. The most that could be understood would be how, if we had good powers of introspective recall, and were very clever at detecting and analysing some rather subtle forms of regularity in the course of our sensory experience, we might come to construct and accept some theory of an unperceived external reality as a way of accounting for the sensory facts in question. And, whether or not we have the requisite recollective and investigative skills, this is not our actual situation.

V

AT looked, at first sight, promising. But it has been found to be problematic on two counts. In the first place, it is out of line with what seems to be indicated by an introspective analysis of the situation—with the fact that, even when we consider the nature of our experiences in an appropriately detached way, we are unable to discern the supposed adverbial character of the sensory core. Secondly, it leaves us without any explanation of how phenomenal experience, in the relevant sense, comes to occur. For if the sensory core is truly adverbial—the sensing *in a certain manner*, rather than the sensing *of a certain object*—it becomes impossible to understand how we manage to experience it as presentationally perceptive, or indeed as perceptive in any way. In the light of these points, I do not see how we can continue to regard the adverbial theory as a serious option.

7 THE SENSE-DATUM THEORY REVISED

I

The twin difficulties with the adverbial account of the sensory core seem to be pointing us, unambiguously, back to SDT. But, if I am right, SDT itself is vulnerable to a fundamental objection. For there is no way of understanding how there could be internal objects of awareness of the kind it postulates—how each sense-datum could be tied, in its existence, to the context of a particular presentational episode. It is no good suggesting that a sense-datum derives its existence from its being presented to the relevant subject on the relevant occasion; for obviously there cannot be anything which derives its existence from facts about itself. Nor is it any good suggesting that, whenever a sense-datum is presented to a subject, the fundamental psychological fact is of a different—not sense-datum involving—kind; for that would be to abandon SDT altogether. The only suggestion which we could begin to take seriously would be that, for sense-data, existence *takes the form of* presentation—that, for each sense-datum x, presented to a subject S at a time t, the existence of x *precisely consists in* the fact that x is presented to S at t. But if we suppose that the existence of a sense-datum just consists in its standing in a certain presentational relationship, there is no way of understanding how the sense-datum can be ontologically available to stand in that relationship. It would only be by its having an existence which transcended its standing in that relationship that there could be something there for the presentational awareness to be directed on to—something left over from the presentational act to form the presented object.

This leaves us in a dilemma. For, without reverting to something already rejected, it is hard to see what alternative there is to the sense-datum and adverbial accounts. Given the failure of the pure conceptualist approach, and our acceptance of the RC-claim, we have to recognize that each phenomenal experience contains a non-conceptual sensory core—a core in which the relevant sensible qualities are genuinely realized—and, in each case, this core will either have to take the form of some kind of relationship, of sensing or sensory awareness, between the subject and a sensibly characterized object, or take some other (non-relational) form. If the form is relational, we seem to have, unavoidably, SDT. If it is non-relational, then we presumably have to say, in accordance with AT, that the sensible qualities only feature in this core as modes of sensing. Admittedly, under the non-relational option, there is the formally available alternative of eliminating the sensory act, and saying that the sensory core just consists in the mental occurrence of the sensibly characterized object. But without the presence of a sensory act—something to render the object *an object of awareness*—there would be no way of understanding how the occurrence of the object could form an element of phenomenal experience, or, indeed, could qualify as mental at all.

We seem to have reached an impasse. If we accept that phenomenal experience has a non-conceptual sensory core, it seems that we have to choose between SDT and AT, and neither option is acceptable. On the other hand, if we abandon the idea of such a core, then we are forced back to an approach which we have already examined in detail, and found wanting. There seems to be no way left of making progress. But there is something quite simple here which we are overlooking. For although the adverbialist alternative has proved a failure, there is another, and much less radical way of revising the sense-datum account as we have so far formulated it—a way which does not disturb the basic structure of a sensory act and a sensory object, and yet does crucially alter the whole situation of the ontological relationship between them. It is the availability of this revised version of SDT which, it seems to me, provides our way of escape from the dilemma.

II

Let us start by taking a fresh look at what, in its present form, SDT is claiming. The theory claims that, given any phenomenal experience, its sensory core takes the form of an episode of awareness. This awareness is stipulated to be non-conceptual, just consisting in the presentation of a certain object (for example, a colour-array or a sequence of sounds) to the subject involved. And the object of the awareness is stipulated to be internal to it, in the sense explained—something whose existence is necessarily confined to the context of its presentation to that subject on that occasion. Now, amongst other things, this internality means that the sensory object shares the *particularity* of the associated sensory act. The sensory act—the episode of presentational awareness—is, like any other mental act or episode, a mental *particular*: it occurs in a single subject on a single occasion, and it is logically incapable of occurring in any other subject or on any other occasion. And because the sensory object is conceived of as internal to the associated act in the way specified—something which is incapable of existing outside the context of that act—it automatically inherits the same particularity. Each such object—each sense-datum—is presented to a single subject on a single occasion, and, as tied to the particular presentational act, is not capable of being presented to other subjects or on other occasions. So the sensory core, thus conceived, is a complex of two entities sharing a common particularity—each entity being tied, in its occurrence, to a unique subject and unique occasion. Even in the abstract, this duplication of coincident particulars within the single sensory event seems strange. It is hardly surprising that, when we try to make sense of the ontological relationship between the entities involved, we are lost for a coherent account.

But the solution, it seems to me, is simply to eliminate the duplication: not indeed, in the manner of the adverbialist, by eliminating the sensory objects altogether, but by reconstruing them as *universals*. We can do this without having to change their qualitative content: they can remain, as they were on the original theory, colour-arrays, complexes of sound, patterns of texture and temperature, and so on. What we alter are the identity-conditions imposed on them. Thus, instead of tying the occurrence of each object to a single act of presentation, and thereby to a single subject-time location, we stipulate that, wherever objects have exactly the same qualitative content, they are—irrespective of the subjects and times involved—numerically the same entity. In this way, at a stipulative stroke, we turn the objects from sensory particulars into sensory universals—each object being now capable of presentational occurrence to any number of subjects and on any number of occasions. Let us refer to these universals as 'sense-qualia'; and when SDT is developed in this new way, with sense-qualia as the new form of sense-data, let us speak of it as the *sense-quale theory* (SQT). A sense-*quale*, in this sense, is not to be confused with a sense-*quality*. Sense-qualia, like the sense-data they replace, are *qualitatively replete* items, with all the quality-elements needed to form complete sensory objects—though this does not preclude cases in which a simpler quale forms a component of a more complex one. In this respect, the kind of sense-qualia I have in mind are like those which featured in the later philosophy of A. J. Ayer, though Ayer's reasons for introducing an ontology of qualia were quite different from my own.[30] It should be stressed that, in taking the sensory objects to be universals, the new theory in no way does violence to the *phenomenological* facts. All that the subject can introspectively detect about the object presented to him is its qualitative content, and this leaves it entirely open as to whether what has this content is something

---

[30] Ayer makes the shift from an ontology of sense-datum particulars to an ontology of sense-qualia in *The Origins of Pragmatism* (London: Macmillan, 1968). On Ayer's reasons for making this shift, see my 'The construction of the physical world', sect. 2, in Lewis E. Hahn (ed.), *The Philosophy of A. J. Ayer* (La Salle, Ill.: Open Court, 1992).

tied to that particular presentational occasion or something with a capacity to be presented to other subjects and at other times. The introspective character of sensory experience leaves us free to decide the issue of particularity–universality in whatever way we find theoretically appropriate.

The adoption of sense-qualia as the sensory objects does not alter the content of SDT in any other respect. The new theory, like the old, represents phenomenal experience as having two components—a sensory core, consisting in the presentation of a sensory object, and an externalist interpretation imposed on this object—and all that was said about the relationship between these components in the original exposition continues to apply. Moreover, by preserving, in these other respects, the content of the original theory, SQT preserves its virtues: it continues to meet the various requirements that we identified for a satisfactory account. But where the new theory has a crucial advantage is in eliminating the problem of internality. By being reconstrued as universals, the sensory objects are no longer tied to any particular presentational acts. Even if a sense-quale is only once presented—to a unique subject on a unique occasion—its ontological nature equips it to be presented to any number of subjects on any number of occasions; nor, indeed, is its presentational occurrence to that particular subject on that particular occasion essential to it. So the aspect of the original theory which caused the problem—the ontological internality of the relevant objects to particular acts of awareness—has simply disappeared. Because a sense-quale is ontologically available for presentation to any subject on any occasion, there is no longer anything puzzling—anything that calls for explanation—about the ontological relationship between an episode of presentational awareness and the sensory object it presents.

It is SQT which, in my view, provides the correct theory of the nature of phenomenal experience. I have already made clear why I think that we need a theory which recognizes the presence of a non-conceptual sensory core; and, given the inadequacies of the adverbialist approach, the only way of understanding the nature of this core is in relational (act–object) terms. Within this framework, SQT is a phenomenologically available option; and only SQT, it seems to me, offers a coherent account—an account which leaves the ontology of the act–object relationship in an intelligible form.

III

I am offering SQT as the correct account of the nature of phenomenal experience. But, to get a proper understanding of the theory, it is crucial that we construe the nature of sense-qualia in the right way. I have already stressed that sense-qualia, as I here understand them, are qualitatively replete items, with all the quality-elements needed to form complete sensory objects. But there are other points that need to be clearly grasped if misunderstanding is to be avoided. In particular, we need to get clear about what is involved in speaking of sense-qualia as *universals*.

I have introduced sense-qualia as a class of *sensory universals*, in contrast with the sense-datum particulars they replace. But they are universals of a very special kind. Standard universals, like properties, types, and natures, are *abstract* entities: the only way in which they can contribute to the composition of the concrete reality is by the occurrence, within that reality, of things which instantiate them; and where an entity E instantiates a universal U, the basic fact involved is not expressed in that relational form, but rather by saying that E is . . ., with some suitable (U-signifying) predicate or sortal term filling the dots. Thus the only way in which, say, squareness or personhood or masculinity can contribute to the composition of the concrete reality is by that reality's containing things which are square or persons or masculine. Now it is crucial that we should not think of sense-qualia as universals of this abstract sort—as entities which only contribute to the composition of the sensory reality by the occurrence of other sensory items which instantiate them. Sense-qualia are not the determinate sensory types which the presented sensory objects instantiate, but the concrete objects themselves, which instantiate such types. In this respect they are exactly like the original sense-data they replace. What makes them universals, and sets them in contrast with the original items, are the distinctive identity-conditions imposed on them. Thus whereas, in the original case, each sensory object was logically confined to a single presentational context, in the case of sense-qualia it is stipulated that qualitative identity suffices for numerical identity, so that wherever there is an instantiation of the same determinate sensory type, there is the very same instantiating entity. Because sense-qualia are concrete entities—concrete ingredients of the sensory reality—there is, of course, no question of recognizing the existence of qualia that never occur as objects of presentation. In the case of the sensory types, it is permissible, and indeed theoretically convenient, to recognize an abstract space of types, which covers both those types that are presentationally realized and other types which are capable of realization, and which can be defined in terms of the same qualitative dimensions. But, in the case of sense-qualia, the recognition of unpresented instances would make no sense. Sense-qualia are not ontologically tied to specific presentational contexts—that is how the problem of internality is avoided.

But, as concrete sensory objects, they have no existence outside the sensory realm. Presentational occurrence remains the form of their existence.

An analogy with the physical realm will help to make the situation clear. Suppose we take a time-slice of a material object—for example, the present momentary stage of the desk at which I am now sitting. Standardly, we would conceive of this entity as a spatiotemporal *particular*, confined, in its occurrence, to this one moment in this one region. But there is nothing which prevents us from construing it, instead, as a spatiotemporal *universal*. We can do this, as in the case of a sense-quale, by imposing the appropriate identity-conditions on it. Thus, in introducing the entity into our ontology, we can stipulate that its identity is wholly determined by its intrinsic qualitative nature—a nature which is logically capable of realization in any number of places and on any number of occasions. And this will ensure that wherever and whenever this nature is realized, the same entity will occur as what instantiates it. In construing the entity as a universal in this way, we leave it, of course, as a concrete constituent of the physical world—as enjoying exactly the same kind of concreteness as the momentary particular it replaces. It continues to be something which is genuinely located in space and time, as a concrete material stage in the history of certain objects at certain moments; and it continues to be something which is incapable of existing in any but a physical—spatiotemporally located—form. All that is involved in its being a universal is that it has the freedom to occur in any number of places and on any number of occasions, and that there is no particular spatiotemporal occurrence, or group of occurrences, which is essential to it. It is universals of this sort which emerge when we replace the sensory particulars of the original version of SDT by the sense-qualia of the new. The sense-qualia retain all the empirical concreteness of the original sense-data—as entities which form the sensory objects of presentational awareness, and which can only exist as thus presented. But they qualify as universals because of their distinctive identity-conditions—conditions which give each quale a capacity for presentation to different subjects and on different occasions, and leave its association with any particular group of subject-time locations as only contingent.

It is crucial that we should recognize the concreteness of sense-qualia, which sets them apart from the kind of universals that feature in standard philosophical discussion. But, in recognizing this concreteness, we must be careful not to confuse them with a certain class of particulars. What creates the opportunity for such confusion is that, given the original domain of sensory particulars—the sense-data of the original theory—there are two quite different ways in which, for a given determinate type of sense-datum, we can recognize an entity which covers all and only sense-data of that type. One way is what we have already envisaged under SQT: we recognize a sensory universal which qualitatively coincides with each of the sense-data taken on its own, but without the particularity of this sense-datum's occurrence. The other way would be to think of the *aggregate*, or *sum*, of all the relevant sense-data—something which we would introduce into our ontology by merely grouping these sense-data together and stipulating that they collectively form a single complex object. Such an aggregate would be a particular rather than a universal: it would not be, like the sense-quale, something which occurred as a complete entity in all the separate subject-time locations of the several qualitatively coincident sense-data; it would be something that was divisible into parts—each with its own distinct identity—which separately occurred at, and collectively covered, these various locations. It is crucial that we should register the clear-cut difference between these two ways of covering the relevant class of sense-data, and avoid confusing the universals of SQT with the scattered particulars of the alternative. In the case of *any* universal, of course, there is an analogous distinction to be drawn between the universal itself and the aggregate of the particulars which instantiate it. But, standardly, the universal in question is of an *abstract* variety, where there is much less risk of confusion with anything in the concrete reality. In the present case, the distinction calls for special emphasis, precisely because of the concrete, empirically immanent, character of the universals involved—just as it would call for emphasis in the case of the concrete *physical* universal that we envisaged in our analogy.

The notion of a concrete universal that I am invoking is a relatively unfamiliar one, and I can anticipate a certain amount of unease, or even outright scepticism, over its introduction. And this unease, or scepticism, would apply as much to the case of the physical analogy as to the sensory case which concerns us. For this reason, I think that it is worth drawing attention to a respect in which our ordinary conceptual scheme for thinking about the physical realm has taken a step in the direction of recognizing such universals. We must start by taking a closer look at the notion of particularity, as it applies to this realm.

A physical entity, to qualify as physical, has to have location in space and time; such location, indeed, is the form of its existence, its mode of being. Now the notion of *particularity*, as it applies to physical entities, concerns the way in which spatial and temporal location relate to numerical identity. The basic point is that, where there is particularity, diversity of identity keeps pace with diversity of location. Thus, given an entity which covers a certain region of space (or a certain scattered aggregate of regions) at a certain time, this entity exhibits full particularity with respect to this spatial spread if and only if, to the extent that the region (aggregate of regions) it covers divides into smaller regions (region-aggregates), it too, correspondingly, divides into smaller entities—its proper spatial parts— which severally cover these regions (aggregates), and which are, in virtue of their distinct spatial locations, numerically distinct. Likewise, given an entity which covers a certain period of time (or a scattered aggregate of periods), this entity exhibits full particularity with respect to this temporal spread if and only if, to the extent that the period (aggregate) divides into smaller periods (aggregates), it too, correspondingly, divides into smaller entities—its proper temporal parts—which severally cover these periods (aggregates), and are, in virtue of their distinct temporal locations, numerically distinct. In short, where there is full particularity with respect to space or time, difference of location entails difference of identity, and entities are divisible into smaller entities to the extent of their locational spread.

Now when we consider our ordinary conceptual scheme for the physical world, we see that the most prominent category of physical entities that feature in it, namely the category of material objects, only meets the requirements for particularity in a partial form. More precisely, we conceive of such objects in a way which renders them fully particular with respect to *space*, but not with respect to *time*. Thus take, as an arbitrary example, the case of Pauline's apple, and, for the sake of simplicity, let us pretend that this is an object with no internal gaps. Then, at each time, the apple occupies a certain three-dimensional region of space, and, to the extent that this region is divisible into smaller regions, the apple itself is, at that time, divisible into smaller objects, which severally occupy those regions and are numerically distinct. But the situation with respect to time is quite different. Thus, although the apple occurs at each moment of a certain period, it does not *extend over* this period, in the way that it extends, at each moment, over a three-dimensional region. Rather, it *persists through* this period—the very same entity existing at each moment—so that whereas it is divisible into numerically distinct parts in respect of its coverage of space, it is one and indivisible in respect of its coverage of time. This means that, in respect of its occurrence in time, the apple has the character of a universal rather than a particular. It is something which, universal-like, preserves its identity across the diversity of its temporal locations. To get something which is particularized with respect to these locations, we should need to replace the apple by the sort of four-dimensional 'worm' which features in Relativity Theory, where time is treated like an extra dimension of space. But while there may be point to such an ontological manœuvre in an attempt to capture the fundamental nature of the physical world, it is certainly not the ontology of our ordinary conceptual scheme.

Now the reason why I have made this digression into the nature of our ordinary physical ontology is because I think it may help to remove some of the strangeness in the notion of a concrete universal. I tried to explain earlier how, by imposing new identity-conditions on a time-slice of a material object (so that its identity comes to be fixed by its intrinsic nature alone), we can transform it into a concrete universal of the relevant kind— an entity whose form of existence is spatiotemporal (existence *within* the physical realm), but which is free to be located in any place at any time. What we can now see is that this move from the particular to the universal is only a more extreme version of a move from the same particular to the persisting object of which it forms a momentary stage. The comparison is especially neat if, in the case of persistence, we focus on an example, such as would presumably occur with a fundamental particle, in which it is necessary for the preservation of the same entity through time that its successive time-slices preserve the same intrinsic character. For this would allow us to see the persisting object as precisely embodying the universality of the envisaged universal in a more limited form. Thus the class of momentary particulars over which the persisting item preserves its identity would become a proper subset of the class of momentary particulars over which the full universal preserves its identity—the full universal covering not only the series of time-slices of the relevant item, but the totality of time-slices (drawn from any object) which have exactly the same intrinsic character. In the case of most objects of our ordinary conceptual scheme, of course, the situation is more complicated. For, although the degree of universality of the persisting thing is limited to the series of its own time-slices, the members of this series are not required to be qualitatively identical. The object is conceived in such a way that the preservation of numerical identity through time is compatible with certain forms of qualitative change. Thus Pauline's apple was able to survive a period of growth prior to the time of her visual encounter with it, and it is equally capable of preserving its identity through some subsequent period of decay. In this sort of case, a full universal, introduced by imposing the relevant identity-conditions on a selected time-slice, would be in one respect more restricted than the persisting object itself. By covering all and only time-slices which were qualitatively identical to the slice selected, it would have the chance of ranging over the stages of other objects, but there would be no guarantee of its being able to range over all the stages of the particular object from which this slice was drawn.

In explaining how we can come to recognize a category of concrete physical universals (formed by imposing the new identity-conditions on time-slices of material objects), and in drawing attention to the partial analogy between such universals and the persisting objects of our ordinary conceptual scheme, I am not suggesting that their actual introduction into our system of physical thought would serve any purpose. In the case of the persisting objects, of course—the objects we already recognize—there *is* a purpose; for such objects reflect and underline forms of spatiotemporal and causal continuity, which impose a genuine unity on the successive momentary items which form their stages. (It is because the persisting objects embody such principles of diachronic unity that there is usually room for the preservation of numerical identity through qualitative change.) But I cannot think of anything that would be gained by the introduction of the relevant universals. What makes these universals interesting, in the context of our present discussion, is that, however marginal their importance to our theorizing about the physical world, they provide an exact and illuminating analogy with the sensory universals that I take to be crucial to our understanding of the nature of phenomenal experience; and, to enable them to serve this purpose, we only have to show that we have a coherent way of coming to acknowledge their existence.

IV

The reason why the introduction of the ontology of sense-qualia is crucial to our understanding of the nature of phenomenal experience is, as I have stressed, that it allows us to avoid the problem encountered by SDT in its original—particularistic—form. Thus it is not true of sense-qualia, as it was of the original sense-data, that if one of them is presented to a certain subject on a certain occasion, then its existence is logically confined to the context of that particular presentational event. And so, for sense-qualia, there is not the problem which there was for the original sense-data, of understanding how that kind of ontological internality can obtain. Sense-qualia are entities which only exist within the compass of the mind; and, like the original sense-data, they can only exist in presentational form. But, being available for presentation to any subject on any occasion, they have the right kind of ontological independence, in relation to the particular episodes of their presentational occurrence, to leave no problem as to how they can serve as genuine objects of awareness.

PART FOUR

THE PROBLEM OF PERCEPTION

1 INTRODUCTION

Since the start of Part Three, we have been working on the assumption of the truth of the broad version of the representative theory (BRT). This theory makes two claims. First, it asserts the truth of physical realism: it claims that the physical world is something whose existence is logically independent of the human mind, and something which is, in its basic character, metaphysically fundamental. Secondly, and in effect in the framework of its acceptance of physical realism, it claims that our perceptual contact with the physical world is, in all cases, psychologically mediated. That is to say, it claims that, for any subject S, physical item x, and time t, if S perceives x at t, then there is a psychological state (type-state) Σ, such that Σ is not in itself x-perceptive, and indeed not essentially physically perceptive at all, and such that S's perceiving of x breaks down into (is constituted by the combination of) two components: one component consists in S's being in Σ at t; the other comprises certain additional facts, though ones which do not involve anything further about S's psychological condition at t (anything, that is, over and above his being in Σ). Within the framework of physical realism, BRT contrasts with the strong version of direct realism (SDR). This too accepts a realist view of the physical world, but insists that, where the perceiving of a physical item is Φ-terminal (there being no other physical item which is more immediately perceived), the perceptual relationship is something psychologically fundamental, and thus not subject to the sort of decomposition postulated by BRT. The reason why we have been working on the assumption of the truth of BRT is that we are taking ourselves to have refuted SDR in Part Two, and indeed to have shown that the SDR-account of the perceptual relationship is wrong in all instances; and, within the framework of physical realism—a framework which we have had in place from the outset of our discussion—BRT is the only remaining option.

Now this acceptance of BRT left us with two areas for investigation, corresponding to the two components into which each fact of physical-item perceiving is supposed to break down. First, it left us needing to determine the precise nature of the relevant (mediationally involved) psychological states. BRT stipulates that these states (the Σ-states) are not in themselves perceptive of the relevant physical items, and indeed not essentially physically perceptive at all, but otherwise leaves their nature unspecified. Secondly, it left us needing to determine the nature and role of the additional facts—the facts which supposedly combine with the realization of the psychological states to secure perceptual contact. BRT stipulates that these facts should not involve anything further about the subject's psychological condition at the relevant time, but does not specify what sorts of fact they are or how they play their role in the securing of perceptual contact.

Our subsequent discussion, in Part Three, dealt in detail with the first area of investigation, at least in so far as it bears on the conditions for Φ-*terminal* perception; and, having systematically explored the various options, we now have, in the form of the sense-quale theory (SQT), an established account of the nature of those psychological states (the phenomenal-experiential (PE) states) which are mediationally involved. Thus, according to SQT, these states have two components. One component is the presentation of a sense-quale, which is a sensory item in the mind. Sense-qualia are just like the sense-data of the traditional sense-datum theory (SDT), except that they are sensory *universals*—each quale being capable of occurrence in any number of subjects and on any number of occasions. The other component is an element of experiential interpretation, which represents the sense-quale as something external—as something existing in a three-dimensional space in which the subject himself is located. With SQT as the account of the relevant psychological states, our acceptance of BRT, which is in itself the *broad* version of the representative theory, has become an acceptance of NRT, which is the *narrow* version. In other words, the claim is not just that perceptual contact with physical items is always *psychologically* mediated, but that this psychological mediation is also a kind of *perceptual* mediation, in which the relevant psychological state involves the occurrence of a perceptual object in the mind. Admittedly, in our previous characterizations of NRT, we worked on the assumption that the perceptual objects in question would be internal objects of awareness in a strong sense, so that each object was confined in its existence to a single episode of awareness. With the introduction of sense-qualia as the relevant perceptual objects, this aspect of our understanding of

NRT has to be revised. In fact, of course, we explicitly allowed for this revision when the NRT option was first introduced in Part One.[1]

We have dealt in detail with the first area of investigation. What we still need to address is the second. Here the quest is to determine the nature and role of the additional facts—the facts which supposedly combine with the realization of the psychological states to create perceptual contact with the physical world. It is to this topic that I now turn.

2 THE EMERGENCE OF THE PROBLEM

I

In basic outline, the way we should approach this further issue is already clear. Thus suppose we have a subject, S, who is in a PE-state Σ at a time t, and M is some momentary physical item which is earlier than t; and we want to know what sort of additional facts would enable this realization of Σ to psychologically mediate a Φ-terminal perceiving of M, so that S Φ-terminally perceives M at t, and his perceptual contact with M is constituted by the combination of his being in Σ at t and these facts. Then it is clear that, to have any chance of achieving this result, the additional facts would have to do at least two things.

In the first place, they would have to be such as to render S's Σ-experience representationally appropriate, to an adequate degree, to the relevant environmental situation—the situation of the presence of M in a certain spatial relationship to S at t. In part—indeed in large measure—such appropriateness would be simply a matter of there being certain forms of agreement between the type of environmental situation which Σ represents and the actual situation of M in that relationship. So, if Σ is a visual PE-state, and if the situation-type which it represents is, or is in part, that of there being an item of a certain shape, size, and colouring, at a certain distance and in a certain direction, the representational appropriateness of S's experience to the actual (M-involving) situation would have partly to stem from respects in which the character of M and its spatial relationship to S coincided with that representation. However—and in effect this is something which we noted in our earlier discussion[2]—representational appropriateness is not entirely a matter of such representational accuracy. For it is also, in certain respects, a matter of conforming to what is normal, or

---

[1] Part One, Section 2, II.
[2] Part Two, Section 5, V.

normative, for the relevant conditions of observation. Thus when a straight stick, which is half-immersed in water, looks bent, this bent appearance, though not veridical, is, for perceptual purposes, representationally appropriate to the stick's actual shape, since it is exactly how a straight object *should* look *in those conditions.* And, given our Lockean account of the ES-qualities—an account which excludes their realization in the physical world—we can see that the representational appropriateness of such qualities in the content of phenomenal experience is a matter of conformity to some dispositional norm, rather than a matter of straight veridicality. Thus if Σ is the PE-state involved in the Pauline case, and M is the relevant (Φ -terminally seen) time-slice of the apple's surface-portion, what makes the sensory colour in Σ representationally appropriate (if it *is* appropriate) to M's pigment (or appropriate to M's pigment relative to Pauline's colour-system) is not that it literally resembles it, but that it is this colour whose sensory realization this pigment is, in such conditions of observation, disposed to produce (or disposed to produce in Pauline). (Arguably, we might also need to insist that, for a sensory colour to be representationally appropriate to a physical pigment, the dispositional correlation between them has to be part of a general system of such correlations, and that this general system is such as to allow qualitative similarities and differences in sensory colour to reflect, in certain respects and up to a certain degree, qualitative similarities and differences in pigment, or in the effects of pigment on the reflection and absorption of light.)

The second thing that the additional facts would have to do is ensure that M played an appropriate causal role in the production of the realization of Σ in S at t.[3] The relevance of this causal role to the securing of perceptual contact becomes clear when we focus on a case in which the subject's phenomenal experience is representationally appropriate to his environmental situation, but has been brought about by a process which this situation did not affect. Thus, going back to the example of the radio-controlled device (the device attached to, and determining the firings in, the subject's optic nerves),[4] we can envisage a case in which, with the subject blindfolded and the device operating under the control of some pre-fixed programme (a programme not responsive in any way to the relevant environmental factors), a visual experience occurs which, purely by

---

[3] It was H. P. Grice who first drew attention to the need for this causal role in his classic paper 'The causal theory of perception', in *Proceedings of the Aristotelian Society*, Suppl. Vol. 35 (1961), 121–52.

[4] See Part Two, Section 2, I.

chance, is representationally appropriate to the subject's (relevant) environmental situation (that earlier situation which would have been visible to him at that time if his eyes had been open and his visual system working in the normal way). It is clear that, just because this situation played no causal role in the genesis of the visual experience, the experience cannot be regarded as perceptive of it. The experience is a mere hallucination, despite its representational appropriateness to the situation in question.

In fact, in order for S's Σ-experience to qualify as a Φ-terminal perception of M, it is necessary not only that M should play *some* causal role in the production of the experience, but that it should play a causal role of a special—perceptually appropriate—kind. For it is not hard to think of cases in which we have both representational appropriateness (to the fullest degree) and a causal route from the relevant situation, or situational item, to the experience, but where the causal process is not of the right sort for perceptual contact. Thus if, on a particular occasion, the radio-controlled device happened to produce an experience as of seeing such a device, in a suitably magnified form, and attached to the optic nerves in the relevant way, the experience would still be hallucinatory, despite its representational appropriateness to the thing which caused it. Exactly what is needed for the causal process to qualify as perceptually appropriate is a complicated question, and not one which we could hope to settle without detailed investigation.[5] But two requirements, at least, seem reasonably clear. The first is that the causal process should be fine-grained in relation to the various respects of representational appropriateness involved, so that each representationally relevant feature of the perceived item should be distinctively causally responsible for the corresponding representational feature of the experience. The second is that the process should exemplify—be an instance of—a reliable general system by which environmental items of a certain general kind bring about representationally appropriate experiences in that fine-grained way. Neither of these requirements, of course, would be met in the example of the device above.

It is clear, then, that, if they are to enable S's Σ-experience to qualify as a Φ-terminal perceiving of M, the additional facts must at least be such as to ensure two things: first, that the experience be, to an adequate degree, representationally appropriate to the M-involving situation (the situation of

⁵ For some interesting discussions of this, see P. F. Strawson, 'Causation in perception', in his *Freedom and Resentment* (London: Methuen, 1974); David Lewis, 'Veridical hallucination', *Australasian Journal of Philosophy*, 58/3 (1980), 239–49 (reprinted in J. Dancy (ed.), *Perceptual Knowledge*); and Christopher Peacocke, *Holistic Explanation* (Oxford: Oxford University Press, 1979), ch. II.

the presence of M in the relevant spatial relationship to S at t); and secondly, that M play an appropriate causal role in the bringing about of this experience. To ensure representational appropriateness, the facts will obviously have to include ones which cover the relevant aspects of the relevant situation (facts which relevantly characterize the nature of M and its spatial relationship to S at t). And, to ensure causal appropriateness, they will obviously have to cover relevant aspects of the causal process from M to the experience. But, as well as these, there will also, on both counts, have to be certain *general* facts about the lines of causation from environmental items to experiences of the relevant sense-modality. For such facts are relevant both to the ensuring of representational appropriateness (e.g. by fixing the dispositional norms in the case of the ES-qualities), and to ensuring—what is needed for causal appropriateness—that the causal process from M to the experience exemplify a reliable general system of causation from environmental items to representationally appropriate experiences.

II

The above account seems to provide a promising framework for pursuing the relevant topic of investigation—for determining the precise nature and role of the facts which combine with the realization of the relevant psychological states (the PE-states) to secure Φ-terminal perceptual contact. It indicates the general lines on which we would seek to characterize the main facts involved in any particular case, and highlights the basic themes of representational and causal appropriateness that would be crucial to our understanding of what these facts contributed. Our next task, it seems, must be to provide the details and fine-tuning. This would be partly a matter of developing a more detailed account of these two forms of appropriateness, and partly a matter of seeing, in the light of that fuller account, whether any other (less obvious) factors are involved as well. None of this promises to be straightforward: there are, in particular, delicate issues concerning the exact conditions for causal appropriateness. But granted the truth of BRT, and assuming that our basic approach is sound, we can presumably expect things eventually to fall into place.

But all this is to ignore a fundamental problem which now arises for BRT itself. Throughout our discussion so far, we have been working on the common-sense assumption—made explicit at the end of Part One—that we do, in some way or another, perceive physical items; and the aim of our investigation has been to try to establish the precise nature of this perceptual relationship, as it presents itself in psychological terms. Given our rejection of SDR, and our continuing allegiance to the framework of physical realism, this assumption—let us refer to it as the *perceptualist assumption*—inevitably turned into our present assumption of the truth of BRT. But the trouble is that, now that we have established SQT as the right account of the relevant psychological states—the states that are supposed to feature in the psychological mediation postulated by BRT—it seems that the perceptualist assumption itself has been undermined. For let us take a cool look at the facts, as SQT represents them. The objects immediately presented to us, in cases of supposed physical-item perception, are sense-qualia, which only exist in the mind. Although existing in the mind, we experientially interpret these sense-qualia as external items, existing in a three-dimensional space in which we ourselves are located, and it is this which gives us the impression that we are perceiving, and indeed presentationally perceiving, things in the environment. In combination, the presentation of the sense-quale and its externalist interpretation form the subject's phenomenal experience; and if there are any cases of physical-item perception, the occurrence of this experience is the only aspect of the subject's psychological condition at the relevant time which, at least at the point of Φ-terminality, contributes to the securing of perceptual contact. But if these are the facts, it is very hard, on reflection, to think that we are able to perceive physical items at all. The situation seems to be, rather, this: the only objects of which we are genuinely aware, in cases of supposed physical-item perception, are the sense-qualia occurring in the mind; and we ordinarily, but mistakenly, suppose ourselves to have perceptual access to an external reality, because we ordinarily, but mistakenly, take the qualia themselves to be elements of such a reality. So given SQT as our account of the nature of phenomenal experience, it seems that the project of providing a BRT-account of physical-item perception has to be aborted. Exactly the same situation, of course, would arise under the *original version* of SDT, in which the sensory objects were construed as particulars. What creates the problem is simply that the immediate objects of awareness are ones whose occurrence is in the mind, rather than in the physical world.

In a sense, this problem is just the fully fledged version of a worry that has hung over the BRT-approach from the beginning, and indeed that I explicitly highlighted at the start of our discussion in Part Two. BRT claims that, whenever someone perceives a physical item, his perceptual contact with it breaks down into two components, one of which is the subject's being in some more fundamental psychological state—a state which is not in itself physically perceptive—and the other of which comprises certain additional facts, but ones which do not involve anything further about the subject's psychological condition at the relevant time. But, given that the relevant psychological state is not in itself physically perceptive, then, whatever its nature, there is a prima facie difficulty in understanding how the subject's perceptual awareness can reach beyond the boundaries of his own mind. According to the theory, this outreach is achieved by the addition of certain further facts. But if they do not introduce anything additional about the subject's psychological condition, it is quite unclear how these facts could turn a psychological situation which does not involve the perceptual awareness of a physical item into one that does. And this is so irrespective of whether, as SQT claims, the psychological situation involves the awareness of a *non*-physical item in the mind.

What the establishing of SQT does, or indeed any version of SDT, is to give this general difficulty a specific and much sharper form—a form which turns what is no more than an initial worry into a clear-cut and seemingly decisive objection. In fact, the acceptance of SQT (SDT) affects the situation in three ways.

The first and basic point is that, by introducing an ontology of non-physical items as the immediate objects of awareness, SQT seems to be, *quite transparently*, in direct conflict with the assumption that we have perceptual access to the external reality. For it seems just obvious that, even if these items serve to convey information about this reality, the subject's perceptual awareness does not reach beyond them. It seems just obvious that, if the sensible object immediately before his mind is a sense-quale, and if the only other relevant aspect of his current psychological condition is the accompanying experiential interpretation, then the subject's awareness stops at the quale itself and does not make contact with anything external. So while there may be, in any case, a general worry about how perceptual access to the physical world can be secured in the framework of BRT—a difficulty in envisaging what could serve to extend the reach of the subject's awareness beyond the boundaries of his mind—SQT seems to rule out, in advance, any possibility of an answer. It seems to establish, unequivocally, that the only objects which are accessible to perceptual awareness are confined to the mind.

The second way in which SQT affects the situation is concerned with the relationship between perception and identification. When an item is genuinely perceived, the perceiving of it must surely, for a subject with the appropriate conceptual resources, render that item, or at least some part or stage of it, available for direct demonstrative identification—identification not just (indirectly) as whatever it is, of a certain sort, that stands in a certain relationship to something else (something more immediately identified), but straightforwardly as *this* thing, of a certain sort, manifest in its own right. But it seems clear that, if our relationship with the external reality is as SQT represents it, the external items involved do not become available for identification in this way. On the one hand, the subject can, in this direct demonstrative fashion, identify the presented *sense-quale*; and, given the way in which the quale is experientially interpreted, this identification will ordinarily *seem* to him to be the identification of something external. But since the occurrence of the quale is within his own mind, this impression of an externalist identification is just an illusion. On the other hand, if the subject reflects on the situation philosophically, and comes to recognize that what is presented is only in his own mind, he can try to identify the relevant external item as that to which his phenomenal experience stands in a certain relationship—for example, as that to which it has a certain representational appropriateness and which contributes to its causation in a certain way. But, even if this is successful, it is precisely not the direct form of identification required for perception. What SQT does not seem to allow is an identificatory access to the external reality which is both genuine and relevantly direct. It seems clear that, once sense-qualia have been introduced as the immediate objects of awareness, posing as external items in the perspective of their experiential interpretation, the only genuine identificatory access to the external reality, or at least the only one made available by the occurrence of the relevant forms of experience, is indirect—an access mediated by the identification of something in the mind.

The third point is that, as well as seeming to entail that we do not have perceptual access to the external reality, SQT independently discredits the factors which ordinarily persuade us that we do. What ordinarily leads us to assume that we perceive external things is, of course, that this is the impression which our phenomenal experiences themselves convey: it is what these experiences invite us to believe. But what SQT reveals is that this experiential impression embodies a systematic error. For it involves the interpretation of things that are internal to the mind (the presented sense-qualia) as themselves external—as ingredients of a three-dimensional world in which the subject himself is located; and while such a system of interpretation is both natural and useful—reflecting and encapsulating the themes and regularities of sensory experience—it is undeniably mistaken. So, in this way, the SQT-account undermines the basis on which we ordinarily take ourselves to be percipients of the external reality, and it does this irrespective of whether—as it seems—it also succeeds in showing, quite directly, that this ordinary view is false. One consequence of this, of course, is that we no longer have the option of simply digging our heels in on the perceptualist assumption as something whose truth is just obvious. Even in the face of the objections brought against the assumption, this common-sense response may retain a certain appeal. But it is no longer available if the basis on which we ordinarily hold the assumption, and from which the appeal of the response would ultimately stem, has been independently discredited.

We spent the whole of Part Three trying to find the right account of the psychological states that are mediationally involved in physical-item perception. We thought that, with the eventual emergence of SQT, we had found that account; and we were ready to move on to the second phase of the BRT-project, where we have to determine the nature and role of the facts which combine with the realization of the relevant psychological states to secure perceptual contact. But what we now seem to have discovered is that, with SQT in place, the whole project of providing an account of physical-item perception is doomed. There are, it seems, no facts whose combining with the relevant psychological states will suffice to secure perceptual contact with physical items. For, with sense-qualia as the immediate objects of awareness, any such contact seems to be excluded.

3 AN ARGUMENT FROM ANALOGY

I

Assuming that he retains the commitment to SQT, there is now, I think, only one way in which the BRT-theorist could, with any plausibility, try to defend his position and justify the continuation of the project envisaged. It involves appealing to an analogy between the account of perception which he is forced to accept in the framework of SQT and something which we are in any case happy to accept within our ordinary framework of thought, where we take the perceptualist assumption for granted. Specifically, it involves insisting that the way in which the presentation of a sense-quale should be thought of as mediating perceptual contact with an external physical item is of the same general kind, and enjoys the same acceptability, as the way in which, in this ordinary framework, we happily take our contact with one physical item to be perceptually mediated by our contact with another.

The relevant notion of perceptual mediation was defined in Part One.[6] Thus given a subject S, a time t, and two items x and y which S perceives at t, S's perceiving of x at t is perceptually mediated by his perceiving of y at t if and only if two conditions are satisfied. First, S's perceiving of x at t breaks down into (is constituted by the combination of) his perceiving of y at t and certain additional facts. Secondly, these additional facts do not involve anything further about S's perceptual condition at t; in other words, in combining with the fact of S's perceiving of y, they do not add further perceptual facts, about S at t, to the constitutive base. Along with this definition, we also provided, by reference to the case of Pauline, what we took to be two straightforward examples of such mediation. Thus Pauline's seeing of the apple was held to be perceptually mediated by her seeing of the relevant portion of its surface (breaking down into her seeing of this portion and the additional fact that this latter item is a portion of the apple's surface). And similarly, her seeing of this surface-portion on any given occasion was held to be perceptually mediated by her seeing of a particular momentary stage of it (breaking down into her seeing of this stage and the additional fact that this latter item is a stage of that portion). Both these examples are ones in which the perceptual mediation is in the physical domain—the perceiving of one physical item mediated by the perceiving of another. And, in offering them as examples, we were taking for granted our perceptual access to the physical world, so that there was no problem over the assumption that the item represented as the more immediate object of perception was genuinely perceived.

The line of defence which this makes available to the BRT-theorist is not hard to discern. In our ordinary framework of thought, where we take for granted our perceptual access to the physical world, our intuitions allow us to acknowledge cases of perceptual mediation in the physical domain: they allow us to recognize cases in which the perceiving of one physical item breaks down into the perceiving of another physical item and certain additional facts of the relevantly restricted kind. But if there is no difficulty, in this ordinary framework, in recognizing cases of such mediation within the physical domain, why should we not be able to extend this recognition to the kind of mediation which the theorist postulates in the framework of SQT? After all—as we noted earlier—this kind too is a form of perceptual mediation, in which the presented quale plays the role of what is immediately perceived. Thus the situation envisaged is one in which there is a subject S, a time t, a sense-quale Q, and a physical item x, such that: (1) S is

---

[6] Part One, Section 2, I.

presented with Q at t; (2) S perceives x at t; (3) S's perceiving of x at t breaks down into S's presentational awareness of Q at t and certain additional facts; and (4) these additional facts (covering such things as the interpretative component of the phenomenal experience, and the causal and qualitative relations between the phenomenal experience and x) do not introduce anything other than Q as an object of awareness for S at t. In all this, there is a clear analogy between the way in which the presentational occurrence of a sense-quale is seen as facilitating access to an external physical item and the way in which, in our ordinary scheme of thought, the perceiving of one physical item (perceptually more immediate) is seen as mediating perceptual access to another physical item (perceptually more remote).

It is just this analogy, then, that the theorist can try to exploit in warding off the objection to his position. In particular, he can point to the fact that, in our ordinary scheme of thought, Φ-terminally perceived physical items can give perceptual access to other physical items, despite the fact that, within the physical domain, they alone are immediately perceived, and, at the fundamental level of description, they alone are represented as perceptual objects at all. And he can claim that when, in the light of this, we reflect on the situation he postulates, we can see that sense-qualia too are able to give perceptual access to the physical world, despite the fact that they alone are the immediate objects of awareness, and that, at the fundamental level of description, they alone are represented as objects of awareness at all. In other words, he can claim that once we focus on the similarity between what he postulates and what we ordinarily accept for the physical domain, our intuitions about the acceptability of his position will change, and we shall no longer see the perceptualist assumption as under threat.

This, at least, is a clear-cut line of defence. And, as far as I can see, it is the only one which offers the theorist any hope of a successful outcome. What we now need to investigate is whether it withstands critical scrutiny.

II

At first sight, the proposed line of defence seems quite plausible. There is no denying the overall analogy between what the BRT-theorist is postulating and what we ordinarily recognize with respect to the physical domain. And if we only focus on this analogy *in a general way*, it may seem to be adequate for the theorist's purposes. But the problems emerge when we start trying to develop the proposal *in detail*—focusing on particular cases of supposed perceptual mediation in the physical domain, and trying to set out both how they work in their own terms and how they can serve as a model for what is envisaged under BRT. Indeed, it seems to me that, once we adequately reflect on any specific type of case, we always find that there is something which undermines its use in the context of the analogical argument. *Either* it turns out that, within the overall analogy, there are crucial points of *dis*analogy—points which explain why what the theorist envisages is more problematic—*or* it turns out that we cannot, after all, legitimately construe the case as one of perceptual mediation at all.

The first thing we should stress—and no doubt this was obvious all along—is that the two examples of perceptual mediation which we have so far cited, as illustrative of its occurrence in the physical domain, are quite unsuited to serve as models for the sort of mediation postulated by the theorist. In the latter case, the immediate objects of awareness and the physical items to which they supposedly give access are ontologically separate, the former occurring in the mind, the latter forming elements of the external, extra-mental reality. And it is just this ontological separation which creates the prima facie problem, since it is difficult to see how the subject's awareness can be thought of as reaching beyond the internally occurring objects to the items that lie without. But what enables the Pauline examples to work so smoothly—the seeing of the apple being mediated by the seeing of the relevant portion of its surface, and the seeing of this portion being mediated by the seeing of the relevant portion-stage—is that the perceptual objects involved are not ontologically separate in this way. There is no difficulty in understanding how the event of Pauline's seeing the surface-portion qualifies as an event of seeing the apple, since contact with the portion is precisely contact with the apple itself at a particular spatial part. Nor is there any difficulty in understanding how the event of her seeing the portion-stage qualifies as an event of her seeing the persisting portion, since contact with the stage is precisely contact with the portion itself at a particular moment in its history. In short, there is no problem with either of these examples precisely because, unlike what is envisaged by the SQT-version of BRT, the mediations involved do not represent the subject's perceptual awareness as reaching to something which is ontologically beyond the item whose perception plays the mediating role. And this means, of course, that the theorist cannot hope to make use of such examples in pressing his argument from analogy. Moreover, there are a number of other sorts of case which have to be excluded for the same reason. Some of these cases are simply variants of the Pauline cases. For instance, if someone is holding an object, his tactual perception of it will be perceptually mediated by his perception of a portion of its surface; and this case works in exactly the same way as the analogous cases in visual perception. But there are other sorts of case as well. Thus suppose someone knocks on my door, causing me to have the relevant kind of auditory experience. Setting aside any general worry about perceptual access to the physical world, we want to say that I hear the sound of the knocking, and that, by hearing this sound, I gain auditory access to the knocking itself—to the striking of the fist on the door. But, again, what makes this case straightforward is that we do not think of the relevant perceptual objects as ontologically separate. In accepting that I genuinely hear the knocking, we think of the sound as an element or aspect of this event, so that the knocking itself can be said to be loud or soft, deep-pitched or higher-pitched. This case too, then, is of no help to the theorist in developing his analogical argument; and obviously there is a whole range of auditory cases of the same general sort.

If his argument is to work, the theorist will need to find cases of perceptual mediation in the physical domain which, though still unproblematic, exhibit the same kind of ontological separation as creates the prima facie problem in the cases envisaged by his theory. As far as I can see, there are only two kinds of case that might be thought to satisfy this requirement, and I shall consider them in turn. In presenting these cases, it will be convenient to use the term 'I-item' to refer to whatever it is that forms the more immediate object of perception, and to use the term 'R-item' to refer to the putative perceptual object which is more remote. I shall also, in this context, ignore the philosophical challenge to the perceptualist assumption itself. For what is now at issue is not whether the subject genuinely perceives the I-item, but whether, granted that he does, this perceiving succeeds in giving mediated perceptual access to the R-item, and does so in a way which provides the theorist with a suitable analogy.

III

The first type of case answers to the following specification. There is a subject S, a time t, and two physical items x and y, which are ontologically separate, such that: first, S perceives y at t in a way which is (by ordinary standards) absolutely straightforward—the sort of way in which, for example, I now see this sheet of paper in front of me or feel this pen in my hand; second, we are happy, for ordinary purposes, to speak of S as also perceiving x at t; third, in speaking of S as perceiving x, we accept that S's contact with x is perceptually mediated by his perceiving of y; and fourth, we see this mediated contact with x as crucially depending on both (i) the fact that the subject recognizes the presence of y as an indicator of the presence of x, or something of x's kind, and (ii) the fact that x plays a certain causal role in the production of y.

Examples of this type of case are not hard to find. Thus imagine a radar operator who sees a certain signal on his screen and thereby knows that an enemy missile is approaching. For ordinary purposes, we are happy to say that the operator has not only seen the *signal*, but seen the *missile itself*. But obviously we would intend this latter perceptual claim to be understood in perceptual-mediational terms, and these terms would meet the conditions of the specification. Thus we would think of the visual contact with the missile as constituted by the seeing of the signal, together with certain facts of the relevantly restricted kind; and we would take these facts to consist in, or crucially include, the two that the specification mentions—of the operator's recognizing the signal as an indicator of the presence of a missile, and of the missile's playing a certain causal role in producing the signal. Or, to take an example from a different sense-realm, imagine someone in an apartment who hears the bell ring in his sitting-room and knows that someone is pressing the relevant button on the front door below. We are again happy, for ordinary purposes, to speak of the subject as not only hearing the sound of the bell, but as hearing the person who is ringing it. And once again, we would intend this perceptual description to be understood in a perceptual-mediational way, in accordance with the specification. Thus we would think of his auditory contact with his visitor as constituted by his hearing of the bell, together with other facts of the relevantly restricted kind, and would take these facts to consist in, or crucially include, facts about what he takes the sound of the bell to signify and about the causal role of the other person in producing it. It is easy to think of a whole range of other examples of the same general kind. Thus, to cite but a few, we may speak of someone smelling a fire by smelling the smoke it emits, or of seeing the wind by seeing the swaying of the trees, or of hearing the approach of the Pope by hearing the applause of the crowd; and these cases too will fall under the same general specification as the two examples above. In all these examples, of course—again in line with the specification—the I-items and R-items involved are ontologically separate: the existence (or occurrence) of the thing which is more immediately perceived (the photic event on the screen, the sound of the bell, the smoke, . . .) is quite distinct from the existence (occurrence) of the item which is said to be mediately perceived (the approach of the missile, the person at the door, the fire, . . .). This is crucial. For, as I have stressed, it is just this ontological separation that the theorist requires. He is looking for a form of perceptual mediation in the physical domain which can serve as a model for what he envisages as holding quite generally, when he takes the occurrence of sense-qualia in the mind to mediate perceptual access to the external reality.

In this respect, then, the relevant class of cases complies with what the theorist needs for the purposes of his analogical argument. And it meets these purposes in a further respect as well. For the I-item involved is always something whose occurrence causally derives from the occurrence of the relevant R-item, and this too mirrors the situation envisaged by the theorist, where the presentation of the quale is brought about by the presence or activity of the external item supposedly perceived. But the trouble is that the cases fall foul of the theorist's purposes in another and more basic way. For it only takes a moment's reflection to see that, although the relationship between the subject and relevant R-item is mediated in the way envisaged (constituted by such factors as the perceiving of the I-item, the evidential significance which the subject attaches to this item, and the causal role of the R-item in producing it), it is not genuinely *perceptual*. It is just obvious that, from a strict standpoint, the perceptual awareness stops at the I-item; and this is confirmed by the fact that the only way in which the experience equips the subject to identify the R-item, or any part or stage of it, is in terms of its relationship to the I-item, which he can identify directly. In short, by perceiving the I-item, the subject is able to *detect* the R-item, but he does not truly *perceive* it.

This, indeed, is something which we recognize even at the level of our ordinary thinking. It is true that, in the context of ordinary discourse, we are happy to *describe* these cases as ones in which the R-item is perceived, and, in this way, to *represent* them as cases of perceptual mediation. But, even in our ordinary thinking, we do not take the perceptual claim *seriously*. Thus suppose the radar operator reports to his commanding officer that he has just seen (spotted, caught sight of) an enemy missile. And suppose that the officer corrects him, on the grounds that what he has seen is not the missile, but only something which signals its presence. No doubt we would regard such a response as pointlessly pedantic. But we can hardly deny that its content is, strictly speaking, correct: the operator has not genuinely *seen* the missile, though he has detected its presence by visual means. Likewise, in our second example, if the subject announces that he can hear the person at the door, it would be pedantic for anyone to challenge him on the grounds that he can only hear the sound of the bell. But again, we can hardly deny that such a challenge would be, strictly speaking, correct— that it is only the ringing sound in the sitting-room that is genuinely heard.

In short, in all the cases of this sort, we are happy, for ordinary purposes, to *speak* of the subject as perceiving the R-item in question. But we regard this as a mere *façon de parler*, whose real meaning, or informational content, is just that the subject detects the presence of the item, or an item of that sort, through the evidence supplied by his perception of something else. We do not think of the subject's access to this item as perceptual in the strict sense.

The upshot is that, notwithstanding the advantage of ontological separation, the class of cases we are considering does nothing to help the theorist's cause. The theorist is trying to defend a certain account of physical-item perception—an account which represents our perceptual access to the external reality as mediated by the occurrence of sense-qualia in the mind—and he is looking for some suitable form of perceptual mediation in the physical domain to serve as a model. But the kind of cases envisaged cannot serve as a model, because they are not ones in which the R-items are genuinely perceived. They are ones where we *speak as if* the R-items are perceived, and perceived through the perceiving of the I-items. But this perceptualist talk does not represent the true situation. And, even in our ordinary thinking, we do not suppose that it does.

IV

As I indicated, however, there is a second type of case to which the theorist might appeal in developing his analogical argument. This type too meets the requirement of ontological separation. And, like the cases we have been considering, it involves a causal process from the R-item to the I-item. But it also seems, on first inspection, to have a much better prospect of serving the theorist's purposes in other respects. I shall introduce the type by means of an example.

Think of the situation of someone watching a live football match on television. In some ways, this situation is like that of the radar operator. Both subjects are looking at a screen. Both have visual experiences which are caused, in the normal neurophysiological way, by light which comes from this screen. In both cases, these experiences, in their sensory (sense-quale) elements, register and reflect the patterns, and sequences of patterns, which occur on the screen. And, in both cases, the experiences furnish the subject with information about physical circumstances and events which are ontologically separate from these patterns, and not visible to him by ordinary means. But there is also a crucial difference. In the case of the radar operator, this information becomes available purely by inference, from his more basic information about what the screen itself displays. Thus the operator sees, say, a certain pulse of light, or a sequence of pulses, on the screen, recognizes it as such, and infers from its character the presence of a missile. The inference need not take the form of a conscious step of reasoning: the operator may well reach his conclusion *automatically*, without having to reflect on the situation. But, whether the process is automatic or consciously reflective, he only reaches this conclusion because he cognitively registers the character of the signal and gauges its evidential significance. The situation with the television viewer is quite different. It is true that the viewer may—almost certainly will—make certain inferences from the information which he visually acquires. But, even in its most basic form—the form in which it is directly drawn from how things sensibly appear—this information is not about the two-dimensional pattern of colours on the screen, but about the three-dimensional colour-arrangement of the football scene itself. This is because the visual experience includes not just the visual registering of the screen-pattern (though it does include that), but also the interpretation of that pattern in three-dimensional terms, making it experientially seem to the viewer as if he is watching the match from a location in the football stadium—though, of course, he will know that this is not so. In other words, the subject visually registers the pattern on the screen, but sees it not as such a pattern, but as the three-dimensional scene available to a spectator watching the match directly. It is only when the television goes wrong, and the pattern loses its representational quality, that he sees it as a mere pattern—a pattern, indeed, which now seems to obstruct his view of the scene that was earlier displayed.

Now, granted our perceptual access to the physical world, it is, on the face of it, plausible to characterize this television viewer as seeing the football match; and, unlike the case of the radar operator, where the subject's access to the relevant R-item is at best inferential, we find it plausible to say that the relationship involved, while of a distinctive kind, is one of *genuine* seeing—not just something which we are prepared, within the loose conventions of everyday discourse, to *describe* in perceptual terms. At the same time, taking account of the distinctive character of the televisual process, we also find it plausible to say that, if there is this perceptual relationship, it is mediated, and in effect perceptually mediated, by visual contact with the patterns on the screen. For it seems clear that, for any occasion when the viewer sees some momentary stage of the match, the fact of his seeing this stage breaks down into (is constituted by the combination of) his visual registering of the relevant pattern and certain additional facts of the relevantly restricted kind—facts which crucially include the way in which he experientially interprets the pattern and the causal role of the stage in producing it. So, putting both points together, the BRT-theorist has, here, a further type of case to which he can appeal in pursuing his analogical argument. The type, of course, is not just restricted to the specific case of the viewer and the match. It covers other television cases which work in the same general way. And it will cover a range of further cases as well. For example, it will cover the case of someone who is listening to a live radio broadcast and hears the sounds from his loudspeakers as the voices of people in the studio; and, arguably, it will cover the case of a doctor who is looking at the pictures coming from an ultrasound scan, and sees a certain shape as a baby.

The theorist has this further type of case to which he can appeal. And, at first sight, it seems to be *exactly* the type of case that he needs. For, as well as its appearing to meet the basic requirements—of exhibiting perceptual mediation with ontological separation—it seems to serve the purposes of the envisaged analogy in every respect. Thus, continuing to focus on our example, we can see that the way in which the pattern on the screen features in the television story is, point by point, exactly parallel with the role which the theorist assigns to the sense-quale in ordinary visual perception. So, (i) like a visual sense-quale, the screen-pattern is a kind of two-dimensional coloured array; (ii) just as the occurrence of a visual quale is (in the standard situation) caused by a process whose initial phase takes the form of light from the environment entering the eye, so the occurrence of a pattern on the screen is caused by a process whose initial phase takes the form of light from the environment entering the television camera; (iii) just as the quale-array, thus caused, reflects the relevant three-dimensional arrangement of colours in the subject's environment, relative to the projection of that arrangement on to the viewpoint of the eye, so the pattern, thus caused, reflects the relevant three-dimensional arrangement in the camera's environment, relative to the projection of that arrangement on to the viewpoint of the lens; and (iv) just as the total experience of a normal visual subject includes not just the presentation of a sense-quale, but also its externalist three-dimensional interpretation, so the total experience of the television viewer includes not just the visual registering of the pattern on the screen, but also its interpretation as the relevant type of three-dimensional scene. The extent of the analogy is striking. So long as we can accept that there is perceptual mediation in the television case, which seems reasonable, there really does seem to be a strong case for accepting the theorist's comparable claim about visual perception in general.

In fact, however, the situation is not so simple. For although there seem, at first sight, to be reasonable grounds for accepting that there is perceptual mediation in the television case, these grounds vanish when we examine the issue more closely. The basic problem is this. The claim of perceptual mediation divides into two component claims, one asserting that the relationship between the subject and the match is that of genuine seeing, the other asserting that it breaks down into further factors in the relevant mediational way; and, of course, both these claims have to be true if the example is to play its role in the context of the analogical argument. But while each claim, taken on its own, and considered in a certain light, can strike us as plausible, a little reflection reveals that they cannot be plausibly combined. It cannot be plausibly claimed *both* that the subject genuinely sees the match *and* that the fact of his doing so is subject to the relevant kind of decomposition.

Let us start by considering the perceptual claim—that the viewer genuinely sees the match. As I have said, we find this claim initially plausible. But the reason why we do is that, when we initially focus on its credentials, we think about the situation in the perspective of the viewer himself. The viewer experiences (experientially interprets) the screen-pattern not as what it is—something *on* the screen—but as a three-dimensional scene of the relevant kind, thereby gaining the impression that he sees *through* the screen to the events on the football field. And, in our initial, common-sense, thoughts about the situation, we directly draw on our own experience of television viewing and adopt the same perspective. Thus we find it natural to think of the viewer as genuinely seeing the match because it always seems *to us* that we are genuinely seeing the relevant televised events when we are in that kind of situation. There is an obvious parallel here with the way in which, quite generally, our common-sense belief that our senses give us perceptual access to the physical world reflects the subjective feel of the phenomenal experiences involved.

Now the first and most obvious point to be noted here is that the adoption of this experiential perspective—of how things subjectively seem to the television viewer—while natural enough in our initial, common-sense consideration of the matter, is not what is needed for the achieving of an objective view. To achieve an objective view—and, of course, it is this that, as philosophers, we seek—we need to *stand back from* the perspective of the viewer and focus on his experiential condition *from the outside*. It is not appropriate just to endorse the way things seem to him—to evaluate the perceptual claim from the standpoint of what his experience invites him to believe. We need to raise the question of *why* things seem that way, and whether that way of seeming is, in reality, *veridical or illusory*. It follows that the plausibility of the perceptual claim, when discerned in the experiential perspective, cannot be of help to the theorist in the development of his analogical argument. Before the claim can be accepted philosophically, its truth has to be confirmed by what emerges when things are examined from an objective standpoint.

But there is also a further and quite independent reason why the theorist needs to move the issue to the objective standpoint. For when we confine ourselves to the experiential perspective, where we find it natural to think of the viewer as genuinely seeing the match, we are not in a position to recognize this perceptual link as *mediated* by the visual registering of the screen-pattern in the relevant sense. Of course, we recognize that the seeing *depends on* the television, and, in particular, on the visual exposure of the screen to the subject. We know full well that if the set were to be switched off, or if someone else were to stand in front of it, contact with the match would be lost. But we regard this dependence on the working of the set and the visibility of the screen as *causal*, rather than *constitutive*: we do not think of the visual contact with the match as *breaking down* into the visual registering of the pattern and the relevant additional facts. The reason is not hard to discern. In the experiential perspective, we are endorsing the way things subjectively seem to the viewer; and to the viewer, who experiences the screen-pattern as itself the three-dimensional scene, it seems that contact with the match is not only genuinely perceptual, but perceptually direct. Indeed, to the viewer, it seems that this contact is directly presentational. So it turns out that the theorist has a double reason for rejecting the experiential perspective and trying to look at things from an objective standpoint. Not only is the objective approach what philosophical enquiry demands; but also, without such an approach, he has no chance of being able to represent the case of the viewer as one of perceptual mediation, and so no chance of being able to appeal to it in his pursuit of the analogical argument.

Now when we consider the situation in an objective way—reflecting on the viewer's condition *from the outside*, and identifying the factors which make it *seem* to him that he is in visual contact with the match—we do indeed come to recognize a strong case for the mediational account. Thus we find it hard to deny that the relationship between the subject and the match is constituted in the way envisaged—that, whatever kind of contact is made with the match, it is secured by, and nothing over and above, the visual registering of the pattern on the screen, its experiential interpretation, the causal process from the match to the pattern, and other facts of the relevantly restricted kind. After all, the only thing which could tempt us to suppose that the seeing is perceptually direct is that this is how it subjectively seems to the viewer himself. But when we consider things from the objective standpoint, the subjective appearance of directness is explained away—explained by the presence of the interpretative element which forms part of the whole experience. We no longer feel any temptation to endorse this appearance, because we see that the factors which create it do not provide any grounds for thinking it true.

Now, this objective way of considering the situation is, as I have just said, precisely what is needed to reach a proper philosophical verdict about it. And so the fact that it enables us to discern a strong, indeed seemingly conclusive, case in favour of the mediational account is something which the theorist could hope to exploit. But the problem now is that his purposes are blocked at the other point. For when we approach things in this way, and recognize the case for acknowledging mediation, we find it correspondingly difficult to accept that what is thus mediated is genuine seeing. Thus if the only fundamental form of visual contact is with the pattern on the screen, and if the only other factors fundamentally involved are such things as the experiential interpretation of this pattern and its causal origin, it seems just obvious that, strictly, the subject does not see the match at all, and that his visual awareness does not reach to anything beyond the screen itself. In other words, once we detach ourselves from the perspective of the viewer, and recognize that the putative perceptual relationship decomposes in the specified way, exactly the same problems beset the perceptual claim in this case as seem to beset all claims to physical-item perception in the framework of SQT. The result, indeed, is the emergence of an exact analogy with what the BRT-theorist postulates in this framework. But it is an analogy which, so far from serving the theorist's purposes, only serves to emphasize the apparent weakness of his position.

It turns out, then, that, however we look at it, the case of the television viewer does not help the cause of the analogical argument. When we first consider the case in common-sense terms, we find it plausible to suppose that the viewer genuinely sees the televised scene. But we only find this plausible because we are focusing on the situation in the perspective of the viewer himself—the perspective of what it is like, subjectively, to have the televisual experience. And not only is this the wrong perspective for the purposes of philosophical enquiry, but it is also one in which we take the seeing to be perceptually direct. On the other hand, once we approach things from an objective standpoint—the standpoint suitable for philosophical enquiry—and come to recognize that the relationship between the viewing subject and the televised scene is mediated in the relevant way, the case becomes exactly analogous to that postulated by the theorist, but in a way which shares, rather than dissolves, the latter's problems. For we are no longer able to suppose that the subject really does see the match, or that his own impression of seeing it is anything more than an illusion.

We have focused exclusively on the case of someone watching football on television. But obviously the conclusions which we have reached apply to all other cases of the same general type.

V

This, as far as I can see, is the end of the road for the whole analogical argument. What the BRT-theorist needs to find, in the physical domain, is a type of case which—ignoring the general problem with the perceptualist assumption—can be unproblematically classified as one of perceptual mediation, and which is similar, in all relevant respects, to what he himself envisages under SQT. But, while there is a variety of possible candidates, none, it seems to me, fits the bill. There are cases, like that of the radar operator, where we ordinarily speak as if there is perceptual mediation, but where we do not take seriously the claim that the R-item is perceived. And there are cases, like that of the television viewer, where we ordinarily take seriously the claim that the R-item is perceived, but where the plausibility of this claim does not survive into that context where, looking at things more objectively, we discern the mediation. The only kinds of case I can think of where there is genuine perceptual mediation—with both the R-item genuinely perceived, and the relationship between the subject and this item relevantly mediated—are those, as with Pauline, where the two perceptual objects are ontologically linked. And, as we stressed at the outset, these cases are quite unsuited to serve as a model for what is envisaged under SQT, where the relevant R-items and I-items are ontologically separate.

4 A DEEPENING OF THE PROBLEM

I

Given the failure of the analogical argument, and the truth of SQT, we are brought to the conclusion that we do not have perceptual access to the external reality. Our perceptual awareness does not reach beyond the sensory items which occur in our own minds, and we only suppose that it does because we experientially interpret these items as themselves external. If I am now, as I believe, writing on a sheet of paper, the paper is not something which I genuinely *see* and the pen is not something which I genuinely *feel*. Nor do I genuinely *hear* the sound of the children playing nearby, or *smell* the aroma of what is cooking in the kitchen, or *taste* the coffee that I sip. Nor are these items things which I, or anyone else, ever could perceive. It goes without saying that all this is both counterintuitive and deeply disturbing. We ordinarily just take it for granted that we have perceptual access to the physical things around us, and it is very hard to adjust to the idea that such a fundamental element of our ordinary ways of thinking has to be abandoned.

The loss of the perceptualist assumption is indeed disturbing. But before we reflect any further on this, we need to notice that the potential problem runs even deeper. For, as well as being hard to accommodate in its own terms, the denial of the perceptualist assumption threatens our ordinary ways of thinking at three further points. If these additional threats are realized, what we face, overall, is the wholesale collapse of our ordinary understanding of the nature of the external reality and our relationship to it.

The first threat is to our conception of the external reality as forming *our world*—the world in which we are located, and within which we live our daily lives. In part, this conception turns on the fact that we think of ourselves as *embodied*: it is the thought that, by possessing bodies, we are concretely present in the external reality, and in some sense form part of it. But the conception also involves the thought that the external reality is something *phenomenologically immanent*: it is something within which we have a perceptual viewpoint, and whose contents are, in appropriate circumstances, perceptually accessible to us in the perspective of that viewpoint. And, in respect of how we ordinarily think about the reality, and its relationship to us, it is surely *this* aspect of our conception which plays the dominant role. As a result, it is not easy to see how, once we have rejected the perceptualist assumption, we can continue to regard the external reality as forming our world in any but a highly attenuated sense.

The second threat is to our conception of the *character* of the items which the external reality contains. We have a rich stock of concepts by which we ordinarily classify the things we believe to be found in the physical world—concepts like *tree, river, mountain, house, car, pen*, and so on. But, on the face of it, such concepts involve thinking of the objects to which they apply as disposed, in suitable conditions, to reveal their presence to us under certain forms of sensible appearance; and, of course, an object cannot have a sensible appearance except to someone who is *perceiving* it. Thus to think of something as a *tree*, or at least as a tree of a typical sort, it seems that we have to think of it as something which is disposed to reveal itself, perceptually, under certain characteristically tree-type forms of appearance—something, for example, which would look a certain (arboreal) way when viewed from a certain distance, or whose various portions would, according to their specific shape and texture, feel in certain ways when held or handled. And the same general pattern seems to hold for all the other familiar sortal concepts of this kind. This does not mean, of course, that the objects which fall under these concepts possess the relevant dispositions to sensible appearance *essentially*—that they are logically incapable of existing without them. Obviously, an object's possession of a phenomenal disposition depends on a number of factors (including our own physiological and psychological constitution) which are not essential to its existence. But that still allows the dispositional modes of appearance to be crucial to whether, in the actual world, the objects count as being of the relevant types. To take an analogy, it is not essential to the individual Moses that he did any of the things attributed to him in the Bible. But we can hardly count anyone in the actual world as Moses—as satisfying our identifying concept of Moses—unless he did at least some of these things, and perhaps even certain of them in particular. In a similar way, it seems that we lose our conceptual grip on what it is to be a physical object of one of these familiar types unless we are able to think of the object as the sort of thing which is equipped to perceptually manifest itself to us in certain sensible ways. And if this is really so, then the conclusion that we have no perceptual access to the external reality entails that this reality does not contain such things at all.

The third threat is to our ordinary belief that we are able, through our sensory experiences, to gain *knowledge* of the external reality—to acquire information about the world that we ordinarily take ourselves to perceive. The denial of perceptual access does not *immediately* commit us to denying epistemic access: there is no self-evident contradiction in insisting that, while our experiences are not physically perceptive, they still serve to furnish us with physical information. But, for obvious reasons, the denial of perceptual access does call our possession of epistemic access into question. For we normally take it for granted not only that we perceive external items, but that it is precisely *through* such perception that we gain, directly or indirectly, all our information about them. We assume that it is *because* the external reality is perceptually open to scrutiny that we can discern the existence and character of what it contains.

This epistemological issue is, I think, the most important. Moreover, it could well prove to be crucial to our handling of the other two. For if we could find some satisfactory way of eliminating the threat in this area—of showing that we do, after all, retain a rich epistemic contact with the external reality—then the other two threats might be seen as correspondingly diminished, or their consequences mitigated. Thus if it turns out that our sensory experiences still serve to supply information about the external reality and our place within it, then this reality might still be thought of as *our world* in some decent sense—and maybe a sense which at least takes us some way in the direction of our ordinary conception of the reality as ours *phenomenologically*. And even if the external objects are not capable of having a genuine sensible appearance (being inaccessible to perception), the fact that they reveal their presence through the experiences they cause, and that these experiences (or the experiential states which they instantiate) represent certain types of sensible situation, might be viewed as some kind of substitute—maybe even sufficient to allow the objects to qualify as instances of the familiar kinds. The preservation of epistemic contact would also, presumably, do something to mitigate the psychological disturbance of relinquishing the perceptualist assumption itself. For although it remains difficult to adjust to the idea that we do not have the perceptual capacities we normally take for granted, this adjustment would at least be easier if we knew that the lack of perceptual access did not affect our epistemic access. At least we would not have to think of our situation as like that of someone who had lost his powers of sensory perception *in the normal sense*—for example, someone who, as a result of some degenerative disease, had lost the use of all his sense-organs.

But all of this is, at the moment, purely hypothetical. What we have to do first is to look into the epistemological issue in its own terms, and try to establish exactly what epistemic links with the external reality remain in place now that perceptual access has been blocked. Granted this loss of perceptual access, in what ways, if at all, do our experiences still serve to provide us with knowledge of (with genuine information about) the external situation?

II

The first thing we need to realize, in approaching this epistemological issue, is that there are two quite different questions that we could be raising. Both questions are concerned with the issue of what kind of epistemic access to the external reality we can justifiably think of ourselves as possessing, now that we have been obliged to deny the existence of perceptual access. But they differ in respect of how we envisage the psychological situation of the subjects—ourselves as the *objects* of our philosophical investigation—about whom this issue is raised.

One of the questions is this. Granted our lack of perceptual access, in what ways, if any, do our experiences serve to provide us with knowledge about the external reality *in our normal, pre-philosophically-reflective, state*— the state in which we assume ourselves to be genuine percipients of the physical things around us? In raising this question, we would be envisaging a sharp contrast between our psychological situation as philosophical investigators and our psychological situation as the subjects under investigation. As investigators, we would know that the external reality is beyond the reach of perception. But as the subjects under investigation, the perceptualist assumption, and all the other endowments of common-sense thought, would still be in place. So the aim of the investigation would be to find out what kind of epistemic access to the external reality we, from the standpoint of philosophical enlightenment, would be justified in attributing to ourselves at the point of common-sense naivety, where we take perceptual access for granted.

The other question we could be raising is this. In what ways, if any, do our experiences provide us with knowledge about the external reality *once we have come to recognize the truth about our perceptual situation*? Here, we are precisely not envisaging a contrast between our psychological situation as philosophical investigators and as the subjects whose epistemic capacities are at issue. What is being investigated is not the nature of our epistemic capacities when the lack of perceptual access is combined with our retention of the perceptualist assumption, but the nature of our capacities when the lack of perceptual access is combined with our acknowledgement of that lack. In other words, having arrived at this stage in our philosophical enquiry, in which we have come to recognize that the external reality is beyond the reach of perception, we would now be trying to determine what we can take ourselves to know, or to be capable of finding out, about it *in our enlightened condition*.

Both these questions are philosophically important, and relevant to our concerns. What is crucial is that we should not confuse them. And such confusion is all too easy, precisely because the subjects whose epistemic capacities are under investigation and the subjects who are conducting the investigation are one and the same. So, with the distinction clearly before us, let us look at the two questions in turn—beginning with the question of the nature of our capacities in our ordinary, naive psychological state, where perceptual access is taken for granted.

To give us a point of focus, we can turn again to the case of Pauline and the apple. Pauline has a visual experience as of seeing an apple, or, more narrowly, an apple-type colour-patch, at a certain distance in front of her. This experience takes the form of the presentational occurrence of a visual sense-quale, together with an externalist interpretation imposed on it—an interpretation which represents the quale as an external colour-patch, presented to her in a certain perspective. Pauline, in her pre-philosophical innocence, endorses this interpretation, and believes herself to be seeing, and presentationally seeing, just such an item. This belief is false. But, in holding it, she also believes that there is such an item currently in front of her; and, given a suitably liberal understanding of 'current' (so that we do not quibble over the fact that there is an interval between the relevant time-slice of the apple and the visual experience which reflects it), and given a Lockean account of what is involved in the item's possession of the relevant colour (so that we take this to consist in its disposition to affect human colour-experience in certain ways), this second belief is true. The question now is: can we think of this further environmental belief (understood as true) as an item of genuine knowledge—genuine information—supplied to Pauline by the occurrence of her visual experience and its links with the environment? This question is only explicitly focused on one particular case. But the answer we give will extend to other situations of the same general type, and thereby imply a general answer to the issue which concerns us—of how our epistemic capacities fare, given both our lack of perceptual access and our naive assumption that we have it.

There is an obvious case for returning a *negative* answer—for saying that Pauline's environmental belief does *not* meet the requirements for genuine knowledge. Pauline acquires this belief on the basis of her perceptual belief—her belief that she sees an item of the relevant type in front of her. In saying that she acquires it *on this basis*, I do not mean that she *consciously infers* the truth of the environmental proposition from the truth of the perceptual; it may well be that she does not consciously think of these propositions at all, let alone perform a conscious act of inference. But even so, it is only because her experience invites her to believe that the relevant type of environmental situation is perceptually present that it invites her to believe that it currently obtains, and only in so far as she responds positively to the former invitation that she responds positively to the latter. And, in that sense, the acquiring of the environmental belief is entirely covered by, and dependent on, the acquiring of the perceptual. But, of course, the perceptual belief is, we are assuming, false. It is the appropriate belief for her to acquire, given the nature of her experience and her acceptance of the perceptualist assumption; but we have already agreed that the external reality is not accessible to perception. So the situation is one in which Pauline has acquired a true belief on the basis of one that is false. And, for familiar reasons, this seems to rule it out as a case of genuine knowledge: it seems to be just a special case of the notorious Gettier-type situation, in which the epistemic credentials of some true and properly evidenced belief are impugned by the falsity that lies behind it.[7] Thus it seems to be of the same general kind as a case in which, say, John believes, on good evidence, that his brother Albert is in France, and so believes that some member of his family is in France, when it so happens that (1) despite the evidence, Albert is *not* in France, and (2) by chance, and unbeknown to John, his sister Alice *is*. John's belief that some member of his family is in France is then true, and held on good evidence (the evidence that Albert is in France), but, given the falsity of its basis, is not a case of knowledge. Likewise, it seems, Pauline's belief that there is the relevant sort of item in front of her is true, and, at least relative to her common-sense framework, held on good evidence (the evidence of her senses), but, because of the falsity of the perceptual belief on which it rests, is not a case of knowledge. The only difference seems to be that, with the right kind of rational reflection, Pauline could, in principle, discover the falsity of her perceptual belief without recourse to further evidence. But this ability could hardly be thought of as improving the epistemic credentials of her situation.

It might be countered that the apparent analogy with Gettier cases is only superficial. In the Gettier examples, or at least the ones that tend to dominate the literature, it is just good fortune that the relevant false belief, which forms the basis, leads the subject to the acceptance of a truth. Thus if John's sole reason for believing that a member of his family is in France is his belief that Albert is in France (which is false), and if Alice's presence in France has no influence on his acquisition of either belief, then the fact that the first belief turns out to be true is purely fortuitous: it is just a coincidence—a lucky accident—that the conclusion which his false belief logically forces on him happens to fit the facts in the way it does. But, in the case of Pauline, it is *not* just a lucky accident that her erroneous perceptual belief leads her to the environmental truth. In the first place, it is precisely because there is an item of the relevant type in front of her, and affecting

---

[7] See E. Gettier, 'Is justified true belief knowledge?', *Analysis*, 23 (1963), 121–3.

her visual system in the appropriate way, that Pauline comes to think that she sees such an item: if there had been a different sort of item present, then (with her visual system working in the same way) the content of her perceptual belief, and the environmental belief it gave rise to, would have altered accordingly. And secondly, the way in which the environmental belief has been brought about in this particular case is an instance of the operation of a general causal system, whereby the character of the subject's environment reliably gives rise to a true environmental characterization within the content of a false perceptual belief. And so, as well as its causal dependence on the particular circumstances that make it true, her acquisition of the environmental belief exemplifies a general system of truth-reliable acquisition. These two factors—the causal dependence on the truth-making circumstances and the truth-reliability of the general system—are absent from the standard Gettier cases. Thus John's belief that some member of his family is in France does not causally depend on the state of affairs that makes it true; nor, in the relevant respect, is the general system by which John has reached this belief truth-reliable, since it will tend to result in falsity in cases where the mediating belief is false. The absence of these factors in the standard cases might be thought crucial to their failure to qualify as cases of knowledge. And correspondingly, their presence in the case of Pauline might be thought to secure its epistemic credentials, notwithstanding the falsity of the perceptual belief involved.

This is a tempting idea, but nonetheless mistaken. There is no denying that the case of Pauline and the standard Gettier cases do differ in the ways we have specified. And it may also be true (this is not an issue which I want to pursue here) that the distinctive factors in the Pauline case—the causal dependence of her belief on the truth-making circumstances and the truth-reliability of the general system involved—have some crucial role to play in securing the epistemic status of beliefs that qualify as knowledge, or at least have such a role in some significant range of cases. But it would be quite wrong to suppose that it is the absence of these factors which is the central point about the Gettier situation and what underlies our intuition that the cases involved are epistemically defective. For what makes these cases defective, and prevents our classifying them as cases of knowledge, is something much simpler and less controversial. It is that knowledge, whatever else, must be of the *truth*—an awareness, an intellectual grasp, of *how things are*—and that where a belief is based on a false belief, then, as a claimant to count as an awareness of how things are, it shares in, and is undermined by, that falsity. Thus consider again the case of John's belief that some member of his family is in France. What immediately reveals to us that this is not a genuine instance of knowledge is not that it does not have the right sort of causal dependence on what makes it true (that it would have occurred even if Alice had been elsewhere), or that the general system of belief-acquisition involved is not truth-reliable. What reveals its epistemic deficiency is simply that, because it is only held on the basis of another, stronger, belief which is false (the belief that his brother Albert is in France), we see the truth of the belief as a kind of sham: it is a truth which pertains to the proposition on to which the belief is directed, but does not reflect any quality of veracity in the believing itself. The proposition is, in itself, true: a member of his family is indeed in France. But John's believing it is, in effect, an instance of error, since it amounts to no more than, and reflects no insights beyond, his holding of the erroneous belief on which this believing is based. In short, we reject this as a case of knowledge simply because, as soon as we dig beneath the surface, we see it as, in substance, an instance of falsity rather than of truth. But if so, then the same point will carry over to the case of Pauline too. It is not purely accidental that Pauline reaches a true belief about her environment, in the way that it is accidental that John comes to believe a true proposition about his family. But what is crucial is that, in the context in which it is held, this belief amounts to no more than, and reflects no insights beyond, the false belief that a certain sort of item is perceived. And because it amounts to no more than this false belief, it has no better claim to count as knowledge.

We must conclude, then, that the epistemic credentials of the Pauline case are no better than those of Gettier cases in general. And this assessment will extend to all other cases of the same general kind, where the subject acquires a true belief about his environment on the basis of a belief about what environmental situation he perceives. It follows that the only way in which it might still turn out that we have epistemic access to the external reality would be if we have methods of finding out about this reality that do not rely on such perceptual beliefs—methods that we can employ in the context of an explicit recognition that the perceptualist assumption is false.

III

This brings us to the second of our two epistemological questions. Given the Gettier point, we know that, in so far as we rely on the perceptualist assumption, or the specific perceptual beliefs which entail it, knowledge of the external reality is blocked. But what is our epistemological situation in our state of philosophical enlightenment, where we have corrected our ordinary naive view, and accepted that external items are not accessible to sense-perception? Is there some other way in which our experiences can serve to provide us with knowledge of the existence and character of these items?

Let us, for the moment, continue to focus on the case of Pauline, but a Pauline who, having already gone through the appropriate philosophical reasoning prior to her encounter with the apple, has reached the conclusion that neither she nor anyone else has perceptual access to the physical world. In this enlightened state, she then has the relevant visual experience. This experience, embodying how things sensibly appear to her, carries the impression of being presentationally perceptive of an apple-type sensible item, located at a certain distance in front of her. But, bringing her philosophical knowledge to bear on the case, she concludes that this impression is illusory: the only item genuinely presented is the sense-quale, which occurs internally, and the impression that she sees something external is due to the fact that, as an integral part of the experience, the quale itself is interpreted as external. Equipped with this insight, she avoids the mistake of *automatically* acquiring the corresponding environmental belief—acquiring it by a simple endorsement of how things subjectively seem. So the question now is: can she, in some less direct way, use her knowledge of the character of the experience to acquire a knowledge of the relevant environmental situation? Or more generally, can she use this experiential knowledge to find out at least *something* about the nature of the external reality?

Well, this knowledge, *on its own*, does not tell her anything. But, of course, Pauline comes into this situation already equipped with a whole stock of beliefs—items of putative information—about the physical world and her place within it. Although she has been forced to relinquish her former assumption of perceptual access, this putative information might make it reasonable for her to believe that, in her case, visual experiences tend to be more or less representationally accurate (or to be so with appropriate adjustments for time and for the Lockean account of the secondary qualities). And it might also make it reasonable for her to believe that, in the present instance, the likelihood of accuracy is particularly high—with nothing to suggest that the normal tendency has been disturbed, and with the representation involved being consonant with what she independently knows about her environmental situation. On this basis, she might come to the conclusion that things are environmentally as her experience represents them, and that, consequently, there is (was fractionally earlier) an item of the relevant sort in front of her. If she reaches this conclusion, should we then count it as *epistemic*—as something which Pauline gen-uinely *knows*?

It only takes a little reflection to see that we should not. To begin with, given the nature of the reasoning on which it is based, the most that Pauline is entitled to believe is that the relevant conclusion has some *likelihood* of being true. And even if this likelihood happens to be high, it does not suf-fice to turn the conclusion into something genuinely *known*. This is not because genuine knowledge requires Cartesian indubitability, where the subject is incapable of even envisaging a way in which his belief could turn out to be mistaken. But obviously a subject cannot be said to *know* some-thing if the basis on which he accepts it does not even purport to *settle* the issue. And, in the case envisaged, the basis of the belief clearly does not pur-port to settle the issue, being merely a matter of the general *tendency* of the subject's visual experiences to be representationally accurate and the *like-lihood* that this tendency is operative on the particular occasion. However much support for the conclusion these factors provide, we cannot think of Pauline as *knowing its truth*, any more than we can ascribe knowledge to someone who, having bought a lottery ticket, and accurately calculated the chances, comes to believe (correctly) that he will not win first prize.

But there is also a more far-reaching point. We are supposing that Pauline arrives at her conclusion, about the current (fractionally earlier) state of her environment, by combining her knowledge of the character of her visual experience with all the things she already believes about the physical world and her place within it. And we have so far noted that, at best, this would entitle her to regard the conclusion as something whose truth is *likely*, rather than something whose truth has been *settled*. But what also needs to be stressed is that this stock of background beliefs itself fails to meet the conditions for knowledge. These beliefs, after all, have not been acquired by a priori reasoning or by divine revelation: they have been built up, over the years, in response to phenomenal experience perceptually con-strued—by the subject's constant accumulation and processing of items of purportedly perceptual information. For the Gettier reason already high-lighted, we cannot count these beliefs as genuine knowledge because of the perceptualist error which systematically underlies them. Moreover, in her philosophically enlightened state, Pauline herself is in a position to see this. She knows that she has no perceptual access to the external reality, and she has already used this insight to avoid an automatic acceptance of the envi-ronmental proposition which her current experience invites her to believe. She only has to apply this same insight to the origins of the relevant back-ground beliefs to see that their epistemic credentials are undermined. And, of course, once she has rejected their epistemic status in this way, she will no longer be able even to take their truth for granted: recognizing that the beliefs have been developed on the basis of false perceptual beliefs, in the general framework of the false perceptualist assumption, she will recognize that she is not entitled to rely on them until some new grounds for holding them have been found.

The upshot is that, in her philosophically enlightened state, Pauline is not only forced to abandon any claim to be the acquirer of perceptual information, but finds herself, for that very reason, confronting a radical sceptical challenge to all her physical beliefs. Prior to recognizing the falsity of the perceptualist assumption, she regarded these beliefs as items of knowledge, reflecting her capacity to perceptually register environmental states of affairs and gauge their significance. With the recognition that she has no perceptual access to the physical world, she is forced to concede that these beliefs do not meet the requirements for knowledge, and that she no longer has any rational entitlement to accept the propositions involved until some new justification—not depending on claims to perceptual knowledge—is produced. And, of course, Pauline here stands in for all of us in our state of philosophical enlightenment. Once he has recognized the falsity of the perceptualist assumption and applied that recognition to his own system of physical beliefs, each of us is forced to reject the epistemic status of these beliefs, and look for some new way of establishing their credentials if he wants to retain them at all.

Given that we can no longer assume the truth of our ordinary physical beliefs, we can neither use them as a source of knowledge about the external reality nor combine them with items of experiential knowledge to reach conclusions about it. The questions we now have to consider are: Do we have any other way of acquiring information about this reality? And do we have a way which will restore the credentials of what we ordinarily believe?

Two things, I think, are clear. First, since we can no longer take anything physical for granted, any way of trying to gain information about the external reality will have to rely, for its evidence, exclusively on facts about our own mentality. And, of course, these facts will have to be ones which can be formulated without presuppositions about the contents of the physical world; they cannot, for example, include facts about how subjects are mentally related to physical items, such as the fact of someone's remembering a certain physical event, or of his aiming to reach a certain physical destination. Indeed, in practice, the relevant facts will have to be free from externalist presuppositions altogether, since, with the complete loss of physical information, there are no aspects of the external situation which can be assumed at this stage. Secondly, given these restrictions on the nature of the evidence, our only hope of reaching well-founded conclusions about the external reality would be by inference to the best explanation—by reasoning that certain externalist claims are worthy of acceptance, or of acceptance as probably true, because they best explain the psychological facts in question.[8] The most obvious line of approach here would be to appeal to the distinctive character of human sensory experience. Thus we might begin by pointing to the fact that the course of such experience exhibits certain themes and regularities—ones which, taken at face value, systematically suggest the presence of a three-dimensional world of the sort whose existence we ordinarily accept. We might then insist that these themes and regularities call for explanation—that they are too pervasive to be credibly attributed to chance. And finally, we might claim that the appropriate way to explain them is by supposing that the sort of world which they suggest, and in which we ordinarily believe, actually exists and constrains human experience to reflect its character. Given that this is the kind of reasoning on which we would have to rely—from facts about human mentality to conclusions about how they should be explained—what we now have to determine is whether we can employ it effectively. Can we use such reasoning to give us significant access to the external reality? And can we thereby use it to give us a rational entitlement to our ordinary physical beliefs?

Well, if what has to be achieved is *knowledge* of the external reality, it is clear that we cannot. For, whatever the merits of this kind of reasoning, any conclusions it yields are bound to be, to some degree, *conjectural*—conclusions which may enjoy some high level of *plausibility*, but cannot be regarded as *established*. There is already bound to be an element of conjecture in the supposition that the relevant psychological facts call for explanation: the suggestion that there is nothing further which accounts for them may be very implausible, but can hardly be excluded altogether. But the main point is that, even if we grant the need for explanation, there are going to be alternative forms of explanation available; and although there may be reasons for regarding some explanatory hypotheses as more credible than others, we have no way of *establishing*, and thereby coming to *know*, that a given hypothesis is correct.

---

[8] I am aware, of course, that some philosophers have tried to move from the psychological evidence to externalist conclusions by deductive reasoning alone. Descartes, in his *Meditations*, is an obvious (and notorious) example. These attempts all seem to me to be vulnerable to clear-cut objections, though I do not have space to discuss the matter here.

To illustrate, suppose we are minded to press the line of argument envisaged above, where we appeal to the themes and regularities of human sensory experience, claim that these call for explanation, and explain them by postulating the existence of the sort of world which they at face value suggest. We can think of this explanation as the *standard* one, since the kind of external reality which it postulates is the one in which we ordinarily believe. But it is not difficult to devise alternative (non-standard) explanations, which postulate a different kind of external reality, but accord it the same influence on human experience. For example:

1. We could suppose that, instead of containing a *single* three-dimensional space, the external reality contains *two* such spaces, which, between them, cover the same ground. And, to explain why the sensory factors *suggest* the existence of a single space, we could suppose that, although separate, the two spaces are nomologically organized, in respect of both their internal processes and the effects of these processes on human experience, as if they were adjacent parts of a single space—a space in which a certain two-dimensional boundary of one of them coincides with a certain two-dimensional boundary of the other. This would mean, for instance, that when an object pursuing a straight-line course in one space reaches the relevant boundary, it gradually disappears into it, to be replaced by the simultaneous emergence of an exactly similar object at the corresponding place on the relevant boundary of the other—an object which then continues on a straight-line course in the appropriate direction. And it would mean that, whenever such a two-space process occurs, nothing results in the realm of human experience to give the slightest indication that it *is* a two-space process, rather than the continuous movement of a single object in a single space.

Or again:

2. For simplicity (and this is just to keep the details of the example manageable), let us assume that, in its scientifically developed form, the standard account takes the fundamental external reality to consist of a three-dimensional space, certain types of mobile particle distributed over space and time, and certain laws of nature governing this distribution. Then, as an alternative, we could suppose that the external reality comprises a collection of (non-human) minds; and to explain how this reality generates the relevant themes and

regularities in human sensory experience, we could suppose that these minds are nomologically organized, in respect of both their own mentality and the effects of this mentality on human experience, in a way that structurally mirrors the organization which the standard account ascribes to the particles in space. There are various ways of doing this, according to the kind of mentality involved and the kind of way in which the quasi-spatial organization is imposed on it. One neat way would be to suppose that there are three loudness-degrees X, Y, and Z such that: (1) at each time, each of the relevant minds has an auditory sense-experience consisting of the occurrence of three simple sound-qualia: a pitch at X, a pitch at Y, and a pitch at Z; (2) relative to a correlation of pitch-triples with triples of co-ordinates for spatial position, and relative to a suitable correlation between types of mind and types of particle, the laws which govern the distribution of sound-qualia over the relevant minds at times exactly match the laws which, under the standard account, govern the distribution of spatial positions over particles at times; and (3) relative to these same correlations, the ways in which types of auditory situation and process in this domain of minds are disposed to affect human experience exactly match the ways in which, under the standard account, we would need to think of types of spatial situation and process in the domain of particles as disposed to affect human experience.

These are just two of a whole range of non-standard hypotheses which we could entertain. There may be factors which make such hypotheses less plausible than what we ordinarily believe (this is an issue which we shall address presently). But even if we can show them to be less plausible, this does not amount to showing that they are *false*, and that the standard account is *true*. And assuming that the hypotheses are internally coherent, and accurately cover the course of human experience, it is clear that the kind of reasoning envisaged is not equipped to settle the issue in that way.

The fact that we have to rely on inference to the best explanation to reach conclusions about the external reality, and that any conclusions of such reasoning are bound to be, to some degree, conjectural, means that *knowledge* of the external reality is beyond our reach. And this already, on its own, settles the epistemological issue in the form in which it was originally posed—of whether, and if so in what ways, such knowledge is available to us in our philosophically enlightened state. The most that we can now hope for is that, by employing the explanatory form of reasoning envisaged, we can reach conclusions about the external reality which, while not *established*, are at least *well supported*, and that these conclusions will allow us to regain some reasonable level of confidence in our ordinary physical beliefs. Such an outcome, of course, would not be without value: it would at least provide some compensation for the loss of genuine knowledge.

However, even with respect to this more modest aspiration, it turns out that we can make no progress, and that the form of reasoning envisaged can deliver nothing of significance.

The first point to note is that, even when we restrict our attention to the domain of our own mentality, there are severe limits on the kinds of facts that we can use as evidence. For a great deal of what we ordinarily take ourselves to know about the composition of this domain is only available on the assumption that our epistemic access to the physical world is already in place. And knowledge which is dependent on that assumption is precisely *not* available in the present context.

The most obvious aspect of this stems from the fact that the mentality in question is distributed over a large number of distinct subjects, and that each subject only has direct access to his own mental states and activities. Thus Pauline is immediately conscious of the visual experience she is currently undergoing, and can no doubt recall, in an introspective fashion, some of her experiences, and other mental states, on earlier occasions. But, in so far as she has information about the mental lives of others, this is because their mentality is in some way *physically* revealed to her—in the basic case, by her being able to identify other subjects by their bodies, and gauge their mentality by their behaviour and utterances. Without epistemic access to the physical world, she would lose the whole epistemological framework in which her putative knowledge of such mentality is acquired and retained. And this, of course, is the situation for each of us: for information about the mental lives of others, each of us depends, at every point, on information about how things stand physically. The consequence is that, instead of being able to invoke our knowledge of the mentality of others to help sustain conclusions about the external reality, we find that the sceptical challenge to our physical beliefs extends to our other-minds beliefs as well. These too turn out to be beliefs which we are not rationally entitled to retain until we find some new and independent justification for holding them.

But, in fact, the evidential possibilities are even more constrained. As we have said, the most obvious way of trying to reach conclusions about the external reality would be by appealing to the distinctive themes and regularities in human sensory experience. And it might seem, at first, that even if each subject only has initial access to his own mind, there is still, for each, the prospect of being able to appeal to these factors in his own case. But the trouble is that, as well as depending on physical knowledge for his information about the mental lives of others, a subject also depends on such knowledge for the bulk of his information about his own experiential past. Certainly this is how things stand with me. In my pre-sceptical state, I believe that my past experiences have collectively exhibited the relevant themes and regularities. But the reason I believe this is not that I possess, or possess anything remotely approaching, a comprehensive recollective record of my past experiential biography, and can discern the relevant factors by directly surveying its contents. It is rather that, not having much in the way of a direct record of this biography, I nonetheless find myself with a rich stock of beliefs about the physical world and my place, as a predominantly veridical percipient, within it; and, on this basis, I assume that my experiences, being predominantly veridically perceptive, have exhibited the themes and regularities which this would require. The knowledge of my experiential past that I now possess independently of my present physical beliefs is relatively meagre and, divorced from the framework of these beliefs, of little evidential value. Even where I can directly recall a past experience, or experiential sequence, I rely on my putative knowledge of the physical circumstances of its occurrence to determine its temporal relations to my experiences on other occasions and its remoteness from the present. There is no way in which I could develop a plausible explanatory inference on the basis of the experiential knowledge that remains, once everything that depends on my physical beliefs has been subtracted. And I assume that other subjects will find themselves in a similar situation.

These twin restrictions on the kinds of psychological evidence to which we can appeal already make it hard to see how, in practice, an effective explanatory inference could be constructed. Without access to the mentality of others or to the bulk of one's own experiential past, the evidential base is bound to seem rather thin in relation to the inferential weight it will have to bear—even allowing that we are only wanting it to provide *good support* for the relevant externalist claims, rather than to *establish their truth*. There seems to be no real prospect of being able to use such a restricted domain of evidence to achieve anything of significance.

But there is also a further reason why the possibility of an effective explanatory inference is excluded; and this is a reason which applies *in principle*, and irrespective of the extent of our access to the psychological facts that might be evidentially relevant. As I have already stressed, whatever psychological facts are cited as evidence, there is bound to be a range of alternative hypotheses which could be advanced to explain them. To provide good grounds for accepting a particular hypothesis, or for accepting it as probably true, we would need to do two things. First, we would need to show that the relevant psychological facts call for explanation— that there is a strong, and perhaps overwhelming, case for assuming that there is something further which accounts for them. And secondly, we would need to show that the hypothesis in question is significantly more plausible than its rivals, and indeed than the totality of its rivals disjoined. But even if it is possible to meet the first of these requirements, a little reflection reveals that there is no prospect of meeting the second, or coming anywhere near meeting it.

The problem is that, in the context in which we are presently considering things, there is hardly anything to which we can appeal to gauge plausibility. In normal cases where we are trying to settle questions of plausibility, we take for granted our knowledge of the basic structure of the external reality, and the modes of causation that are naturally possible within it. And in trying to decide between rival explanations of a certain phenomenon, we are able to rely on this knowledge for guidance: we are able to judge that one hypothesis is more plausible than another because it accords better with the information we already have about how the world works. But, in the present context, where the nature of the external reality is initially concealed, no such guidance is available. The only principles of plausibility on which we can rely will have to be of purely *a priori* kind— endorsed by reason alone. This is a very severe limitation. Indeed, assuming the coherence of the hypotheses whose relative merits are under consideration, the only factor to which I think we could now appeal would be that of *simplicity*: one hypothesis would be deemed to be more plausible than another because it represents things as structured and organized in a simpler way. For example, if we are looking for an explanation of the themes and regularities in human experience, the first of the non-standard hypotheses we mentioned earlier, in which the external reality is taken to contain two spaces, organized as if they were one, is, in an obvious sense, a more complex theory (representing things as structured and organized in a more complex way) than the standard hypothesis, which postulates a single space. And, on these grounds, the standard hypothesis might be thought more plausible.

Now considerations of simplicity may be of help in certain areas. But what is also clear is that they do not suffice to solve the whole problem. In the example just mentioned, the rival hypotheses share a common approach: both are offering an explanation of the relevant features of sensory experience in terms of an external spatial reality. There is a straightforward sense in which the explanation in terms of two spaces is more complex than the explanation in terms of one. And there is a correspondingly straightforward way in which we can think of this difference as making the standard account more plausible than the alternative. For the additional complexity of this alternative is *needless—gratuitous—*relative to the approach it exemplifies. The alternative hypothesis is, as it were, just a deliberately complexified version of the standard hypothesis, and it seems perverse to introduce this complexity when the experiential phenomena do not require it for their adequate explanation in spatial terms. But, in addition to having to adjudicate between alternative hypotheses *within the framework of a common approach*, there is also the need to adjudicate *between alternative approaches*—approaches which seek to explain the relevant data in ways that are radically different. And, in this area, considerations of simplicity are of no assistance. There is often no clear-cut sense in which one approach qualifies as simpler than another. And, more crucially, in so far as we are able to make comparisons of simplicity at all, there is no rationale for thinking that the outcome has any bearing on the issue of plausibility. For any difference in simplicity that may emerge is, in effect, an incidental consequence of a more fundamental difference which needs to be evaluated in its own terms.

We can already see this in the case of the second of the two non-standard hypotheses mentioned earlier, where we envisage the external reality as consisting in a collection of minds, whose mentality is organized in a way which structurally mirrors the organization of particles in space. We can think of simpler and more complex ways of developing this hypothesis, according to the precise method by which the quasi-spatial organization is mentalistically realized, and perhaps the simpler versions should be deemed more plausible. But there is no way in which considerations of relative simplicity could reveal whether this hypothesis is more or less plausible than the quite different approach of the standard account, which postulates an external space. To begin with, there is not even a clear-cut answer to the question of which approach has the greater simplicity. Looking at things in one way, we might say that the non-standard approach is simpler, since, by substituting minds for particles, it is able to dispense with the spatial medium. Looking at things in another way, we might say that this hypothesis is more complex, since, precisely by dispensing with this medium, it requires a more complex way of covering what is standardly covered by spatial position. But, however we might care to resolve the issue of simplicity, it is in any case clear that the issue of plausibility cannot be settled in these terms. If there is nothing else which counts against a spatial explanation of the experiential phenomena, the increase in ontological complexity incurred by postulating a spatial medium does not put the standard account at a disadvantage. And likewise, if there is nothing else which counts against the mentalistic explanation, the increase in complexity involved in the substitute for spatial position creates no problems for the non-standard account. Considerations of relative simplicity simply have no relevance at this point.

An even more striking illustration is the issue between the standard explanation of the experiential phenomena and the theory proposed by Bishop Berkeley. All the explanations which we have so far considered have been *mechanistic*: they have involved postulating an external reality whose internal processes and effects on human experience are controlled by *laws*. But Berkeley held that our sensory experiences are directly caused by divine volition, and that the world-suggestive themes and regularities they exhibit have been chosen by God to fulfil his purposes for our lives. We can compare the simplicity of Berkeley's theory with that of theories of a similar (supernatural-agency) kind. For example, we can rate it as simpler than a theory which replaces God by a team of deities, who have to combine their volitional efforts before an experiential outcome is produced. And there is at least a case for concluding that its greater simplicity renders Berkeley's account more plausible than this polytheistic alternative. But there is no prospect of being able to appeal to simplicity to settle whether the Berkeleian account is more or less plausible than what we ordinarily believe. It is even harder than in the previous case to find any objective basis for making a comparison of relative simplicity across such an ideological gulf. And it is just obvious that, whatever we can achieve by way of comparison, any attempt to use this as the means of reaching a verdict about plausibility would be wholly inappropriate.

Considerations of simplicity, then, do not enable us to decide between radically different explanatory approaches—as in the issue between the spatial approach of the standard account and the postulation of particle-simulating minds, and the issue between the mechanistic approach of the standard account and the theistic position of Berkeley. And, in the present context, where we are not allowed to assume anything in advance about the nature of the external reality, nothing, as far as I can see, will serve to settle issues of this kind. If the non-standard approaches tend to strike us as intuitively less plausible, this is simply because the standard approach is what coincides with our ordinary beliefs, and it requires a special intellectual effort to stand back from these beliefs and look at things in a properly neutral way. Since different approaches represent the external reality in quite different ways—sometimes, as in the contrast between the standard and the Berkeleian accounts, in *utterly* different ways—it follows that there is no prospect of being able to use the kind of explanatory reasoning envisaged to establish even the likely truth of any significant claim about the external situation. And this is so, whatever the extent of our access to the relevant psychological evidence.

This brings our epistemological investigation to its cheerless conclusion. Throughout, we have been trying to determine the nature of our epistemological situation in our state of philosophical enlightenment, where we have come to recognize that we do not have perceptual access to the external reality. And we have been concerned to characterize this situation both in the narrow respect of our capacity to achieve *knowledge* of this reality, and in the broader respect of our capacity to reach conclusions about it which are *well supported*. The nature of the situation, in its various aspects, is now clear:

1. With the recognition that we have no perceptual knowledge of the external reality, we are forced to give up reliance on our ordinary physical beliefs.

2. Without the framework of these beliefs, our only evidence concerning the nature of the external reality comes from what we know about our own mentality; and our only chance of successfully moving from such evidence to externalist conclusions is by inference to the best explanation.

3. This kind of reasoning, on this kind of evidential base, is not equipped to yield *knowledge*, since its conclusions are bound to be, to some degree, *conjectural*.

4. Nor, however, can we even get it to yield, in any significant form, conclusions which are *well supported*, both because of the restrictions on the scope of the psychological evidence to which we can appeal, and, more crucially, because, where there are radically different explanatory approaches, there is no rational way of deciding between them.

In short, in our state of philosophical enlightenment, we are forced into a position of almost total scepticism: we can find no rational basis for retaining our ordinary physical beliefs, nor for reaching any significant conclusions at all about how things externally are, or are likely to be. With the recognition that we cannot monitor it perceptually, we are forced to acknowledge that the external reality is almost wholly inscrutable. Clearly, this is a very disturbing outcome, and how we should ultimately respond to it has yet to be determined.

Before we turn to that question, there is one final point which I want to underline, to help bring the outcome itself into proper perspective.

The sceptical conclusion to which we have been led has stemmed from the recognition that we do not have perceptual access to the external reality. But there is another and more familiar form of sceptical argument, which does not depend on a prior rejection of the perceptualist assumption. Rather, it rests on the weaker point that the subjective character of our phenomenal experiences does not logically guarantee their representational accuracy, and that it is logically possible that, even in their totality, these experiences should be subjectively just as they are, but there be no external reality remotely like the one which they collectively suggest. The way this generates a sceptical challenge is obvious enough. Since we have no way of investigating the external reality except through our experiences, and so have no independent way of checking on their representational accuracy, it is hard to see how we can be justified in putting any trust in what they purport to tell us. And once we have relinquished our trust in them, then, for the reasons we have elaborated, it is hard to see how we can reach any significant conclusions at all about the external situation. In effect, this is the sceptical challenge posed by Descartes's *First Meditation*.

Now it seems to me that, in the dialectical context in which it arises, there is a straightforward way of meeting this traditional challenge. For because it is made purely on the basis of the logical gap between the subjective facts and the external facts, and does not require us to reject in advance the perceptualist assumption, we are in a position to dig our common-sense heels in at the crucial point. We can insist that we just *know* that we have perceptual access to the external reality, and that this access is a rich and reliable source of information about it. And offered in that dialectical context—where nothing has been done in advance to impugn the perceptualist assumption—I think that this is an appropriate response. It might be objected that such a response just ignores the sceptic's point. For how *could* we know that we have perceptual access to the external reality if this is not revealed by the subjective character of the experiences through which that access is supposedly achieved? After all, if the sceptic's envisaged scenario obtained, in which there was no external reality of a kind to match our experiences, we would be none the wiser. So how can we tell that this is not our actual situation? But this rejoinder itself just begs the question. It is true that once we concede that we can only achieve know-ledge of the external reality by appeal to how things stand subjectively, then there is, indeed, no way of establishing the true situation. Our only hope of gauging this situation would be by an inference to the best explanation, and this, as we have seen, does not yield a decisive outcome. But the point about the common-sense response is that it refuses to make this concession. For it claims that the nature of our situation—our perceptual access to the physical world and the perceptual scrutability of its states of affairs—is something *independently clear*: clear without our having to draw inferences from the subjective evidence. Of course, it is not claiming that the occur-rence of our experiences and their subjective character play no role in mak-ing this situation clear; obviously, the situation is only apparent because we have phenomenal experiences, and because they give the impression of being presentationally perceptive of external items. But that does not mean that we have to appeal to the subjective facts as *evidence*. And the sceptic's argument, as we are presently envisaging it, has not succeeded in showing that we do.

No such way of dealing with the sceptical challenge was an option in the context of our own discussion. For what generated this challenge was not the logical gap between the subjective and external facts, but the denial of the perceptualist assumption itself. And so the point where we are able to stand our common-sense ground against the Cartesian sceptic was never available. In effect, with the loss of the perceptualist assumption, we were forced to approach the epistemological issue in the sceptic's own terms—abandoning all our ordinary procedures for finding out about the external reality, and relying entirely on what we could infer from knowledge of our own mentality, narrowly conceived. And, as the argument showed, once we are forced into that dialectical position, we are epistemologically doomed.

IV

With the denial of the perceptualist assumption, we are left with no epis-temic access to the external reality. This, we have seen, is true in two ways. On the one hand, in our ordinary, pre-philosophical state, where we take the perceptualist assumption for granted, our physical beliefs do not qual-ify as knowledge. For, being founded on perceptual beliefs (which are in all cases false), they fail the Gettier test: they do not meet the condition that knowledge must be not only *of* the truth, but *not based on anything but the truth*. On the other hand, in our state of philosophical enlightenment, where we recognize that the external reality is not open to perceptual scrutiny, and are seeking some new basis on which to acquire information about it, knowledge is blocked by the fact that no new basis is available. Indeed, there is no basis even for well-supported conjecture.

This is a bleak conclusion. And it surely further means that we have lost our only form of protection against the other two ways in which the denial of perceptual access was seen as threatening. Thus, once we take the external reality to be beyond the reach of both perception and knowledge, I do not see how we can continue to think of it as *our world* in anything approaching the ordinary sense. We can continue to think of it as the reality to which we corporeally belong—containing those substances (our bodies) with which our mentality has direct causal links. But we cannot come anywhere near thinking of it as the world in which we live and move and have our phenomenological being, in the way we ordinarily suppose. Nor, surely, can we continue to think of the reality as containing physical objects of the familiar types—objects such as trees, mountains, houses, and cars. Without perceptual access, it was always going to be difficult to think of these types as externally realized, since our very conception of them seems to involve thinking of the things which they characterize as having forms of sensible appearance. But, with the additional loss of epistemic access, we cannot even invoke the form of substitute we earlier envisaged, whereby the external items (though incapable of sensible appearance in the strict sense) reveal their presence by causing experiences which represent certain types of sensible situation. Putting everything together, it seems that, as we earlier feared, we face the wholesale collapse of our ordinary understanding of the nature of the external reality and our relationship to it.

In fact, in one respect, our situation has turned out to be worse than we anticipated. We might have thought, initially, that, whatever the problems over epistemic access to the *external* realm, we at least possess a rich knowledge of how things stand in the realm of *our own mentality*. In particular, we might have assumed that we have a rich knowledge of those experiential facts which ordinarily make it seem to us that we are perceptive inhabitants of a physical world, and so know that, even if our physical beliefs turn out to be unwarranted, they at least reflect genuine aspects of how our experience is organized. But, as we have seen, no such knowledge is in fact available. For our access to the mental realm itself depends, to a large degree, on our possession of physical knowledge. Both in our acquisition of beliefs about the minds of others and in most of what we take ourselves to know about our own experiential pasts, we crucially rely on our capacity to acquire and retain information about the physical world. So, with the loss of epistemic access to the physical realm, we lose it, in large measure, to the mental realm as well.

5 TAKING STOCK

It looks as if our whole investigation is now at an end. We set out to discover the nature of physical-item perception. Curiously, what we seem to have discovered is that there is no such phenomenon to be investigated. There is no account of what it is for a subject to perceive a physical item, because, with sense-qualia as the immediate objects of awareness, perceptual access to the external reality is excluded. To make matters worse, we also seem to have discovered that, in lacking *perceptual* access to the external reality, we lack *epistemic* access too. We lack this access both in our naive state, where we take for granted the perceptualist assumption, and in our state of philosophical enlightenment, where we have come to accept that this assumption is false. Finally, we seem to have established that, in our enlightened condition, we not only lack *knowledge* of the external reality, but also lack any rational basis for reaching significant conclusions about it; and this, of course, would mean that we lack any rational basis for retaining our ordinary physical beliefs. These are not the conclusions which we expected at the outset of our discussion; nor are they what we would have hoped for. But, given our acceptance of SQT, there seems to be no way of avoiding them.

This outcome is bad enough. But it also leaves us with a further problem. There is no denying that these negative conclusions about perception and knowledge are both surprising and disturbing: they undermine the whole basis on which we ordinarily form our beliefs and conduct our lives. But given that they *are* the conclusions—seemingly established by our philosophical arguments—the expectation must be that we shall now, however reluctantly, accept them. But the fact is that we do not. We acknowledge that the arguments *seem* to show that there is no perceptual or epistemic access to the external reality. But we find that our belief in such access remains intact. Nor is this just a matter of how we cognitively respond at the level of our *ordinary thinking*—the fact that we continue to take our perceptual and epistemic capacities for granted in the course of *everyday life*. For we also continue to endorse this common-sense view at the level of *philosophical reflection*, where we are fully aware of the case against it. This, at least, is what I find in my own case. Despite the arguments I have advanced, I remain convinced that I see, feel, and in other ways perceive physical items, and that these perceptual encounters provide me with a wealth of genuine information about their character and physical setting. And I can only assume that this will be the typical response of others who reflect on the situation.

Now this response, of course, does not count as an *argument* against the conclusions to which our discussion has brought us. For all we have shown, our failure to accept these conclusions might stem from some special feature of our psychological makeup. Perhaps we simply lack the psychological capacity, even in our reflective thinking, to accommodate such a radical and destructive departure from our natural ways of thought. And indeed, it would not be difficult to understand, whether in evolutionary or in creationist terms, why the common-sense outlook should be protected in this way. But what is also clear is that, given the nature of our cognitive response, we have no choice but to think that the issue of perception is not yet settled. If we cannot, even on reflection, eliminate the conviction that we are inhabitants of a physical world, whose ingredients are perceptually accessible to us, and whose character is revealed through perceptual encounter, we cannot avoid thinking that there is something wrong with the philosophical arguments which purport to show that that conviction is false. And, if we think that the arguments have somewhere gone astray, we are bound to feel a corresponding pressure towards trying to identify the place (if it exists) where this has happened.

PART FIVE

THE IDEALIST SOLUTION

1 THE NEW OPTION

I

So far, our investigation into the nature of perception has focused exclusively on two rival general approaches, and the more specific theories which fall under them. One approach is that of the strong, or full-blooded, version of direct realism (SDR). This accepts a realist view of the physical world—taking the world to be something whose existence is logically independent of the human mind, and something which is, in its basic character, metaphysically fundamental. And, in the framework of that realism, it asserts that, whenever a subject Φ-terminally perceives a physical item (i.e. perceives it, without there being any other physical item which he perceives more immediately), his perceptual relationship with it is something psychologically fundamental. The other approach is the broad, or flexible, version of the representative theory (BRT). This too accepts a realist view of the physical world, but, in contrast with SDR, insists that, whenever a subject perceives a physical item (and even when the perceiving is Φ-terminal), his perceptual relationship with it breaks down into (is constituted by the combination of) two components, one of which consists in the subject's being in some more fundamental psychological state—a state which is not in itself physically perceptive—and the other of which consists in certain additional facts, but ones which do not add anything to the subject's psychological condition at the relevant time.

If my arguments have been correct, neither of these approaches allows the development of a satisfactory account. The problem for SDR is over its handling of phenomenal content (the phenomenal manner in which the relevant physical item is perceived). If such content is taken to be just the presentational imprint of the external situation on the percipient's mind, cases of non-veridical perception (where sensible appearance is at variance with the external situation) are—incorrectly—excluded. But if such content is construed in the internalist way (so that the featuring of a quality in the content is ontologically separate from its external realization), the only way of making sense of its involvement in perceptual contact is in mediational terms, which is just what SDR rules out. The problem for BRT, in contrast, is concerned with the issue of perceptual contact. If the psychological states which are fundamentally involved in cases of supposed perception are not in themselves physically perceptive, it is hard to see how the subject's awareness can be thought of as reaching beyond the boundaries of his own mind; and it is quite impossible to see how there could be a reaching to anything external when BRT assumes the SQT (SDT) form which I have defended. The upshot is that, if these are the only positions available, and if my arguments have been correct, we do not have perceptual access to the physical world at all. And this further means that we do not have epistemic access either. What makes these conclusions so awkward is not just that they are unpalatable, but that we cannot bring our actual convictions into line with them—not even when we endeavour to consider the issue from the most objective, philosophically reflective, standpoint.

The situation is looking bleak. But there is still one possibility which we have not yet considered. So far, we have conducted the whole of our investigation within the framework of a realist view of the physical world; and, within that framework, SDR and BRT are the only available options. What we have still not explored is the possibility that this realist view is itself mistaken, and that its being so is what has led to our present difficulties. Adopting the framework of realism in our previous discussion was, of course, entirely reasonable. On the face of it, the realist view is the only position which does justice to our basic understanding of what a physical world is; and it is simply taken for granted in almost all current philosophical writing. It was only natural that we should begin by confining our attention to realist theories of perception, with the expectation that we would be able to reach a satisfactory outcome in these terms. But what is now inescapable is that the outcome in the realist framework has *not* been satisfactory. Our project of providing an account of the nature of perception has collapsed, and we are left with conclusions to which our philosophical reasoning commits us, but which we cannot bring ourselves to accept. In the light of this, it is clear that we can no longer avoid raising the question of whether the realist framework should be abandoned and an account of perception be sought along quite different lines.

II

We must begin by considering in more detail what physical realism involves. As we have formulated it, the realist thesis is the conjunction of two claims: that the physical world is something whose existence is logically independent of the human mind (the *mind-independence* claim); and that the physical world is, in its basic character, metaphysically fundamental (the *fundamentalist* claim). Before we can approach the question of whether realism should be abandoned, we need to know how these two claims are to be understood.

The mind-independence claim is relatively straightforward. It means that facts about the human mind do not logically contribute to the existence of the physical world. But there are two points that need to be noted in this connection. The first is that when I speak here of 'facts about the human mind', I mean facts about the *potential*, as well as the *actual*, occurrence of human mentality, and I mean facts about the potential occurrence of mentality in *potential*, as well as *actual*, human subjects. So if someone thought that what logically creates the physical world, and the various facts it includes, is some set of general psychological laws—laws which concern some area of human mentality, but whose obtaining does not require the existence of human subjects—he would not be endorsing the independence-claim in the relevant sense, or have any chance of qualifying as a realist. The second point is that the claim of mind-independence should not be thought of as extending to *every aspect* of the physical world. Even a realist will recognize that certain physical facts are, for special reasons, logically dependent on the human mind—for example, facts about the secondary qualities of objects, construed in a Lockean fashion, and facts involving concepts like *car* and *landmark*, which imply that the objects in question are either of human design or serve certain human purposes. All that the realist is insisting is that the *primary core* of physical reality is mind-independent. This core will include, in particular, the existence of physical space, and the presence within it of the various forms of space-filling material object, characterized in primary-quality and non-anthropocentric terms. In case it is not obvious, I should stress that whenever, in the context of the present discussion, I speak of *mind*-dependence, or *mind*-independence, I always mean dependence on, or independence of, the *human* mind.

The fundamentalist claim is a little more complicated. A fact is *metaphysically fundamental* (or simply *fundamental*) if and only if it is consti-

tutively basic, i.e. not constituted by other facts; and a fact F is *constituted by* a fact or set of facts F′ if and only if it obtains in virtue of, and its obtaining is nothing over and above, the obtaining of F′. Now, irrespective of how the philosophical issues are to be resolved, it is undeniable that there is a wide range of physical facts which are not metaphysically fundamental in the relevant sense. And, indeed, this range will include many facts that belong to the primary core of physical reality which the realist takes to be mind-independent. For instance, the fact that one chunk of matter contains more atoms than another will belong to this primary core; but there is no denying that it is constituted by the combination of the relevant facts about the numbers of atoms in each chunk. It is because not all physical facts could be thought of as metaphysically fundamental that the realist claim is limited to the 'basic character' of the physical world. What is being asserted is that there is some non-empty set of physical facts which are metaphysically fundamental (constitutively basic), and that any other physical fact is ultimately constituted by some complex of facts drawn from this basic set, or by some such complex together with certain non-physical facts. Although this basic set will not include *all* the facts which the realist takes to be logically independent of the human mind, it will obviously be *confined* to them.

Even with its restriction to the *basic character* of the physical world, there is a theoretical risk that the fundamentalist claim, in its present form, will not serve the realist's purposes. This is because the realist might want to allow for the possibility that constitution within the physical realm is, in certain areas, infinitely regressive, so that there are some physical facts which are neither constitutively basic nor constituted by facts which are constitutively basic; and, indeed, he might want to allow for the possibility that this is so quite generally. In other words, while insisting that there is no reality more fundamental than the physical world—nothing non-physical which constitutively underlies it—he may want to allow for the possibility that, in certain areas, or perhaps quite generally, the physical world does not have a character which is basic in the relevant sense. To allow the realist this option, we would need to formulate the fundamentalist claim in a different way. We would need to express it as the claim that physical facts are never wholly constituted by non-physical facts. This would preserve the spirit of the original claim, since it would imply that there is nothing with a more fundamental status than the physical realm. But it would leave open the possibility that there is no level of physical reality that is not less fundamental than some other.

For a realist who wants to leave room for a regress of physical constitution, formulating the fundamentalist claim in this way is what is strictly required. But, in my own discussion, I shall simply ignore this complication and retain the claim in its original form. In doing this, I am not limiting the significance of the conclusions I shall reach. The various points that I am going to make could all, with care, be re-expressed in a way that takes account of the possibility of regress. But the discussion will be altogether simpler and clearer if we set this possibility aside, and work on the assumption that the lines of physical constitution ultimately terminate. In any case, this assumption seems to me to be very plausible.

Because physical realism is the conjunction of these two claims, there are three ways in which we could think of rejecting it. Thus we could reject it by either (1) retaining the fundamentalist claim, but denying the claim of mind-independence, or (2) retaining the claim of mind-independence, but denying the fundamentalist claim, or (3) denying both claims.

The first option, it seems to me, can be quickly dismissed, since I cannot think of any remotely plausible way in which it could be developed. If we deny that there is even a primary core of physical facts which are logically independent of the human mind, we obviously have to offer some account of why this is so. How is it that facts about the human mind logically contribute to the existence of physical space and the presence of material objects within it? The obvious explanation would be that physical facts are, quite generally, constituted by non-physical facts, and that facts about human mentality form, or systematically feature in, the non-physical facts involved. But this explanation is explicitly excluded by the continued endorsement of the fundamentalist claim. The difficulty now is in seeing what viable alternative is left. The only possibility I can think of would be to say that the physical world, or some essential component of it, can be literally equated with something in the realm of human mentality. But there is nothing along these lines which even begins to make sense. The only suggestion which even comes to mind would be the crudest application of Berkeley's doctrine of *esse est percipi*—an application in which physical objects are identified with collections of human sensory ideas (in my terminology, collections of occurrences of sense-qualia). But such an identification would simply not leave the objects involved as *physical* objects in any recognizable sense. In particular, it would neither allow them to possess anything approaching the full complement of their qualities, nor allow them to form elements of a spatially unified whole. Even Berkeley, as I interpret him, was led to develop his doctrine in a more subtle way, to avoid the obvious objections.[1]

The second option, in which we reject the fundamentalist claim, while retaining that of mind-independence, can also be set aside, though here the reason is quite different. Our interest in the possibility of rejecting realism has arisen in a specific dialectical context. Thus we have been looking for a satisfactory theory of perception, and have found that, in the framework of realism, no such theory is forthcoming. Our interest in the possibility of a non-realist approach is with a view to solving this problem. Our hope is that, by abandoning realism in the right way, we shall be able to offer a radically new account of what physical-item perception involves, and thereby be able to show how perceptual access to the physical world is possible. Now what created the problem, in the framework of realism, was the combination of three factors: first, that, in cases of what we ordinarily take to be perception, the immediate objects of awareness are sense-qualia; second, that there is no way of understanding how perceptual awareness can reach beyond these qualia to items in the external, mind-independent reality; and third, that, from the standpoint of realism, perceptual awareness would *have* to reach to such items if it was to make contact with the physical world. But obviously, the abandoning of realism cannot help with this problem if it preserves the claim of mind-independence. For if the world has an existence which is logically independent of the human mind, we get exactly the same obstacle to perceptual access, irrespective of whether we keep the fundamentalist claim or not. Taking physical facts to be constituted by non-physical facts will not be of any assistance to the cause of perception unless it moves the physical world closer to the realm of human mentality.

It follows that, given our investigative concerns, we can confine our attention to the third option, in which physical realism is rejected in both its claims—in which we both deny that the existence of the physical world is logically independent of the human mind, and deny that it is, in its basic character, metaphysically fundamental. Even here, of course, there is a wide range of options available. But, from now on, I shall focus exclusively on a single non-realist position, which seems to me to offer the only real prospect of providing both a satisfactory account of the physical world and a satisfactory solution to the problem of perception. The position

---

[1] See my essay 'Berkeley on the physical world' in J. Foster and H. Robinson (eds.), *Essays on Berkeley*.

in question is a form of idealism—idealism of a broadly phenomenalistic kind. And since it is the only form of idealism that I shall be concerned with, I shall simply refer to it here as 'idealism' or 'the idealist position'. Let me start by offering a brief exposition of what this position involves.

III

As I have often stressed, human sensory experience is characterized by themes and regularities suggestive of the existence of an external three-dimensional spatial world and our own location as mobile percipients within it.[2] This world-suggestive order can be thought of as stratified into a number of successively dependent levels, so that, at the base, we have themes and regularities which apply to sensory experience directly; at the next level up, we have themes and regularities which characterize the notional world whose existence is suggested by the base-level aspects of order; and so on. This stratification can be represented in different ways, according to how finely or crudely we distinguish the levels. But we can conveniently think of the whole series of levels as dividing into three broad phases. Thus, covering the base and near-to-base levels, there is a primary phase, in which the themes and regularities suggest the existence of a purely sensible world—a world consisting of a three-dimensional space, and, for any time, an arrangement of sensible qualities within it. Then, resting on that basis, there is a secondary phase, covering the middle ground, in which the themes and regularities of the sensible-quality arrangements thus suggested suggest, in turn, the existence of the physical world of our everyday beliefs—the world of ordinarily observable and sensibly characterized material objects. Finally, there is a third phase, in which the themes and regularities of this notional material world suggest the truth of certain scientific theories about its ultimate nature—a nature very distant from the perspective of our everyday beliefs. It may seem forced to speak of the aspects of order which emerge in the second and third phases as *character-izing sensory experience*, since it is not *directly* in terms of such experience that they are defined. But the point is that it is ultimately due to the way things work out at the level of sensory experience that these higher-level aspects obtain. The themes and regularities at the third phase are those which are directly fixed by the character of the notional material world

---

[2] I am here ignoring, because it is irrelevant to my expository purposes, the sceptical challenge that was thought to arise for this claim as a result of the problem of perception. (See Part Four, Section 4, III.)

which the second-phase themes and regularities suggest, and those at the second phase are directly fixed by the character of the notional world which the first-phase (directly experiential) themes and regularities suggest.

Now the fact that sensory experience is, in this phased way, characterized by such themes and regularities is presumably not accidental: it presumably reflects the fact that there is some unitary system of constraints which control the course of experience and oblige it to be orderly in this world-suggestive way. I shall speak of this system of constraints as the 'sensory organization'. In the framework of physical realism, the presence of this organization (this system of constraints) would be ultimately explained in terms of the existence of the physical world itself and the manner in which human subjects are functionally embodied within it: sensory experience would be organized (constrained) in the world-suggestive ways because the physical world existed as something logically independent of the human mind, and, by its causal control of our experiences, imposed a reflection of its character on them. What is distinctive about the idealist position is that it sees the lines of dependence as running in the other direction. Thus, rather than taking the physical world to be what is responsible for the organization, it takes the presence of the organization to be, or to be a central component of, what logically creates the physical world. In other words, it claims that the very existence of the physical world, and all the facts which make up its specific character, are constituted by the obtaining of the sensory organization, or by some richer complex of non-physical facts in which this organization centrally features. The basic idea is that, whether on its own, or in the context of some richer complex, the sensory organization creates a physical world by disposing things to appear systematically world-wise at the human empirical viewpoint; and it creates all the details of its specific character by disposing things to appear world-wise in the relevantly specific ways. Since the sensory organization ensures a series of successively dependent levels of world-suggestive order, there is provision for the physical world to have a corresponding series of levels of composition, beginning with a purely sensible composition, and terminating in what is revealed by the most penetrating forms of physical science. For the idealist, of course, there is no question of eliminating or downgrading the sensible aspects of the physical world in favour of the scientific. For he will see these sensible aspects as directly sustained by the non-physical factors which he takes to be metaphysically fundamental. Even the ES-aspects, which are vulnerable to elimination in the framework of realism, will take their place as basic ingredients of the physical world—idealistically underpinned by the relevant aspects of the sensory organization. So the idealist will have no difficulty in endorsing our common-sense beliefs that ripe tomatoes are genuinely characterized by the redness of their standard look, and that sugar genuinely possesses the sweetness of its standard taste. This is of crucial importance epistemologically, as we shall see presently.

It might seem that the assignment of ES-qualities to the physical world violates the realization-exclusion (RE) claim which I defended in Part Three—the claim that the ES-qualities are not capable of realization outside the content of sensory experience.[3] For even though the physical realization of these qualities is not, from the idealist standpoint, something logically independent of facts about their sensory realization, even an idealist (of the kind I am envisaging) does not want to equate physical realization with a form of sensory realization. And indeed, he wants to allow that an ES-quality could be physically realized, in virtue of the relevant aspects of the sensory organization and whatever other facts may be needed, but there be no associated sensory realization at all. However, this conflict with the RE-claim is only superficial. For, in the context in which we advanced the claim—a context in which we were taking physical realism for granted—we were simply not interested in the possibility of a realization of the ES-qualities that was not *fundamental*, and so any question of an idealistically sustained mode of realization was irrelevant. In retrospect, and with the option of idealism now before us, we can simply reformulate the claim as asserting, more weakly, that the ES-qualities are not capable of *fundamental* realization outside the content of sensory experience. This claim still stands, and can be thought of as a more precise formulation of what the original argument was trying to establish. Likewise, and without disturbing the efficacy of the earlier argument, we can reformulate the realization-conferment (RC) claim to read, more strongly, that the appropriate featuring of an ES-quality in the content of sensory experience suffices for its *fundamental* realization.

Idealism takes the physical world to be logically created by the sensory organization, or by some richer complex of non-physical facts in which this organization centrally features; and this organization is the system of constraints on human sensory experience which oblige it to be orderly in the relevantly world-suggestive ways. In theory, it would be possible for the idealist to think of these constraints as autonomous natural necessities within the sensory realm. Thus, assuming that he has some way of thinking of different human subjects as forming an experiential community

---

[3] See Part Three, Section 4.

independently of their possession of a common physical world, then, in theory, he could construe the sensory organization as a law, or set of laws, requiring the sense-experiences of this community collectively to exhibit themes and regularities of the relevant sort. But, in practice, the suggestion of fundamental laws of this kind, with such a complex prescriptive content, and controlling events in what almost seems a purposive way, is hard to take seriously. And, for this reason, it is almost inevitable that the idealist will see the sensory organization as imposed on human subjects by something outside the sensory realm, and indeed outside the realm of human mentality altogether. In other words, he will suppose that there is some form of external reality—a reality which is separate from, and logically independent of, the realm of human mentality—which causally controls the course of human sensory experience, and whose modes of control form the sensory organization. In this respect, the idealist will find himself in agreement with the realist, who also accepts that there is an external reality which plays this causal role. But whereas the realist *equates* this reality with the physical world, the idealist takes it to be something which *underlies* the physical world—something which sustains the constraints on experience by which, wholly or in part, the physical world is created.

There is a variety of different forms which the idealist's external reality could take. But, given the special way in which sensory experience is constrained—the world-suggestiveness of the themes and regularities that the sensory organization ensures—it is plausible to suppose that this reality in some way 'encodes' the character of the relevant type of world, and that this encoding expresses itself through the ways in which the reality exerts its control over sensory experience. There are two contrasting ways in which such an idea could be developed. On the one hand, the idealist could take the external reality to be something which functions, both internally and in its causal control of human experience, in a purely *mechanistic* way— something which is governed, and linked with the human mind, by natural laws. Here the character and organization of the world suggested by sensory experience would in some way reflect the character and organization of the external reality itself—though the method of reflection may not be straightforward. On the other hand, the idealist could think that what directly controls our sensory experiences and ensures their world-suggestive character is a powerful rational agent (or conceivably team of agents), who (which) has a plan of the kind of world that he (it) wants the course of experience to suggest, and who (which) executes this plan by causing us to have experiences of the appropriate sorts. This, famously, was the approach of Bishop Berkeley, who took the external rational agent to be the Christian God. The first view of the external reality would, of course, bring the idealist into still closer agreement with the realist, who also takes the external reality to work in this mechanistic way. Indeed, curiously, it could lead to a situation in which there was no difference at all between the realist and idealist over the nature of the fundamental facts. Both might think that, at the level of what is fundamental, there is a certain kind of law-governed external reality, with a certain type of structure, and certain types of interactive link with human mentality, and they might agree in detail about the precise form that all this takes. The only difference would then be that, according to the realist, this external reality is what *forms*, in its basic character, the physical world, while, according to the idealist, it is what *underlies* it.

We have been thinking of the various ways in which the idealist might understand what is involved in the obtaining of the sensory organization; and we have noted that, in practice, he is almost certain to think of this organization as imposed by some form of external reality—a reality which is logically independent of the human mind, and whose causal control of human sensory experience forms the relevant system of constraints. What we should also notice is that there is a further way in which the recognition of an external reality may feature in the idealist's account. The opportunity for this further featuring arises from the open-ended way in which the idealist thesis has been formulated, as I shall now explain.

I did not define idealism as claiming that the physical world is logically created by the sensory organization, but as claiming that it is logically created *either* by this organization, *or* by a richer complex of facts in which it centrally features. So there is room for a range of more specific idealist accounts, according to whether the organization is taken to be creatively sufficient on its own, and, if it is not, what kind of richer complex is thought to be involved. One issue here will be concerned with whether, in addition to the organization, the idealist should think that there are certain further aspects of *human psychology* that contribute to the creation of the physical world—for example, the fact that we are disposed to respond to the sensory themes and regularities in certain interpretative and cognitive ways. But another issue will precisely be concerned with the role of the external reality. In one respect, of course, this reality is already directly involved in the idealistic creation, since it is the ways in which it causally controls the course of sensory experience that forms the sensory organization. But the idealist might also want to insist that the *intrinsic character* of this reality is directly involved as well. In other words, he might want to insist that part of what idealistically sustains the existence of the physical world is the fact that the reality which controls our sensory experiences, and ensures their world-suggestive character, is of a certain specific type. To take a simple example, a Berkeleian idealist is likely to insist that, in addition to the way in which God controls the course of sensory experience, the creation of the physical world is partly dependent on the fact that it is the Christian God, with his distinctive attributes and sublimity, who is playing this role. He is likely to insist that any other form of supernatural agent, or team of agents, exercising the same control, would at best create the systematic illusion of a physical world, or would do so unless it was acting under the authority of the Christian God.

One thing which clearly emerges from our recent discussion is that idealism, as I have defined it, is a highly generic position, which can be developed in a number of different ways, according to how certain key issues are resolved. Some of these issues relate to the nature of the sensory organization—to what it is that ultimately ensures the world-suggestive character of human sensory experience. Others concern the nature of the additional factors, if any, which combine with the organization to create the physical world. And, on both these fronts, the topic of the external reality prominently features. Recognizing that it leaves open these further issues is crucial to our understanding of what idealism, in the relevant sense, is. But, in what follows, it will be on the issue of idealism as such, rather than on its different versions, that we shall primarily need to focus.

IV

Idealism takes the physical world to be logically created by the sensory organization, or by some richer complex of non-physical facts in which this organization centrally features. As such, it rejects both parts of the realist thesis. It takes the physical world to be something whose existence is logically dependent on facts about the human mind, and it holds that physical facts are, in all cases, constituted by non-physical facts.

It is not difficult to see how, in rejecting realism in this way, idealism would dispose of the problem of perception. As we noted, this problem arose from the combination of three factors, namely: (1) that the immediate objects of awareness, in the relevant cases, are sense-qualia; (2) that there is no way of understanding how perceptual awareness can get beyond these qualia to items in the external reality; and (3) that, given the truth of physical realism, perceptual awareness would have to reach to external items to make contact with the physical world. The idealist position would immediately eliminate the third of these factors. It would mean that physical items were no longer constituents of a reality that was external to qualia in the relevant sense. Rather, they would derive their very existence from the constraints on the occurrence of qualia, or from some complex of facts in which such constraints centrally featured. It would remain the case that the subject's awareness did not reach beyond the sense-qualia occurring in his own mind. But, on the idealist account, it would not need to reach further to make contact with the factors by which the existence of physical items was constituted, and thereby make contact with the items themselves.

To illustrate, let us go back, once again, to the case of Pauline. We want it to turn out that, at any given time during the period when she photically encounters the apple, Pauline Φ-terminally sees a certain momentary stage of a portion of the apple's surface. In the framework of realism, we cannot understand how this perceptual contact is made. At any time, the only item immediately before Pauline's mind is a certain visual sense-quale, and, in the realist system, the only way in which the occurrence of this quale would be connected with the relevant portion-stage would be by a complex causal process, running through the subject's eyes and brain. It is impossible to see how this causal connection could turn the awareness of the quale into one which genuinely reaches to the external item. But, in the idealist's system, the situation is quite different. There is still a sense in which the contact with the portion-stage is mediated: the occurrence of the sense-quale does not *in itself* qualify as an awareness of the physical item. But, in the new situation, the mediating and mediated objects are ontologically linked. For the occurrence of the quale is itself an instance of the operation of the sensory constraints by which, on their own or in combination with other factors, the existence of the portion-stage is constituted. In such a case, it is no more difficult to see how the presentation of the quale succeeds in giving access to the portion-stage of the apple's surface than to see how the perceiving of this stage gives access to the persisting portion, or the perceiving of this portion gives access to the whole apple. Nor, indeed, is it difficult to see how, despite the mediation, the access to the physical item can—in accordance with the traditional conception of idealism—be thought of as *direct*. Moreover, exactly the same situation will obtain, under idealism, in any other case of what we would ordinarily take to be Φ-terminal perception.

By introducing this kind of ontological link, then, between the occurrences of sense-qualia and the relevant physical item, idealism avoids the problem of perception that arises in the framework of realism. It shows how the subject's awareness does not need to reach beyond what occurs in his own mind to make contact with things in the physical world. Noting this, of course, does not, on its own, provide us with a full account of how physical-item perception works in the idealist's system. Nor, indeed, will I attempt to provide such an account here; for that would require me to elaborate the idealist's system in far greater detail than I have space for in the present work. Nonetheless, there are three basic points about the idealist's treatment of perception that I want to underline.

In the first place, the idealist is claiming that, where there is Φ-terminal perception, the occurrence of the relevant sense-quale is an instance of the operation of the sensory constraints that are involved in the creation of the perceived item, and he rightly sees this ontological link as eliminating the problem encountered by the realist. But he is not claiming that *any form* of such a link would be suitable for the occurrence of such perception. For there is a wide variety of ways in which the constraints that are involved in the creation of a physical item can operate on sensory experience, and only a fraction of these would enable the subject to make Φ-terminal contact, or indeed any kind of perceptual contact, with the item in question. The majority of the ways would, at best, serve to indicate the presence of the item in some less direct fashion—for example, by revealing aspects of its causal influence, within the idealistically created world, on other physical things. Whether a mode of operation would serve to give perceptual access to the item becomes apparent once we consider it in the context of the whole idealistic creation.

Secondly, the perception of a physical item is something which occurs from a location within the physical world. So the idealist has to arrange things in such a way that, given any perception, the factors which idealistically create the physical world, and which, in the context of that creation, provide an appropriate ontological link between the relevant quale-occurrence and the relevant physical item, create the world as something which forms the subject's environment, and which puts the subject and the item into the appropriate environmental relationship. In broad outline, we can see how this would work out. The basic idea of the idealist approach is, as I have said, that, whether on its own or in the context of some richer complex, the sensory organization creates the physical world by disposing things to appear systematically world-wise at the human empirical viewpoint; and, in disposing things to appear systematically world-wise at this (our) empirical viewpoint, it disposes them to appear in ways which are not only suggestive of a certain kind of world, but of a world in which we are located and through which we move. So the idealist can take our location in the physical world to be sustained in the same way as the existence of the world itself. There is still, of course, the question of how anyone could think that the existence of the world was sustained in this way at all. On the face of it, disposing things to appear systematically world-wise at the human viewpoint would at best create a *virtual* world, rather than one that was *real*. But, at present, I am only trying to give an *account* of the idealist position, not to *defend* it.

Finally, even with the subject's location in the physical world in place, and assuming a suitable form on the relevant occasion, the idealist will not want to say that the Φ-terminal perceiving of a physical item depends on nothing more than there being a quale-occurrence which is ontologically linked with the item in a perceptually appropriate way. For, in order for there to be such a perceiving, the subject has to have a complete phenomenal experience, and this means that the occurrence of the quale has to combine with an appropriate level of interpretation—an interpretation which is suitably experiential and which represents the quale as something in the subject's environment. Moreover, relative to the way in which, within the created physical world, the subject, at the relevant time, is spatiotemporally related to the relevant item, and relative to any other aspects of the physical circumstances that may be relevant, the phenomenal experience has to be, to a sufficient degree, qualitatively appropriate to that item. As under realism, such appropriateness will not be entirely a matter of veridicality, but will also take account of what is normal, or normative, for the conditions in question.

By restoring our perceptual access to the physical world, idealism eliminates the problem of perception. And, in eliminating this problem, it eliminates the problem of knowledge which stems from it. It does not do this by supplying us with a new (a distinctively idealist) source of physical information—a way of gauging the character of the physical situation by inference from the character of the non-physical factors which constitutively underlie it. For reasons which we have already made clear, even the sensory aspects of these factors are not ones which we can effectively monitor without prior knowledge of the physical world.[4] Rather, the way in which idealism helps the epistemological situation is by showing how our *ordinary* methods of acquiring putative physical information turn out to be well founded. Thus, by taking the physical world to be logically created in the way envisaged, it ensures our perceptual access to it; and, once we know that this access is in place, we can take physical facts to be open to perceptual scrutiny in the ordinary way. Admittedly, there is one factor in

---

[4] See Part Four, Section 4, III.

the situation which this account does not make explicit. If perception is to be a source of physical knowledge, the basic beliefs which it induces have to be true; and the basic beliefs in question are always, at least in part, about how things *sensibly* stand in the subject's environment. A crucial part of what enables idealism to represent the world as open to perceptual scrutiny, and thereby to vindicate our ordinary methods of acquiring putative information about it, is that—as I stressed earlier—it allows the world to possess a genuine sensible character, and does so even in respect of the secondary qualities which are vulnerable to a Lockean account in the framework of realism.

Idealism eliminates the problem of perception, and the problem of knowledge which stems from it. In default of any other solution, this makes the position very attractive: we would like there to be some way in which we can legitimately think of ourselves as having perceptual and epistemic access to the physical world. But it does not, of course, show the position to be *true*. Moreover, before we can begin to regard idealism as a serious option, there is a fundamental objection to it which needs to be overcome. For, on the face of it, it is essential to our very conception of a physical world that it be something whose existence is logically independent of the human mind. Thus when we consider the nature of the world in its own terms—a world of three-dimensional space and material objects, a world of fields and mountains, planets and stars—it seems to make no sense to suppose that all this derives its existence, wholly or in part, from facts about human mentality. It just seems obvious that we cannot do justice to the nature of the physical entities involved without according them an ontological autonomy in relation to our own mental lives and the ways in which these are organized. In short, no matter how awkward the consequences for our perceptual and epistemological situation, idealism seems to be a non-starter—automatically excluded by our basic understanding of what a physical world is.

This objection seems, initially, very powerful. But, on further reflection, I think we can see that the idealist has a satisfactory answer. The crucial point is that, from an idealist standpoint, the relationship between the physical world and human mentality is to be characterized in quite different ways, according to whether it is what is involved in the idealistic creation itself or what features within the realm of what is thus created. Obviously, as what is involved in the idealistic creation, the relationship is one of logical dependence. The physical world is, in all its aspects, logically created by the sensory organization, or by some complex of facts in which this organization centrally features, and the sensory organization is a system of constraints on human sensory experience. So, in terms of the idealistic creation, the existence of the physical world, and all the facts it contains, logically depend on facts about the human mind. On the other hand, the world which is thus created is not just created *by* facts which involve human mentality, but is created *as* something with which human mentality is intimately linked. It is created as a world which forms our perceptual environment—a world in which we are located and whose ingredients are perceptually accessible to us; and it is also created as a world in which we are functionally attached to human bodies, and in which, through such attachment, our mentality causally interacts with the states of these bodies and with events in the wider environment. In respect of this created situation, the relationship of the physical world to human mentality is *not*, even for an idealist, one of logical dependence. Rather—just as under realism—the two realms of phenomena are interactive parts of a larger psychophysical whole, and, as such, enjoy the same ontological status. In this context, the only way in which the physical is sometimes dependent on the mental—at least, the only way which has a bearing on what the realist would take to be the *primary core* of physical reality—is that human mental events sometimes have a *causal influence* on what happens physically. Indeed, in this context, so far from logically depending for its existence on the sensory organization, the physical world is itself responsible for imposing an organization on sensory experience. For a subject's sensory experiences fall under the causal control of the relevant centres in his brain (the brain of the body to which he is functionally attached), and these centres, in turn, are causally sensitive to the relevant forms of environmental input.

Now this distinction, between how human mentality relates to the physical world in the context of the idealistic creation and how it relates to the world in the context of what is created, gives the idealist a straightforward way of dealing with the objection. When we consider the physical world in its own terms, we consider it in a perspective in which our relationship to it is, in the way just specified, perceptual and interactive; and, in the context of this relationship, as I have just stressed, the existence of the physical world does not logically depend on facts about human mentality. So what the idealist can say is that it is just this fact which makes it seem that our basic understanding of the physical world and his own thesis are in conflict. And if this is what creates the appearance of conflict, then, of course, the appearance is illusory. For the fact that the physical world does not exhibit a logical dependence on human mentality *in that context* is entirely compatible with the claim that it is logically created in the way that the idealist envisages. There is no paradox in the suggestion that human mentality ultimately contributes to the logical creation of the physical world, but that, within the context of what is thus created, also features as something which does not thus contribute. We just need to be careful not to confuse the question of how things stand *within* the psychophysical reality which is idealistically created with the question of how things stand *with respect to that creation.*

This seems to me to be an effective way of meeting the objection. It does not, of course, show that there is no conflict of *any kind* between our basic understanding of the physical world and the idealist thesis; and it remains possible that further investigation will bring such a conflict to light. But what the objection was appealing to was an apparent conflict which is conspicuous when we first consider the issue—a conflict which just seems obvious when we compare our ordinary conception of the physical world with what the idealist is claiming. And what is now surely clear is that this initial appearance of conflict is something which the idealist can, from his own standpoint, adequately explain. He can point out that, even if idealism is true, it is bound to seem initially to be a non-starter simply because of the way in which the physical world and human mentality are related within the reality which is idealistically created—because, within this reality, the physical world exists as an interactive partner with human mentality, rather than as something logically dependent on it.

This disposes of the objection. What we still do not have, of course, is any positive argument in favour of idealism. So far, all we have found in its favour is that it eliminates the problem of perception, and the problem of knowledge which stems from it; and, as I have already conceded, this does not serve to establish its truth. Moreover, the onus of proof is still very heavily on the idealist. The basic idea of the idealist approach is that, whether on its own or in the context of some richer complex, the sensory organization creates a physical world by disposing things to appear systematically world-wise at the human empirical viewpoint; and it creates all the details of the world's specific character by disposing things to appear world-wise in the relevantly specific ways. But, on the face of it, as we have already noted, the most that this disposing would achieve would be the creation of a *virtual* world, rather than one that was *real*. Clearly it is up to the idealist to show why this initial view of the situation is wrong, and how the form of idealistic creation he envisages turns out to be effective.

Before we can be justified in invoking idealism as the answer to the problem of perception, we need, then, a positive argument in its favour. And it is this that I want now to try to provide. I want to try to show that, quite

apart from the problems of perception and knowledge, there are considerations which oblige us to accept the idealist account. These considerations
are ones which I have elaborated in much greater detail in my book *The
Case for Idealism.*[5] In the present context, where the discussion of idealism
only forms the last phase of an investigation into the nature of perception,
I am forced to deal with the issues more briefly, and with greater reliance
on intuition. Even so, I hope to make the argument persuasive.

In developing this argument, I shall put the problem of perception on
one side, as something not relevant to the issues which now concern us. I
shall continue, however, to assume the correctness of the arguments in
Parts Two and Three which created that problem. In particular, I shall continue to assume that we have succeeded in refuting SDR, and in establishing SQT as the correct account of phenomenal experience. Because of our
recent discussion, there is also one respect in which I need to clarify my terminology. As I have stressed, the idealist accepts that, within the ordinary
psychophysical reality—the reality which he takes to be idealistically created—the existence of the physical world is not logically dependent on the
human mind. But, in what follows, whenever I speak of *logical dependence
on (independence of) the human mind,* I shall be referring to how things are
to be characterized when we stand back from this reality and consider the
role of human mentality at the level of what is fundamental. In other
words, I shall be using these expressions, as I have predominantly used
them hitherto, in a way which allows me to say, *without qualification,* that
the mind-independence of the physical world is something which the idealist denies, and hence something about which the realist and idealist have
opposing views.

2 AN ARGUMENT FOR IDEALISM

I

Let us speak of a reality as a *physically relevant external* (PRE) reality if and
only if it is, in all its aspects, logically independent of the human mind, and,
through its systematic causal control of human sensory experience, is what
sustains the sensory organization. The realist is committed to accepting the
existence of a PRE-reality. For he is committed to saying that such a reality
is what forms the physical world in its primary (mind-independent)
core—a core which includes the existence of physical space, and the pres-

---

[5] London: Routledge and Kegan Paul, 1982.

ence within it of the various forms of material object. The idealist too will almost certainly accept the existence of such a reality as a way of accounting for the sensory organization. But, from his standpoint, this reality will not be *identical* with the physical world, but rather something which *underlies* it.

Now we can envisage the possibility that there is a PRE-reality, but that its structure and organization differ, in certain ways, from what all our empirical evidence suggests, and from what, in response to this evidence, we attribute to the physical world in our ordinary and scientific thinking. The issue on which I want to focus is that of how we ought to interpret things physically if we suppose that such a difference obtains. More precisely, I want to focus on this issue for a specific range of cases, where two further conditions are satisfied. First, the difference is not so great, overall, as to lend any intuitive plausibility to physical nihilism—to the view that there is no physical world at all. Thus it is nothing like the difference that would obtain if the PRE-reality consisted of a collection of interacting minds, or if it was of the kind envisaged by Berkeley. Secondly, the reason for the difference is that the PRE-reality is nomologically organized as if it had a different structure from the one which it actually has, and it is this organizationally simulated structure which then gets projected on to the human empirical viewpoint. We shall see in more detail presently just what this involves. I shall speak of cases of this kind as cases of *relevant deviance*—'deviance', because of the way in which how things empirically appear deviates from the character of the external situation, 'relevant', because of the specific conditions to which this deviance conforms.

As I said, the issue on which I want to focus is that of how we should interpret things physically if we suppose a case of such deviance to obtain. It will be best if, in the first instance, we pursue this issue in relation to a particular example.

II

Let us suppose that the PRE-reality, as it is in itself, is composed in the following way. There is an external three-dimensional space, S, and a certain stock of qualities capable of characterizing (of being instantiated by) elements (points, lines, regions) of S at times. The facts which compose the reality then either consist in, or are constituted by: (a) facts to the effect that certain elements of S are characterized by certain qualities at certain times, or over certain periods; (b) facts to the effect that certain causal relationships hold between different spatiotemporal instances of such quality-characterization; and (c) laws of nature (general facts of natural necessity), which govern both the spatiotemporal arrangement of qualities and the obtaining of causal relationships. By restricting what is fundamentally distributed over the elements of S to *qualities*, I am assuming that any persisting objects in S can be thought of as deriving their existence from (as things whose existence is constituted by) facts of quality-characterization, causal relationships, and nomological organization. (Thus, in the simplest case, we might think of the existence of such an object as constituted by the lawlike occurrence of a certain spatiotemporally and causally continuous series of region-moment instances of a certain quality.) But if anyone finds this approach too austere—for example, a realist who wants to include certain kinds of physical particle in his basic ontology—I am happy to expand the ontology of the PRE-reality accordingly. And, indeed, I would be happy to enrich the reality in any other ways that might be demanded. I have kept its basic ingredients to a minimum purely for simplicity of exposition, not because I am trying to set things up in a way that tilts things in favour of what I want to establish. I shall also assume, for ease of exposition, that S is an absolute and ontologically autonomous space, whose points and regions have identities which are both independent of a frame of reference and independent of time. And, so that this should not automatically exclude physical realism, which needs to equate S with physical space, I shall make the same assumption for physical space too. This last assumption, of course, is completely out of line with current scientific theory. But to provide a scientifically accurate account would make the ensuing discussion much more complicated, without affecting the substance of the philosophical issues involved.

In addition to how the PRE-reality is *in itself*, there is the matter of its *relationship to us*, and specifically, its role in sustaining the sensory organization. To take account of this, we have to suppose that there is a system of laws which make provision for, and regulate, forms of causal interaction between aspects of the PRE-reality and the realm of human mentality. A plausible supposition would be this: there is a certain class of complex persisting objects in S—the S-equivalents of human biological organisms—and a one–one correlation between these objects and human subjects, such that, for each such correlated pair, there is a set of laws prescribing ways in which the condition of the S-object is empowered to directly affect the mentality of the subject, and ways in which the mentality of the subject is empowered to directly affect the condition of the object. Of particular relevance here will be the laws which ensure that certain kinds of process in the S-objects cause the correlated subjects to have certain kinds of sensory experience. For the operation of these laws will form the final link in the chain whereby the makeup of the PRE-reality determines the nature of the sensory organization. The laws which connect the PRE-reality with human minds are not, strictly, ingredients of this reality, since the latter is required to be, through and through, mind-independent. But, for convenience, I shall often speak of them as laws of the PRE-reality, and as elements in the larger package of laws which collectively define its nomological organization. I should also make it clear that, in describing the relevant S-objects as the *S-equivalents* of human biological organisms, I was not excluding the option of *equating* them with such organisms. I was simply trying to stay neutral between that (the realist) option and taking the objects to be what *underlie* these organisms.

Now let us suppose that, with one crucial exception, the laws of the PRE-reality, both those that govern its internal workings and those that link it with human mentality, impose the same constraints on events across the whole of S and time. The exception is as follows. Within S there are two separate three-dimensional regions, R_1 and R_2, of the same shape and size, such that everything is nomologically organized, both internally and with respect to human mentality, exactly as if—by the standards of what would be required for organizational uniformity—R_1 and R_2 were interchanged. Thus suppose that there is some kind of mobile process in S whose instances would in general, under the laws, be made to follow a course of uniform motion in a straight line, unless affected by some further force. Then, if an instance of this kind of process comes (in the normal S-time continuous way) to some point on the boundary of R_1, it instantaneously changes its location to the corresponding point on the boundary of R_2, and continues in the corresponding straight line from there. And conversely, if an instance of the process comes (in the normal way) to the boundary of R_2, it undergoes an exactly analogous shift to the boundary of R_1. Quite generally, by the standards of how, in the rest of the space, things behave, interact, and interact with our minds, everything is organized, with respect to the boundaries of the two regions, as if each region had the other's location. We might express the point succinctly by saying that each region is *functionally* located where the other is *actually* located—the functional locations of the regions being the ones which we would need to assign to them to achieve organizational uniformity.

Everything is organized as if R_1 and R_2 were interchanged. And, as I have made clear, this relates not just to the constraints on behaviour in S, but also to the modes of interaction between what occurs in S and human mentality. In particular, then, it covers the ways in which situations in S affect human sensory experience. Crucially, this means that the organizational anomaly in the external reality is wholly concealed at the level of empirical appearance. At the human empirical viewpoint, everything seems to indicate that, within our own world, things behave in a completely uniform way across the whole of space. This, in turn, of course, shapes the character of our ordinary physical beliefs, which are directly responsive to what the empirical evidence suggests. And so the physical world of our empirical beliefs—both those at the level of our common-sense thinking and those which emerge through science—comes to mirror not the external reality as it is, but the reality which would obtain if the relevant regions were interchanged. In the world we empirically construct, the region corresponding to R_1 gets located in the surroundings corresponding to the S-surroundings of R_2, and the region corresponding to R_2 gets located in the surroundings corresponding to the S-surroundings of R_1. In other words, the topology which features in the content of our physical beliefs coincides with the *functional* topology of S rather than with its *actual* topology. For simplicity, let us assume that this is the only point of conflict between the structure and organization of the PRE-reality and those of the world that we empirically construct—the world which our empirical evidence suggests and which features in the physical beliefs that we form on that basis.

To bring the situation into sharper focus, let us make the example more concrete. Thus let us suppose that R_1 and R_2 respectively correspond to what, in the empirically constructed world, qualify as the regions of Oxford and Cambridge. Strictly speaking, of course, even with our assumption of the absolute and autonomous character of physical space, Oxford and Cambridge do not define fixed regions within it, since they are in constant motion. And this means that we can only correctly represent them as corresponding to R_1 and R_2 if we reconstrue the latter as spatiotemporally continuous sequences of regions-at-times. Such a reconstrual would be perfectly feasible, and would not affect the course of the argument. But rather than getting involved in such a complication, I shall simply pretend that the Earth is stationary, and that the two cities occupy the same regions of physical space at all times.

We are supposing that R_1 and R_2 respectively correspond to what, in the empirically constructed world, qualify as the regions of Oxford and Cambridge. And, of course, all the empirical evidence suggests to us that Oxford is in what qualifies as Oxfordshire, and Cambridge is in what qualifies as Cambridgeshire. But, because of the organizational anomaly in the external reality, the situation with respect to R_1 and R_2 is reversed, with the S-surroundings of R_1 corresponding to the relevant portion of Cambridgeshire (i.e. to what remains of Cambridgeshire when the Cambridge-region is subtracted), and the S-surroundings of R2 corresponding to the relevant portion of Oxfordshire (i.e. to what remains of Oxfordshire when the Oxford-region is subtracted). So if someone were to drive from Oxford to Cambridge, the route of his journey in S would have a very different character from the route which was empirically apparent. The external process would begin in R1, the region corresponding to Oxford, but surrounded by what corresponds to Cambridgeshire. But as soon as the driver moved out of the Oxford-region, the process would instantaneously change its S-location to an area just outside R2, corresponding to an area in Oxfordshire normally thought to be just outside Oxford. The process would then continue in a way which coincided with the empirically apparent route until it reached the boundary of R1, when, as the empirical journey would find the driver entering Cambridge, it would once again instantaneously change its location and became a process moving through R2. (See diagram on next page.) So what would seem to the subject to be a spatially continuous journey in physical space would correspond to a process in S-space which became dramatically discontinuous whenever it reached (whether from the inside or the outside) the boundaries of R1 or R2. And of course it is not just that the discontinuities in the external process would not be apparent to the *subject*. Rather, the laws of nature would ensure that they remained completely undetected by anyone, at any time, by any empirical means. All the empirical evidence, past and future, actual and potential, from the most casual observation to the most searching experimental test, would seem to indicate that the external process was (in line with how things experientially appeared to the subject) spatially continuous.

I think that the nature of the case we are envisaging is by now clear. What still needs to be decided is what we should make of it. And one thing which must be conceded in advance is that, taken as a suggestion as to how things may actually be, what is envisaged is not at all plausible. It is not just that, *ex hypothesi*, it runs counter to all the empirical evidence. It is also that there would be something inherently puzzling about a reality which was organized in the way envisaged. If there is nothing which qualitatively distinguishes R1 and R2 from other regions in S—and there has been no suggestion of anything of that sort—it is surely very strange that the laws should treat them in such a distinctive fashion, and even stranger that they should do so in a way which contrives to prevent any empirical trace of what is happening. But none of this affects the role of the hypothetical case in our present discussion. All that presently matters is that what is being envisaged—however improbable—is coherently conceivable. And this is

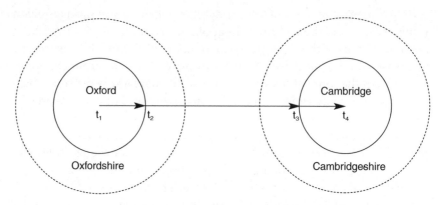

Journey in the empirically constructed world

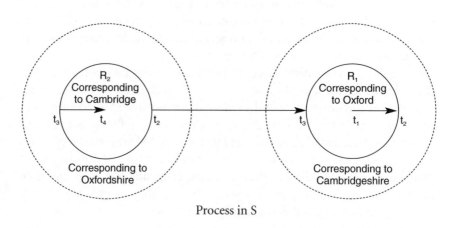

Process in S

surely so. However strange such a situation would be, there is nothing which logically excludes the suggestion that the PRE-reality is organized in this anomalous way.

Given that what is being envisaged is conceivable, the crucial question is how we should interpret it *physically*. How does the peculiar organization with respect to R_1 and R_2 affect the situation of Oxford and Cambridge in the physical world? It is essential, of course, that we should address this question from an appropriately detached standpoint. As we have already stressed, the physical beliefs that we form in the context of our ordinary empirical lives are automatically shaped by the empirical evidence. But the question which we now need to consider requires us to stand back from our empirically formed beliefs, and try to reach a verdict about their correctness when we take into account the external factors which are envisaged as lying behind them.

So, supposing ourselves to know that the PRE-reality is structured and organized in the relevant way, and that it is linked with the world of our empirical beliefs in the ways indicated, what conclusion should we reach about the physical situation? Formally, there are four options available. The first, and most drastic, would be the option of physical nihilism. Here, the discrepancy between how things externally are and how they empirically appear would be seen as excluding the existence of a physical world altogether. The second option, and a sort of modified version of the first, would be to say that, while there is a physical world, it does not contain the regions that we ordinarily think of as Oxford and Cambridge. There are, with respect to these notional regions, 'holes' in the fabric of physical space, and all that empirically suggests their presence, and the presence of objects and processes located in them, is just a form of systematic illusion. The third option would be to say that there is a physical world, and one which is replete with the Oxford and Cambridge regions, and that its structure and organization coincide with those of the external reality. This would involve saying that, contrary to what we ordinarily believe, and to what all the actual and potential empirical evidence suggests, Oxford is really in Cambridgeshire, and Cambridge is really in Oxfordshire. The fourth option would be to say that there is a physical world, and again one replete with the Oxford and Cambridge regions, but that its structure and organization are as they are empirically represented at the human viewpoint. This would involve saying that, despite the positions of R_1 and R_2 in the external reality, Oxford and Cambridge are, physically, where we ordinarily take them to be—Oxford in Oxfordshire, Cambridge in Cambridgeshire.

Now, of these four options, it seems to me that only the last has any plausibility. We can immediately dismiss the first option. It is just obvious that the local organizational quirk with respect to R_1 and R_2, and the resulting effects on empirical appearance, do not suffice to eliminate the physical world altogether. Equally, it only takes a moment's reflection to reject the second. For since, apart from the location of the relevant regions, how things empirically appear with respect to Oxford and Cambridge is accurate with respect to everything that pertains to R_1 and R_2, there is no temptation at all to think that the supposed Oxford and Cambridge portions of the physical world do not exist, and that all the apparent signs of their presence are illusory. But granted that we retain a belief in the physical world, and in those particular portions of it whose physical location is at issue, we surely want to gauge its topology by reference to how things stand empirically, rather than to how they undetectably stand in the external reality. We surely want to say that, when someone travels from Oxford to Cambridge, his journey is, as it empirically appears, genuinely continuous in physical space, and that the concealed discontinuities involved only pertain to the underlying processes in S. We surely want to avoid having to say that, each time the traveller reaches the critical boundary of one of the city-regions, he undergoes an instantaneous but imperceptible transference to another part of the country. We surely want to say that this transference is not with respect to the physical geography of England—the geography that we are trying to characterize in our maps and manuals—but only with respect to the external spatial arrangement which underlies it. In short, we surely want to say that, despite the S-locations of their external correlates, Oxford and Cambridge are physically located where we ordinarily believe and where all the empirical evidence suggests.

The basic point is that, to qualify as the physical world, something has to be *our* world in an epistemologically crucial sense; and to qualify as characterizing *our* world, in *that* sense, the topological arrangement of regions must surely conform to how things are disposed to appear, empirically, at *our* viewpoint. Of course, there can be aspects of this arrangement which we are not, in practice, equipped to detect: the regions to which they relate may be too remote, or the aspects may be too subtle to be captured by current investigative techniques. But what is surely ruled out is the suggestion that something qualifies as our world, in the relevant sense, but that things are so organized as to ensure that, even in an area where we seem fully equipped to monitor the situation, some aspect of its topology is systematically belied by all the actual and potential empirical evidence. If everything is organized so as to ensure that Oxford passes all the empirical tests for being in Oxfordshire, and Cambridge passes all the empirical tests for being in Cambridgeshire, that surely settles the issue of their true physical locations.

It might be objected that, while the physical world has to be our world in an epistemologically crucial sense, this only requires its topology to have a *general* conformity to how things are disposed to appear at our empirical viewpoint, and so allows for exceptional cases where some aspect of the physical topology is systematically at variance with the actual and potential empirical evidence. And this would mean that, in the particular case on which we are focusing, there is no obstacle to concluding that the physical locations of Oxford and Cambridge coincide with the S-locations of R_1 and R_2. I do not find this suggestion at all plausible. But, in response to anyone who does, I would simply develop the example one stage further. Thus, instead of envisaging just one case of a pair of S-regions which exemplify the relevant organizational phenomenon, I would suppose such cases to be a commonplace feature of S. And, if necessary, I would even suppose that, despite the anomaly involved in each case, there was a general pattern to which the various cases conformed—for example, that the pairs of regions were of a constant shape and size, that there was the same distance between the regions in each pair, and that the cases were distributed over S in a uniform fashion. Developing the example in this way would not, it seems to me, affect our judgement that there was still a physical world, and one without gaps. But, even from the standpoint of the objection, it would be impossible to suppose that, on such a scale and in such a regular way, things were organized so as to ensure that the topology of our world was systematically belied by the empirical evidence available at our viewpoint. It would be impossible to avoid thinking that the physical topology coincided with the organizationally simulated (functional) topology of S—in conformity with what all our empirical evidence (actual and potential) suggests.

Bearing in mind that I could always respond to the objection in this way, I shall, for convenience, keep to the example in its original (simple) form, and assume that it is to be physically interpreted in the way I suggested. As I have already said, this interpretation seems to me, in any case, to be the only one that is plausible.

III

We have been focusing on one example of a case of relevant deviance. In such cases, the structure and organization of the PRE-reality differ from what the empirical evidence suggests, and do so in such a way that (1) the difference is not so great, overall, as to lend intuitive plausibility to the conclusion that there is no physical world at all, and (2) the reason for the difference is that the reality is nomologically organized *as if* it possessed a different structure, and it is this organizationally simulated structure which gets projected on to the human empirical viewpoint. There are many other examples of relevant deviance that we could devise (indeed, the potential list is infinite), and any of them could be used to make the same general point. Some of these examples would again be concerned with the geometry of space. For instance, we could suppose that the external reality is organized, in respect of both its internal behaviour and its causal relations with the human mind, exactly as if a certain spherical region of space were rotated by a certain amount in a certain direction. Or again, we could suppose that the external reality is organized, in both respects, as if its space were more narrowly circumscribed, so that its functional boundaries enclose only a portion of what is enclosed by its actual boundaries. Or to take up a case elaborated earlier, we could suppose that the external item corresponding to physical space consists of two separate spaces organized as if they were joined.[6] Other examples might concern different forms of structure, such as relations of qualitative sameness and difference. Thus we could suppose that, for a certain region of the external space, and two qualities, everything is organized exactly as if each quality as it occurs within this region was the same as the other as it occurs outside. Or more elaborately, we could suppose that there are two qualities which exchange their current distributions and functional roles every hour, so that everything is organized as if each of the qualities in hours 1, 3, 5, 7, . . . is the same as the other in hours 2, 4, 6, 8, ... In all these further examples, our intuitions would, it seems to me, follow the same course as in the case discussed: we would say that what is envisaged preserves the existence of the physical world—and a world without gaps—but that the relevant facts of physical structure conform to the organizationally simulated structure of the external reality, rather than to its actual structure. Thus if we supposed the external reality to comprise two spaces organized as if they were joined, our intuition would be that there was only one physical space, reflecting the distinctive (single-space simulating) character of the organization. Likewise, if we supposed that two external qualities exchanged their current distributions and functional roles every hour, we would trace the spatiotemporal paths of the relevant physical qualities in a way which restored organizational uniformity, rather than in a way which matched the external relations of qualitative sameness and difference. Moreover, I think it is clear that this would be our response in all cases of the relevant kind. And running through these responses would be the same underlying thought: that, as characterizing *our* world, in the epistemologically relevant sense, the physical structure must conform to the organizationally simulated structure of the external reality because it must conform to how things are disposed to appear at *our* empirical viewpoint.

All this, I fear, is rather quick. I would like to be able to spend more time elaborating some of these further examples and showing how the common pattern of interpretation applies. But, given the constraints of our discussion, we need, at this stage, to move on to our next investigative task. This

---

[6] I introduced this case in Part Four, Section 4, III.

is to consider how our findings with respect to relevant deviance bear on the issue of physical realism.

IV

If our intuitions have been sound, we know that, in any case of relevant deviance, there is some respect in which the structure of the physical world differs from the structure of the PRE-reality, and, consequently, there is some aspect of physical structure which cannot be equated with an aspect of analogous PRE-structure. Thus, in the example of the two regions, the location of the Oxford-region in Oxfordshire and the location of the Cambridge-region in Cambridgeshire cannot be equated with locational facts about S, since the corresponding S-regions occupy the reverse positions. This already seems to pose a problem for physical realism. Realism is committed to accepting the existence of a PRE-reality, and to equating it with the physical world in its primary core; and this involves taking the structural aspects of this reality to form the corresponding aspects of physical structure. So, for cases of relevant deviance, the correct account of how things stand physically and the realist account are in direct conflict.

This conflict looks awkward for the realist—and may in fact be so—but it does not suffice to show that his position is mistaken. The realist thesis, as we have formulated it, is only strictly concerned with the *actual situation*: it claims that the physical world *is* something whose existence is logically independent of the human mind, and *is*, in its basic character, metaphysically fundamental. But the cases of relevant deviance are, in the context of our discussion, only *hypothetical*: they represent ways in which we can coherently envisage how the situation *might be*. So the realist can still insist that his account of the physical world is right *in fact*. Nor, as things currently stand, would such a response be merely perverse. For, as we noted in the case of the regions, there seem to be good grounds for supposing that the kinds of deviance envisaged do not obtain. Thus, as well as running counter to what all the empirical evidence suggests, there would be something inherently puzzling about a situation in which the external organization was anomalous in this kind of way. So perhaps the realist can afford to concede that cases of relevant deviance are not amenable to a realist construal, but insist that the realist account is correct for how things actually are, or at least for how we are entitled to take them to be.

Whether the realist can really afford to limit the relevance of his claims in this way is, I think, debatable. But, for the sake of argument, let us suppose that he can. Even so, it seems to me that the underlying difficulty for his position remains. For, when we look into the issue more closely, I think we can see that the factors which make cases of relevant deviance resistant to a realist construal carry over, if in a less direct form, to cases to which the realist's approach seems better suited. In particular, they carry over to the case which represents the realist's best scenario, in which there is no conflict at all between how things stand in the PRE-reality and what the empirical evidence suggests. I shall speak of this as the case of *zero deviance*. What makes this case so propitious from the realist's standpoint is that it contains nothing which could even be thought to indicate that there is a qualitative difference between the external and physical structures, and so nothing which presents an immediate obstacle to identifying the two.

We need to begin by noting that, even when we suppose the actual situation to be one of zero deviance, we can envisage ways in which, without altering the external structure, cases of relevant deviance *could have* occurred. Let us confine out attention to deviance with respect to *geometrical* structure. Then the point is that, even when we assume that the geometry of the external space is wholly in line with the actual and potential empirical evidence, we can still envisage ways in which, with this geometry held constant, the laws governing the external reality could have been different, and different in a way which created an instance of the relevant kind of mismatch with how things empirically presented themselves at the human viewpoint. Thus, even when we suppose that, in actual fact, the external organization is entirely uniform with respect to the geometry of the external space, we can see how, without change to this geometry, things could have been organized, both in respect of what takes place within the space and in respect of causal relations with human mentality, exactly as if two regions were interchanged. Or again, with the same supposition about how things actually are, we can see how, keeping the geometry of the external space intact, things could have been organized, in both respects, exactly as if a certain spherical region were rotated by a certain amount in a certain direction. Or yet again, we can see how things could have been organized as if the external space were more narrowly circumscribed—as if its boundaries enclosed only a portion of its true extent. There is no limit to the number of examples that could be offered. We might also note that, as well as being able to envisage such possibilities in the form of what *could have been*, we can envisage them in the form of what *could come to be*. For, in each case, we can envisage the possibility of the laws which have held hitherto changing in the relevant way. But, although these possibilities of future deviance would serve our purposes just as well, I shall continue to focus on the cases of how things would have turned out, if the laws had *always* been different.

Even when we suppose, then, that the external geometry is entirely in line with the empirical evidence, we can envisage ways in which, with the same geometry, but suitably different laws, there could have been cases of relevant geometrical deviance. And just as we earlier raised the question of how the *hypothetical* cases of relevant deviance should be interpreted *physically*—cases where we envisaged the deviance as how, conceivably, things *might actually be*—so we can raise this same question for these *merely possible* cases. If things in the PRE-reality had been organized in a relevantly different way, creating the relevant kind of disparity between the external geometry and what was suggested by all the actual and potential empirical evidence, how would things have turned out for the geometry of physical space?

In the hypothetical cases, we reached our verdict about the relevant aspects of physical structure by appealing to a principle of empirical immanence. Thus, in the example on which we focused, after dismissing the suggestion that the envisaged situation was such as to preclude the existence of the physical world, or affect its repleteness, we were left having to decide between two views, one of which took the physical topology to coincide with the *actual* topology of the external reality, and the other of which took it to coincide with the *organizationally simulated* topology. And what led us to endorse the second of these views was the consideration that, to qualify as characterizing *our world*, the physical topology has to conform to how things are disposed to appear at *our* empirical viewpoint. And this is how we settled the physical interpretation of such cases of deviance quite generally. Now we cannot just assume that, because this consideration was decisive for the *hypothetical* cases of deviance, it will be decisive for the *merely possible* too. After all, there are many instances where something which is a conceptual requirement of a certain type of item *in the actual world* does not hold of that type *in all possible worlds*. For example, to qualify as water in the actual world, something has to be the sort of stuff that we standardly find in rivers and rain; but it is easy to imagine a possible world in which the stuff of rivers and rain is something quite different. Or again, to qualify as Moses in the actual world, someone has to satisfy a reasonable amount of what is recorded of 'Moses' in the Bible; but this does not mean that the person who does qualify as Moses could not have perished in the womb. Accordingly, it could still be suggested that considerations of empirical immanence only play a role in picking out what qualifies

as physical structure *in the actual world,* and that it is then the nature of
what is thus picked out, rather than any need to preserve conformity to the
empirical evidence, which enables us to identify instances of physical structure *in merely possible worlds*—including those worlds which involve the
envisaged forms of deviance.

However, I think it is clear that our intuitions about the hypothetical
cases of relevant deviance do, in fact, carry over to the possible cases as well.
Thus, continuing to focus on deviance with respect to geometrical structure, we surely want to say that if the external reality had been organized as
if two of its regions were interchanged, then the locations of the corresponding physical regions would have coincided with the functional locations of these regions, in accordance with all the actual and potential
empirical evidence. Likewise, we surely want to say that if the external reality had been organized as if its space were more narrowly circumscribed,
then, in line with all the empirical evidence, the extent of physical space
would have been correspondingly diminished. And this, it seems to me,
would be our reaction in any case of this general type. In each such case,
we would take the true physical geometry to be what shows up empirically
at the human viewpoint, rather than what coincides with the concealed
geometry of the external reality. In effect, our response would be to evaluate the physical significance of these merely possible cases as if they were
actual. One way in which we can reinforce this point is by considering the
same issue in reverse—taking the actual situation to be one of relevant
deviance, and then raising the question of how things would have stood
physically if this deviance had been eliminated. Thus suppose we take the
actual situation to be one in which the external reality is organized as if two
of its regions were interchanged, or as if the extent of its space were more
narrowly circumscribed—obliging us to think of the physical geometry as
coinciding with the organizationally simulated geometry—and then consider how things would have stood physically if, with the geometry of the
external space held constant, the organization had been wholly in line with
it. In this sort of case, there is nothing that could even *tempt* us to deny that
the physical geometry would have been correspondingly different—coinciding with the external geometry, in accordance with the new (and
deviance-eliminating) organization. And consistency demands an analogous response when the move from the actual situation to the possible one
is, in terms of deviance, the other way round.

The merely possible cases of relevant deviance are to be interpreted,
then, in the same way as the hypothetical, so that the physical geometry is
taken to coincide with the geometry which the external organization simu-

lates and projects on to the human empirical viewpoint. But this has crucial consequences for our evaluation of physical realism. To begin with, it means that, even in the case of zero deviance, where we can take the physical and external geometries to be qualitatively the same, the obtaining of the physical geometry logically depends on more than just the obtaining of the external geometry. It depends, in addition, on aspects of the external *organization*; for if this organization had been suitably different—though without change to the external geometry—the physical geometry would have been different too. In effect, the obtaining of the physical geometry depends not just on the external geometry, but on the fact that the latter is 'endorsed' by the external organization, and its character thereby translated into how things empirically appear. It follows that, even in the case of zero deviance, the facts of physical geometry cannot be equated with the facts of the external geometry. For if they could, their obtaining would not involve any additional factors. Moreover, the additional factors involved are not just to do with how the PRE-reality is organized *internally*. They also concern the ways in which it is organized *in relation to human minds*. In particular, they concern the ways in which the reality is nomologically disposed to affect human sensory experience; for it is these dispositions to affect sensory experience that determine the character of the geometry which presents itself at the human viewpoint. So, as well as being distinct from their external counterparts, the facts of physical geometry are logically dependent on facts about the human mind. And this means that they cannot even be assigned to the PRE-reality in a derivative form—as facts constituted by more basic PRE-facts—since this reality (as it is in itself) is wholly mind-independent. The same form of reasoning could be used to reach analogous conclusions about other kinds of structure, such as relationships of qualitative sameness and difference. But, for the purposes of our discussion, the results for the geometrical case will suffice.

The relevance of these results to the issue of realism is already clear. The realist, as we have said, is committed to accepting the existence of a PRE-reality, and to equating it with the physical world in its primary (mind-independent) core; and this involves taking the structural aspects of this reality to form the corresponding aspects of physical structure. As we have also noted, the scenario which is most favourable to the realist's cause is that of zero deviance, where we can at least take the physical and external structures to coincide *qualitatively*. It now turns out that, even when it is applied to this case, the realist account fails, and fails comprehensively. The physical and external geometries may coincide qualitatively. But they differ in their concrete existence, since the obtaining of the former depends on more than just the obtaining of the latter. Nor, indeed, can the facts of physical geometry be assigned to the PRE-reality in any way at all, since the additional factors on which their obtaining depends are partly concerned with human mentality. Finally, we can see that, with the exclusion of the physical geometry from the PRE-reality, *all* physical facts are excluded. For the exclusion of the physical geometry entails the exclusion of physical space; and all physical facts essentially involve the existence of physical space, being either facts about its character (or the character of certain of its elements), or facts about what exists or occurs within it. In short, even for the case of zero deviance, we are forced to conclude that the PRE-reality is wholly non-physical.

Because the case of zero deviance represents the realist's best scenario, the failure of realism for this case is enough to show its failure quite generally. But, for completeness, I should stress that the argument which we have employed for zero deviance could also be employed for any other type of case where an anti-realist argument is needed—any type of case where we envisage a PRE-reality, and where it is not obvious from the start that it is incompatible with the realist view.

V

From this refutation of physical realism, it is now only a short step to the endorsement of the idealist alternative. Indeed, this endorsement is already implicit in the points that have emerged.

The realist thesis comprises two claims: the mind-independence claim, to the effect that the existence of the physical world is logically independent of the human mind, and the fundamentalist claim, to the effect that the physical world is, in its basic character, metaphysically fundamental. The argument that we have brought against realism is, in itself, an argument against the first of these claims: it shows that there is not even a primary core of physical facts which can be assigned to an external, mind-independent reality. But, as we noted earlier, there is no prospect of being able to reject the mind-independence claim without rejecting the fundamentalist claim too.[7] For the only way of accounting for the mind-dependence of the physical world is by supposing that the world is logically created by facts of a different kind, and that its mind-dependence is a consequence of its mode of creation. In other words, to account for the mind-dependence, we have to suppose that physical facts are, in all cases,

---

[7] See Part Five, Section 1, II.

constituted by non-physical facts, and that facts about human mentality form, or systematically feature in, the non-physical facts involved.

We already know, then, that the physical world is logically created by facts of a different kind, and ones which at least partly concern human mentality. But it is also clear that, whatever precisely these facts are, they have in some way to cover the obtaining of the sensory organization. This is clear from the considerations which showed the physical world to be mind-dependent. Thus we saw that, even in the case of zero deviance, the facts of physical geometry logically depend, for their obtaining, on aspects of the external organization, and that these aspects are at least partly to do with the dispositions of the external reality to affect human sensory experience. In effect, we saw that what determines the character of the physical geometry is not the external geometry on its own, but the fact that this geometry is 'endorsed' by the external organization, and its character thereby projected on to the human empirical viewpoint. And, in this respect, *zero* deviance is just the limiting case of *relevant* deviance. For, with relevant deviance, the character of the physical geometry is determined by the fact that the external organization *simulates* a certain kind of geometry, and thereby projects it on to the human viewpoint. Moreover, although our focus was on the geometrical case, these results, as I made clear, carry over to other forms of structure as well. Now, in the present context, we cannot make any assumption about the character of the PRE-reality. But it is clear that the only way of doing justice to the results which emerged in that earlier discussion—the only way of accounting for the way in which mind-dependence was seen to characterize physical structure in the situations envisaged—is if we suppose that a crucial part of what equips the facts that create the physical world to play that creative role is that they fix the way things are disposed to appear, empirically, at the human viewpoint. But what directly fixes the way things are thus disposed to appear is, of course, the sensory organization. So, whatever else they involve, the facts which create the physical world must at least cover the obtaining of this organization. They may cover it directly, by simply including facts which are explicitly about the constraints on sensory experience; or they may cover it indirectly, by including a range of facts—for example about the character of the PRE-reality and its nomological links with the human mind—in which the obtaining of these constraints is implicit. But, either way, the covering of this organization will play a central role in both securing the existence of the physical world and determining its specific character.

The upshot is that, in rejecting realism in the way that we have, we are committed to accepting the truth of idealism. We are committed to saying that the physical world is, in all its aspects, logically created (that its exist-ence and all the facts it contains are constituted) by the sensory organiza-tion, or by some richer complex of non-physical facts in which this organization centrally features.

3 THE UNFINISHED STORY

I have tried to establish the truth of idealism. If I have been successful, then, in the context of our larger discussion, this is a welcome result. For it elim-inates the problem of perception. It remains the case that the immediate objects of awareness involved in perception are sense-qualia; and there is no way of understanding how perceptual awareness can reach beyond these qualia to items in the mind-independent reality. But, given our ideal-ist account of the physical world, awareness does not need to reach further than the qualia to make contact with the factors by which the existence of physical items is constituted, and thereby to make contact with these items themselves. In fact, in the context of our larger discussion, the establishing of idealism is a doubly welcome result. For, in eliminating the problem of perception, it also eliminates the associated problem of knowledge. It does this, not by opening up a new route to physical knowledge, but by showing that, with perceptual access to the physical world in place, information about the world can be acquired in the normal, perception-based way. Physical knowledge is now available because the physical world is open to perceptual scrutiny.

I have tried to establish the truth of idealism, but I have not provided, nor come near to providing, a fully elaborated idealist theory. To provide such a theory, there are a number of areas where I would need to develop the idealist account in a more detailed way. One area where I would need to pursue matters further concerns the nature of time. Time is an ingredi-ent of both the physical world and the underlying reality by which the world is created. But does this mean that there is a single time-dimension, occurring at both levels? And if not, how are the separate dimensions related? And, in any case, how are we to understand the nature of time in its pre-physical form? I dealt with these questions at length in *The Case for Idealism*, but am not sure to what extent I would continue to endorse the answers I there gave. Another area where there would be a need for further elaboration concerns the nature of human subjects. Such subjects have to be, in themselves, non-physical, since they feature in the idealistic creation. But there is still the question of the kinds of non-physical things they are.

And there is even the question of whether, in the last analysis, they should be thought of as *things* (substances) at all, or merely as organized bundles of mental items. On all this, I would certainly endorse, point by point, the Cartesian account of the subject that I defended in *The Immaterial Self*. I would also need to say something about how human subjects form a unified group for the purposes of the idealistic creation. The idealism for which I have argued is not solipsistic—a separate created world for each subject. In line with common sense, I have assumed that there is a *single* physical world which is *communally ours*, and a *single* (intersubjective) sensory organization, which contributes to its creation. And this involves thinking of human subjects as forming some kind of communal group independently of what results from the creation of their shared world. At the very least, it involves supposing that there is, pre-physically, provision for certain forms of causal interaction between different subjects, either directly, or via their functional links with a common external reality.

But perhaps the most important area for further investigation is that which arises from the form of the idealist thesis itself. This thesis claims that the physical world is logically created *either* by the sensory organization *or* by some richer complex of non-physical facts in which this organization centrally features. As we noted earlier, there is room for a range of more specific idealist accounts according to how the choices implicit in this formulation are resolved. Should we think of the physical world as created by the sensory organization *on its own*, or by a richer complex of facts? And if the latter, what should we take this complex to be?

The most crucial issues here are concerned with the role of the PRE-reality. To account for the presence of the sensory organization, we can reasonably assume that there *is* some form of PRE-reality, whose causal control of our sensory experiences is what forms the relevant sensory constraints; and, given that this reality is what imposes these constraints, it is directly involved in the creation of the physical world. But, as we noted, there is also the option of saying that the *intrinsic character* of this reality is directly involved as well—that part of what allows there to be a physical world is the fact that the reality which constrains our experience is of a certain specific type. It is not hard to see why we might find such an idea attractive. It is true that, in reaching our idealist conclusion, the crucial consideration was that the physical world has to be something whose structure conforms to how things are disposed to appear at our empirical viewpoint; and if this were the *only* requirement, we could happily think of the world as created by the sensory organization alone. But, in order to be able to think of the created world as a *real* world, we also need to be able to credit it with a certain kind of *objectivity* in relation to us. And the trouble with taking the sensory organization to be the only constitutively relevant factor is that this objectivity would then seem to be lacking: there just does not seem to be a sufficiently significant difference between the presence of a world which is created by the sensory organization alone and there merely being a systematic impression of such a world from the human viewpoint. But if the idealistically created world is to have the requisite objectivity— to amount to significantly more than the way things systematically seem to us—then this presumably has to come from some kind of externalistic underpinning, some way in which the empirical story is underwritten by the external factors which lie behind it. In *The Case for Idealism*, I argued that no such underpinning was necessary—that the sensory organization on its own was sufficient. But I am now inclined to think that this argument was flawed and its conclusion mistaken.

If we do think that the nature of the PRE-reality is needed as a direct contributor to the creation of the physical world, this immediately raises the question of what types of reality would be equipped to play this role. Two things are already clear, and in effect implicit in our earlier discussion. First, the kind of PRE-reality which occurs in the case of zero deviance is suitably equipped. Here, the structure and organization of the reality will coincide with how things empirically appear at the human viewpoint. If the empirical story needs to be appropriately underwritten by external factors in order to yield a matching physical world, it is hard to see how this need could be met in a more clear-cut and comprehensive way. Secondly, the kind of PRE-reality which occurs in cases of relevant deviance is also suitably equipped. In these cases, the structure and organization of the PRE-reality do not coincide with how things empirically appear. But the failure of coincidence is limited in its extent: thus, as we stipulated, it is not so great as to lend intuitive plausibility to physical nihilism. And, even with respect to the area of deviance, the way things appear does, in a less direct way, reflect the nature of the external reality; for the reality is organized so as to simulate the possession of a certain structure, and it is this simulated structure which gets projected, in all its details, on to the human empirical viewpoint. This too seems to meet any need for an externalistic underpinning in a clear-cut and comprehensive way. The delicate questions arise when we consider ways in which the conditions required for relevant deviance could be relaxed. Is it really necessary, for example, to impose some limit on the degree to which the structure and organization of the external reality can deviate from what is suggested by the empirical evidence? Or will any degree of deviance allow for the creation of the physical world—even a deviance which, prior to our acceptance of idealism, would have seemed incompatible with the existence of such a world—so long as the empirical situation is sustained by the external organization in the relevant way? And, in any case, does there have to be this kind of sustainment at all? How, for example, should we respond to the scenario postulated by Berkeley, where human sensory experience is directly controlled by God, and where the sensory organization is formed by the consistent policies of this control? The empirical story would still be, in its way, externalistically underwritten: it would be the story authored, and, in a sense, authenticated, by God. But is this enough for the creation of a real world?

These are intriguing questions, and, along with the issues mentioned earlier, they are ones which any comprehensive study of idealism would need to address. But neither they nor those other issues are matters that I have the space to pursue here. Nor is there any need for me to do so. The relevance of idealism in the present context is that it enables us to bring our study of the nature of perception to a satisfactory conclusion, and this is something which it does irrespective of how these further matters are settled. Just by knowing the truth of the idealist thesis, we know, in its essentials, how the perception of physical items is to be ultimately understood; and, crucially, we thereby know how, despite our account of phenomenal experience, such perception is possible.

BIBLIOGRAPHY

ARMSTRONG, D. *A Materialist Theory of the Mind*. London: Routledge & Kegan Paul, 1968.

—— *Perception and the Physical World*. London: Routledge & Kegan Paul, 1961.

AUNE, B. *Knowledge, Mind, and Nature*. New York: Random House, 1967.

AUSTIN, J. L. *Sense and Sensibilia*. Oxford: Oxford University Press, 1962.

AYER, A. J. *Language, Truth, and Logic*, 2nd edn. London: Gollancz, 1946.

—— *The Origins of Pragmatism*. London: Macmillan, 1968.

BERKELEY, G. *An Essay towards a New Theory of Vision*, in his *Philosophical Works*, ed. M. Ayers. London: Dent, 1975.

—— *A Treatise Concerning the Principles of Human Knowledge*, in his *Philosophical Works*, ed. M. Ayers. London: Dent, 1975.

BROAD, C. D. 'Some elementary reflexions on sense-perception', *Philosophy*, 27 (1952), 3–17.

CHISHOLM, R. *Perceiving*. Ithaca, N.Y.: Cornell University Press, 1957.

—— *Person and Object*. La Salle, Ill.: Open Court, 1976.

CORNMAN, J. *Materialism and Sensations*. New Haven, Conn.: Yale University Press, 1971.

DANCY, J. (ed.). *Perceptual Knowledge*. Oxford: Oxford University Press, 1988.

DESCARTES, R. *Meditations on the First Philosophy*, in *The Philosophical Writings of Descartes*, trans. J. Cottingham, R. Stoothof, and D. Murdoch, vol. 2. Cambridge: Cambridge University Press, 1984.

—— *The Principles of Philosophy*, in *The Philosophical Writings of Descartes*, trans. J. Cottingham, R. Stoothof, and D. Murdoch, vol. 1. Cambridge: Cambridge University Press, 1985.

DUCASSE, C. J. 'Moore's refutation of idealism', in P. Schilpp (ed.), *The Philosophy of G. E. Moore*. Chicago: Northwestern University Press, 1942.

FISHER, G. *The Frameworks for Perceptual Localization*. Department of Psychology, University of Newcastle upon Tyne, 1968.

FOSTER, J. *Ayer*. London: Routledge & Kegan Paul, 1985.

—— 'Berkeley on the physical world', in J. Foster and H. Robinson (eds.), *Essays on Berkeley*. Oxford: Oxford University Press, 1985.

—— *The Case for Idealism*. London: Routledge & Kegan Paul, 1982.

—— 'The construction of the physical world', in L. Hahn (ed.), *The Philosophy of A. J. Ayer*. La Salle, Ill.: Open Court, 1992.

—— *The Immaterial Self*. London: Routledge, 1991.

GETTIER, E. 'Is justified true belief knowledge?', *Analysis*, 23 (1963), 121–3.

GRICE, H. P. 'The causal theory of perception', *Proceedings of the Aristotelian Society*, Suppl. Vol. 35 (1961), 121–52.

HUME, D. *Enquiries Concerning Human Understanding and Concerning the Principles of Morals*, ed. L. Selby-Bigge, 3rd edn. revised P. Nidditch. Oxford: Oxford University Press, 1975.

—— *A Treatise of Human Nature*, ed. L. Selby-Bigge, 2nd edn. revised P. Nidditch. Oxford: Oxford University Press, 1978.

JACKSON, F. *Perception*. Cambridge: Cambridge University Press, 1977.

LEWIS, D. 'Veridical hallucination', *Australasian Journal of Philosophy*, 58/3 (1980), 239–49.

LOCKE, J. *An Essay Concerning Human Understanding*, ed. A. Campbell Fraser. New York: Dover, 1959.

McDOWELL, J. 'Criteria, defeasibility, and knowledge', *Proceedings of the British Academy*, 68 (1982), 455–79.

MILL, J. S. *An Examination of Sir William Hamilton's Philosophy*. London: Longmans Green, 1867.

PEACOCKE, C. *Holistic Explanation*. Oxford: Oxford University Press, 1979.

PITCHER, G. *A Theory of Perception*. Princeton: Princeton University Press, 1971.

PRICE, H. H. *Perception*, reprint of 2nd edn. London: Methuen, 1954.

PUTNAM, H. 'The meaning of "meaning"', in his *Mind, Language, and Reality*. Cambridge: Cambridge University Press, 1975.

QUINTON, A. 'The problem of perception', *Mind*, 64 (1955), 28–51.

ROBINSON, H. 'The general form of the argument for Berkeleian Idealism', in J. Foster and H. Robinson (eds.), *Essays on Berkeley*. Oxford: Oxford University Press, 1985.

—— *Perception*. London: Routledge, 1994.

SELLARS, W. 'Phenomenalism', in his Science, Perception, and Reality. London: Routledge & Kegan Paul, 1963.

—— *Science and Metaphysics*. London: Routledge & Kegan Paul, 1968.

SNOWDON, P. 'Perception, vision, and causation', Proceedings of the Aristotelian Society, 81 (1980–1), 175–92.

STRAWSON, G. *The Secret Connexion*. Oxford: Oxford University Press, 1989.

STRAWSON, P. F. 'Causation in perception', in his *Freedom and Resentment*. London: Methuen, 1974.

—— 'Perception and its objects', in G. Macdonald (ed.), *Perception and Identity*. London: Macmillan 1979.

TYE, M. 'The adverbial approach to visual experience', Philosophical Review, 93 (1984), 195–225.

WITTGENSTEIN, L. *Philosophical Investigations*, trans. G. E. M. Anscombe. Oxford: Blackwell, 1958.

INDEX